Praise for *Coaching That Counts*

"*Coaching That Counts* is filled with compelling insights on leadership coaching and how to manage this powerful development process to deliver strategic value. A must read for anyone involved in coaching."
—**Ken Blanchard**, co-author of *The One Minute Manager*® and *Customer Mania!*

"This book addresses the three key aspects of a successful executive coaching engagement: the art of coaching, the art of managing coaching initiatives and the art of evaluating coaching results. *Coaching That Counts* is a wellspring of inspiring insights and powerful tools for internal and external coaches around the world.
  Giovanna D'Alessio, Chief Executive Coach of Life Coach Lab srl, Italy

"In the three years since we conducted an ROI study on coaching, the benefits revealed by the study have proven to be strategic and sustainable."
  —**Cindy Dauss**, Leadership Development, Nortel Networks, USA

"*Coaching That Counts* belongs on the shelf of every professional coach and leader who cares about the sustainable development of people. The Andersons portray the impressive results of the marriage between coaching and research by using the data and real life examples of case studies that never fail to ask and answer the relevant questions. *Coaching That Counts* leaves the reader with a deeper understanding of why coaching is of value, what needs to happen for coaching to produce results, the value of an empirically based model for coaching and even how to measure the ROI of coaching. This is truly a book that counts."
  —**Nadjeschda Hebenstreit**, President of the ICF, Germany,
  Founder of TheSuccessClub for Solopreneurs

"This book is a must for anyone who is introducing coaching into an organization or managing a coaching initiative."
  —**Ross McLelland**, Managing Director, Pacific Consulting Resources Pty Ltd,
  Australia

"Learning about the three lynchpins for *Coaching That Counts* is a must for business and Human Resources leaders who are working to make coaching an essential element of their global leadership development capability."
  —**Stephan H. Oberli**, CEO and President SHO Resource Group GmbH,
  Switzerland

"This book is a must read for coaches who are interested in working within organizations, program managers of organizational coaching initiatives, and Chief Learning Officers who need to be able to articulate the value of executive coaching to key stakeholders."

—**Vernita Parker-Wilkins**, Executive Development Learning Manager, Booz Allen Hamilton, USA

"What a powerful piece of work! *Coaching That Counts* makes a significant contribution to the field of coaching and to the organizations that use coaching services. Every coach and corporate executive needs to study this book carefully."

—**Cheryl Richardson**, author of *Take Time for Your Life, Life Makeovers,* and *Stand Up for Your Life*

"Companies today are demanding that international coaching firms provide evidence that coaching is valuable and impacting the bottom line. I found that *Coaching That Counts* provides a framework for how to approach large coaching engagements systematically so clients see the value in coaching. This book is a must have for anyone providing coaching services to large organizations."

—**Barbara Singer**, Vice President of Executive Coaching, Global Lore International Institute, USA

"The Andersons' book of data and practices illuminates how pivotal coaching can be in taking organizations and individuals to their next level of performance, and beyond."

—**Dr. Barbara Walton**, MCC, President of the International Coach Federation, USA

Coaching That Counts

IMPROVING
HUMAN
PERFORMANCE
SERIES

Series Editor: Jack J. Phillips, Ph.D.

LATEST BOOKS IN THE SERIES

Performance Through Learning
Carol Gorelick, Nick Milton and Kurt April

The Leadership Scorecard
Jack J. Phillips and Lynn Schmidt

Bottom-Line Call Center Management
David L. Butler

Bottom-Line Organization Development
Merrill Anderson

The Diversity Scorecard
Edward E. Hubbard

Handbook of Training Evaluation and Measurement Methods, 3rd Edition
Jack J. Phillips

The Human Resources Scorecard
Jack J. Phillips, Patricia Pulliam Phillips, and Ron D. Stone

Managing Employee Retention
Jack J. Phillips and Adele O. Connell

The Project Management Scorecard
Jack J. Phillips, G. Lynne Snead, and Timothy W. Bothell

Return on Investment in Training and Performance Improvement Programs, Second Edition
Jack J. Phillips

Visit **http://books.elsevier.com/humanresources** to see the full range of books available in the series.

Coaching That Counts

Harnessing the Power of Leadership Coaching to Deliver Strategic Value

Dianna L. Anderson, MCC
Merrill C. Anderson, Ph.D.

ELSEVIER
BUTTERWORTH
HEINEMANN

AMSTERDAM • BOSTON • HEIDELBERG • LONDON
NEW YORK • OXFORD • PARIS • SAN DIEGO
SAN FRANCISCO • SINGAPORE • SYDNEY • TOKYO

Elsevier Butterworth–Heinemann
30 Corporate Drive, Suite 400, Burlington, MA 01803, USA
Linacre House, Jordan Hill, Oxford OX2 8DP, UK

 Recognizing the importance of preserving what has been written, Elsevier prints its
books on acid-free paper whenever possible.

Library of Congress Cataloging-in-Publication Data
Application submitted.

British Library Cataloguing-in-Publication Data
A catalogue record for this book is available from the British Library.

ISBN-13: 978-0-7506-7820-2
ISBN-10: 0-7506-7580-2

For information on all Elsevier Butterworth–Heinemann publications
visit our Web site at www.books.elsevier.com

05 06 07 08 09 10   10 9 8 7 6 5 4 3 2

Printed in the United States of America

Contents

Section Two: Managing Coaching Initiatives

Section Three: Evaluating Coaching Success

Conclusion

Foreword

Like so many organizations is today's global economy, Booz Allen Hamilton requires leadership that is diverse in its thinking, strong in business acumen and open to new ideas and opportunities. Founded in 1914, Booz Allen Hamilton is a strategy and technology consulting firm with more than 16,000 staff located on six continents. We have experienced tremendous growth, averaging 20 percent per year, over the past seven years. This growth has stretched our current leaders and created new challenges for developing future leaders.

In order to meet these challenges, we needed a way to implement a development methodology that would build the leadership pipeline with leaders ready to take on expanded roles in the most efficient manner. We also recognized that we needed to supplement our internal succession process by recruiting leaders from outside of the firm. Business growth required us to hire new leaders to build specific markets and functional areas, and these new hires needed to rapidly learn their new roles as well as how to operate in our culture. The Booz Allen culture is highly collaborative and networked and so leaders must be adept at engaging the hearts and minds of team members to work on highly complex strategic change projects, often with globally distributed clients. Successful leaders are those who coach—and not try to control—others.

The Cascading a Coaching Culture initiative was launched to build critical leadership competencies in a way that is an expression of our culture. We realize that we are in this for the long haul. Sam Strickland, Chief Administrative Officer at Booz Allen, continuously reminds us that "success is a journey, not a destination." Our experience with creating a coaching culture has and continues to be a great journey. After we were about two years into this journey, we benchmarked companies known to have outstanding coaching programs. Several themes emerged:

- All companies had dedicated staff to support the initiatives
- Coaching was viewed as part of a strategic initiative of the organization to turn the quality of its leaders into a competitive advantage for the firm
- Coaching was integrated with other leadership development programs and competency growth
- All viewed coaching as an investment in top performers or high potentials.
- External coaches were preferred in order to maintain confidentiality and reduce feelings of vulnerability in the most senior staff

Excited about what we learned, we decided that it was the right time to enhance and expand our coaching initiative. Led by two outstanding specialists in senior executive development, Hazel Solomon and Vernita Parker-Wilkins, we launched our Coaching Program office to centralize the management of coaching. This office was responsible for implementing a coach qualification process, defining the rules of engagement and conduct, conducting evaluation, as well as cost management and tracking.

In 2003, we decided that it was time to measure the effectiveness and perceptions of the initiative. This is how we came to know Merrill Anderson. Merrill came into Booz Allen and helped us to first determine what our senior leaders expected from the coaching initiative. This was a crucial step. Expanding the coaching initiative required added investment and our senior leaders were expressing their expectations for a return on this investment. Specifically, their expectations were organized into eight areas of potential business impact: increased productivity, retention of leadership talent, accelerating senior leader promotions, improved team work, increased quality of consulting services, increased diversity, increased team member satisfaction, and increased client satisfaction. These eight areas formed the nucleus of a formal ROI study of our executive coaching initiative. We knew that it was not enough just to show a high ROI, we also had to demonstrate that the value was being produced in the areas that the senior leaders felt were most important for the organization.

Merrill then proceeded with the ROI study. He designed the evaluation approach and then conducted, with several Booz Allen staff, a series of interviews with leaders who had been coached. The eight business impact areas were probed, as well as the impact that coaching had on building critical leadership competencies. Specific examples of what leaders did differently as a result of coaching were documented and, in many cases, the monetary benefits that were produced as a result of these actions were recorded. The study was a real eye opener. Even after adopting the most conservative approach to determining the return on investment, we showed a 700% ROI for the coaching initiative. Moreover, the value was being produced from many of those business areas that the senior leaders expected. Merrill also shared his insights and recommendations that further enhanced the coaching initiative.

Even though I felt good about the results and knew that the return on investment study would solidify the credibility of the initiative, there was still something missing. That's when I was offered the opportunity to read the first draft of Merrill and Dianna Anderson's book, *Coaching That Counts, Harnessing the Power of Leadership Coaching to Deliver Strategic Value.* As I read through the draft, I realized we needed to travel even further into the realm of the strategic value of coaching and find more effective ways to increase its alignment to the business. I also resonated with, as I am sure you will as well, the Leading With Insight model and its four quadrants. This model was something that has been missing from our initiative.

Our coaches, who come from outside our business, are highly skilled and talented coaches. That said, they have been trained in a variety of models and although they appear to be on the road to similar destinations, there are differences amongst their approaches. This book provides a common language and a common roadmap for internal and external coaches to follow. Greater consistency in the approach to coaching facilitates its strategic alignment to the organization. The second section of the book provides companies with practical tools and approaches to managing coaching as a strategic initiative, while the third section describes a roadmap to implement and measure coaching programs. From my own experience, these ideas work and will improve the design, deployment and management of coaching initiatives. Merrill and Dianna provide concrete examples, case studies and draw from their own experience to make each step in the Leading With Insight model come alive. And then they take us further—providing a clear method for documenting the impact of coaching and using those results to gain even greater effectiveness from the coaching initiative.

I know you will enjoy this book as much as I have. Whatever stage you are in your coaching journey, you will find in this book a wealth of practical tools and ideas that will make your coaching initiative count. Best of luck to you on your coaching journey.

Ed Cohen
Senior Director
Center for Performance Excellence
Booz Allen Hamilton

Preface

Writing this book was truly a labor of love. Merrill labored to understand coaching and Dianna labored to understand ROI. What you are about to read is the fruit of our labors. In the past few years or so, leadership coaching has emerged from obscurity to take its place as a premier leadership development process. Coaching has everyone's attention, and yet so little is known about how coaching creates value for the clients of coaching and for the organizations that sponsor coaching initiatives. Dianna writes from the perspective of a Master Certified Coach who has, for the last 10 years, evolved her coaching as the coaching profession has evolved. Merrill writes from the perspective of a strategic change consultant who has, for the past three years, evaluated several coaching and leadership development initiatives. Together, we wrote this book that we believe combines insights and practical experience about how to achieve transformational change through the strategic application and evaluation of leadership coaching.

We had four kinds of readers in mind when we wrote this book. First, to the clients of coaching, we wanted to share with you how others have taken similar journeys. Along the way, we trust that you will recognize a journey that you have taken and perhaps open up new possibilities for additional development. For the coaches, we want you to fully understand the tremendous value you are creating and to better comprehend how to focus this value for even greater strategic advantage for the individuals and organizations you serve. For the managers of coaching initiatives, we present you with a multitude of ideas for gaining maximum value from the investment your organization is making in coaching. We feel it is important for you to not only understand the coaching process, but also to understand how to ensure that coaching delivers the value your senior leaders expect. Senior leaders, please view this book as a clarion call to achieving excellence in your leaders like you have never seen before.

Now, back to the labor of love. We had a wonderful time writing this book. We learned from each other, we challenged each other, and in the process we have created a unique and powerful vision of leadership coaching. We look at coaching from the perspective of the client being coached and the organization sponsoring the coaching initiative. Both the client and the organization have to realize value in order for coaching to be a sustainable leadership development process. We invite both clients and organizations to expect more from coaching. Transformational experiences are inherent in this powerful change process, but you must expect to realize that magnitude of change in order to receive it. Do not settle for less.

As authors, we learned a lot from writing this book and from each other. We trust that our learning has made it into these pages in ways that engage you, the reader, in our learning experience. The first part of this book emphasizes the intuitive intelligence of the reader. A model and process for coaching are described from the perspective of the coaching client and the coach. We talk about the coaching relationship, and it is truly a two-way street. Coaches challenge clients to go where they have never gone before, and clients dig deep to challenge coaches to take them there. The second part of this book shifts to the analytic aspect of coaching. We take a hard look at these coaching relationships and make sure they are delivering the kind of value that senior leaders expect from coaching and that the business needs. By merging these two perspectives—the intuitive and the analytic—a value nexus is created. This value nexus creates transformational value for the coaching client and bottom-line value for the organization.

Thank you for joining us in this journey of discovery. It is a journey that is just beginning. Please view our experiences, models, ideas, and findings as an entry point for gaining greater insights into coaching. We do not intend this book to be the final word; in fact, it is our intention that this book will be the opening question in a greater quest for understanding how to expand the impact that coaching delivers to clients and organizations. Take what you want, use what you can, and make your coaching count.

Merrill Anderson
Dianna Anderson
Johnston, Iowa
September 2004

Introduction to Coaching That Counts™

John and Phil were at a crossroads. John, as the chief learning executive for this global information technology consulting firm, was arguing for a company-wide rollout of coaching. Phil was chair of the partner development committee responsible for developing the bench strength of leaders for the future. Phil's experience with coaching was mixed. Some people really liked it and some people were left scratching their heads about why they were being coached and what kind of value they were supposed to get out of coaching. John pointed to the multitude of voices that supported coaching as evidence that coaching was a powerful developmental tool for building leadership. Phil heard those voices and yet, as a key business leader, his inner voice was asking about the business value of the coaching experience. John and Phil argued their points and neither budged. In a sense, both were right. John was right in that many, if not most, leaders found tremendous value in their coaching experience. Phil was right in the sense that coaching success seemed hit or miss, and it was not clear how the individual value leaders gained translated into business value.

The Coaching Initiative: Developing Leaders and Producing Business Impact

This situation with John and Phil is not unique; in fact, this situation is being played out in countless companies throughout the world. People who are being coached are finding value in the process, but the sponsors or buyers of the coaching services are looking for a return on investment (ROI) for the organization. Successful coaching, therefore, must meet not only the needs of the individual clients being coached but also the needs of the organization.

Coaching That Counts™ represents a model and methodology that does both. For the first time, coaching is described as both a developmental process (for the individual) and a strategic initiative (for the organization). For coaching to be a strategic initiative, it is more than just the sum of the individual coaching relationships. As an initiative, coaching contributes to the achievement of business goals. Coaching initiatives must be managed and create the context for having the coaching relationships each contribute to achieving the strategic business goals. Let's return to our story to see how one company achieved this goal, and in so doing, understand the essential elements that make coaching count. Then we will explore how the organization of this book delves into these essential elements in more detail and provides the reader with the required tools and knowledge to make coaching successful.

John and Phil, both being pragmatic people, decided to conduct a study of coaching and let the data sway their decision about the future of coaching in their organization. This study had two parts. First, the senior partners of the firm would be interviewed to understand the value they expect from coaching. If beauty is in the eye of the beholder, then value is in the eye of the senior leaders. Second, those who had been coached would be interviewed to explore what kind of value—both monetary and intangible—had been produced by their coaching. The ROI would be determined and, perhaps even more to the point, the study would reveal the extent to which coaching was delivering the *kind* of value the leaders expected.

The Coaching Initiative Was Decentralized

First, some words about the coaching initiative. This consulting company was highly decentralized along business lines, so the coaching initiative had little in the way of centralized structure or processes. Leaders throughout the firm were encouraged to utilize coaching as they deemed appropriate. The preferred option was to use the centralized coaching referral service offered by John's corporate university. The key word here is *option*. Leaders could source coaches in any way they wished, and in fact did so. Consequently, many coaches and coaching companies were utilized, which resulted in a mishmash of coaching models, styles, and personalities. Most worked, but some did not.

What the Senior Leader Interviews Revealed

The first part of the study, based on interviews with 10 senior leaders, revealed the value these leaders expected from coaching. The left-hand column of Table 1.1 organizes these expectations by whether they were high, medium, or low on their priority list. Those expectations that were highest on the list mostly related to building the bench strength of leaders. Retaining leadership talent, accelerating promotions, and increasing the diversity of leaders all speak to

Table 1.1   Coaching Expectations versus Deliverables

What Leaders Expected		What Coaching Delivered
Retention of leadership talent Accelerating senior leader promotions Improved teamwork Increased diversity	H I G H	**Increased productivity** Increased quality of consulting services **Improved teamwork**

Increased team member satisfaction
Increased client satisfaction
Increased quality of consulting
  services
Increased productivity
	M
	E
	D
	I
	U
	M
		Increased team member
		  satisfaction
		Increased client satisfaction
		Reduced cost

Increased business development Reduced cost	L O W	Increased business development Retention of leadership talent Accelerating senior leader promotions Increased diversity

increasing the size and quality of the talent base of leadership. The fourth top priority, improved teamwork, referred to the expectation that coaching would increase how well the principals and partners worked with their respective teams to address client issues.

Those expectations that were in the middle of the pack included team member and client satisfaction, quality of consulting services, and productivity. Of course, all of these outcomes are important for a consulting business. The issue here is what the leaders expected from coaching to impact these outcomes. On the low end of the priority scale were increased business development and reduced cost. Coaching was not expected to significantly increase revenue, especially given the long sales cycle for major consulting projects. Cost was not viewed as being as important as the other categories because costs associated with providing consulting services are mostly passed on to the clients.

Business Benefits Delivered by Coaching

The second part of the study examined the business benefits that were actually delivered by the coaching. The right-hand column of Table 1.1 illustrates these benefits, which were both intangible and tangible. The two benefits in bold—increased productivity and improved teamwork—produced the greatest amounts of monetary benefits. Documenting these benefits was done by interviewing all of the coaching clients individually and asking them how they applied what they learned from coaching and how these new behaviors and actions impacted the business.

Comparing What Leaders Wanted and What They Got

Comparing these two columns reveals some glaring disconnects and helps explain how John and Phil saw the value of coaching so differently. First, three of the top four priorities that the leaders had for coaching—retention, promotions, and diversity—were at the bottom of the list for the value the coaching produced. In other words, leaders did not get what they expected from coaching. This is not to say that coaching did not create value, because it did. What this says is that coaching did not create the *kind* of value that the leaders wanted the most. The senior leaders defined success as having their expectations met. These expectations were not met, and therefore, coaching was not viewed by the leaders as being successful.

Managing the Perception of Value

This analysis cleared the air for John, whose entire lens for evaluating the success of coaching was the right-hand column of Table 1.1. John heard so many stories and testimonials from satisfied coaching clients that suggested coaching success. Coaching clients reported increased satisfaction, improved productivity, and improved problem solving. When John compared what was delivered (e.g., the right-hand column) versus what leaders expected (e.g., the left-hand column), he understood why leaders had mixed feelings about coaching. Coaching, for all its virtues, was not meeting the leaders' expectations, and as such, was not *perceived* as being valuable. This analysis also suggested to John how to increase the value—and the perceived value—of coaching. Better integrating coaching within the leadership supply process would address three of those areas that leaders value most: retention, promotions, and diversity. For example, coaching could be targeted to emerging leaders from diverse backgrounds to accelerate their opportunities for promotion. This example illustrates how coaching can meet the individual needs of the leaders being coached as well as the needs of the business.

Three Lynchpins for Coaching That Counts

This story illustrates three key points, which are lynchpins for Coaching That Counts. Incorporating these points into a coaching initiative will maximize the value for both the individuals being coached and for the organization in which the coaching is being conducted.

1. Adopt a Consistent and Proven Approach for Executive Coaching

First, organizations should adopt a consistent and proven approach for executive coaching. One of the challenges that John and Phil faced as they discussed the impact of coaching was the mishmash of different coaching styles and methodologies. Coaches defined coaching differently and adopted different approaches to coaching clients. Some approaches were more successful than others.

Coaching that adds real value focuses on developing clients on multiple levels. Although each coaching relationship is unique, there is a common underlying structure of personal development that creates the foundation for lasting change and is present in all coaching relationships. The coaches who were most effective understood this dynamic and consistently laid the foundation for their clients' continued growth. These coaches encouraged their clients to continuously deepen their own insights and translate their insights into action. Coaching that was less successful was more transactional and focused more on achieving specific outcomes, such as becoming more organized, than on fostering learning. The leaders' expectations for the coaching initiative were complex and required significant learning and development from coaching participants in order to be achieved; such outcomes are not possible through a transactional approach to coaching. The coaching approach must be aligned with the desired outcomes from the coaching intervention.

2. Effectively Manage the Coaching Initiative

One of John's key learnings from the exercise that examined how leader expectations for coaching were realized was just how little was done to effectively manage coaching as a business initiative. For starters, the business context for coaching could have been better established. John's approach had been, more or less, to ring the dinner bell and see who shows up for coaching. This approach was reactive, and little was done to establish the business context for coaching. Several things could have been done differently. John and Phil (and others) could have sat down before coaching was introduced into the organization and agreed on the business objectives that coaching could address. Then specific objectives for the coaching could have been agreed to in advance. John and Phil eventually came to this agreement, but they did so long after most of the coaching had been completed with the leadership group, and therefore, had minimum influence on the management of the coaching initiative.

Conducting a needs assessment is another important aspect of setting the context for coaching. John assumed that coaching was a part of the solution, but when coaching was introduced into the organization, he had little evidence to support that assumption. Eventually, John and Phil agreed that the supply of capable and more diverse leaders needed to be increased. A formal needs assessment would reveal why the current supply of leaders was not adequate and suggest remedial actions. Coaching may have been necessary to address the supply of leaders, but coaching was probably not sufficient by itself to achieve all the supply objectives. Other remedial actions would be required. Improving the recruitment and selection of leaders, for example, may also contribute to the solution. Or implementing a cross-company succession planning process may be a part of the solution. The needs assessment ensures that an integrated and effective solution to a performance issue is identified.

Sponsorship is another area John could have done more to support. Phil was chair of the partner development committee and, thus, was in a position to be a strong supporter—or detractor—of coaching. Phil's issue was building the bench strength of leaders, and he would have been in an ideal spot to sponsor the coaching initiative. John could have worked with Phil to establish Phil as the sponsor for coaching. As sponsor, Phil would have been more involved with the design and deployment of coaching and would likely have offered several ideas about how best to leverage coaching for the business. John would have gained from Phil's perspective and expertise to better manage the coaching initiative. John could also have ridden Phil's coattails to gain credibility for himself and for coaching.

3. Build Evaluation Methodology into the Coaching Initiative

When Phil and John have a meeting of the minds and agree on goals to increase the supply of capable and diverse leaders, they must go to the next step and set objectives for how the coaching initiative will contribute to these goals. These coaching objectives become the cornerstone for managing coaching as a value-added initiative. Achieving the coaching objectives contributes to achieving the business goal. The evaluation strategy goes one step further and describes how these objectives will be evaluated. Evaluation is not a passive process. Developing an evaluation objective is also a test of how strongly the coaching objective is linked to the business goal. If this link is weak or not well-articulated, the evaluation objective cannot be written. This link will then have to be strengthened, and in the process, the potential business impact of coaching will be better understood and communicated.

Coaching objectives can include delivering monetary value and an ROI. A key contribution of Coaching That Counts is the ability to set monetary objectives for coaching and to document the monetary value that is delivered. The evaluation strategy outlines how monetary value will be determined and how the effects of coaching to produce this value can be isolated from other potential influencing factors. Factoring in the cost of the coaching initiative to the accumulated benefits allows the ROI to be calculated. The evaluation strategy will also look into the sources of the monetary value to show specifically how the business value is being produced. As we learned from the story of the consulting company, value can be produced—and a positive ROI realized—but not produce the kind of value that leaders expect from coaching. John may have been able to cite how increased productivity contributed to a positive ROI, but Phil was less interested in productivity gains and more interested in increasing the supply of leaders.

How This Book Is Organized

Coaching That Counts is organized into three sections, each relating to one of the three lynchpins that were just discussed. The first section describes a proven client-centered approach to coaching leaders in an organization with a focus on creating value for the individual client being coached. The second section describes how to effectively manage coaching as a business initiative. The third section provides knowledge, ideas, and tools to effectively evaluate the monetary and intangible value of coaching. Special emphasis is given to determining and isolating the effects of coaching to produce monetary benefits. The concluding chapter delves into the value nexus where organization value and individual value from coaching meet.

Section One: Leading with Insight

Chapter 2 defines the space for coaching. The four-quadrant Leading with Insight™ model is introduced through a case study that illuminates how insight is deepened and translated into action. Donna, an intense, overachieving director of an IT services department, works with her coach to develop a more collaborative leadership style and lead her internal client services team to become valued partners with their clients. Donna progresses through the four levels of insight—reflective, emotional, intuitive, and inspirational—as she learns how to bring more of her considerable talent online. The essential interconnection between insight and action, which is the foundation for the Leading with Insight model, is explored.

The first quadrant of the Leading with Insight model is presented in **Chapter 3** through a case study of Jane, a human resources (HR) manager who is feeling overwhelmed by the demands of a recent merger at her company. Jane's work to create a greater sense of balance and stronger professional focus demonstrates the underlying touchstones or essential areas of personal development for Quadrant 1. The first quadrant is the space where clients increase their personal effectiveness as the foundation for achieving their coaching goals. Coaching tools and approaches to support clients in developing reflective insight and finding focus are offered at the end of this chapter.

Chapter 4 introduces the second quadrant of the Leading with Insight model, where the development of emotional insight supports the realization of coaching goals that involve effectively interacting with others. The essential elements of this quadrant are revealed through a case study of Jack, a client services VP who finds himself in a new role in which he must become a consummate influencer of clients and internally support people to do his job well. The significant shift that Jack makes in his leadership style is founded in his newly developed ability to read and respond to the emotional context of situations. The emotional insight that Jack cultivates through his experiences serves as an anchor for his development of powerful partnerships with key influencers. Coaching tools and approaches to foster emotional insight are offered at the end of the chapter.

Quadrant 3 is mapped out in **Chapter 5** through the case study of Mark, a director of information technology (IT) project management who is responsible for turning around a poorly performing team of IT project managers. As a participant in a new leadership development program, Mark uses his professional challenges to further his own development. A naturally logical thinker, he finds that he must learn to tap into his intuitive insight to craft a leadership style that reflects his values and inspires his team to a higher level of performance. The touchstones—or essential areas of development that form the foundation for intuitive insight—are discussed in this chapter, as are coaching tools and approaches for this quadrant.

Chapter 6 introduces Quadrant 4 of the Leading with Insight model through the case study of Clare, a VP of business development with great ideas, who had difficulty getting the buy-in of her peers. As Clare worked with her coach through each quadrant of development, she learned how to focus her enthusiasm, engage in meaningful dialogues with her peers, and garner support for her ideas. Clare's vision of what was possible for the team to achieve was drawn from inspirational insight. Clare's faith in herself and her ability to build a network of support were tested as she worked to translate her ideas into action. The developmental touchstones, coaching tools, and approaches guide the reader to transfer learning from this case study into practice.

The preceding four chapters clearly demonstrate that coaching is a powerful approach for developing the talents of individuals, but what about delivering results for the organization?

Section Two: Managing Coaching Initiatives

Chapter 7 builds on the value that was realized for the individuals and looks at how coaching also delivers value to the organization. One conclusion made is that harnessing the power of coaching to the strategic requirements of the organization is required to drive value. Failure to do so leaves a lot of value on the table. The case is made for the strategic management of coaching initiatives, and this chapter looks ahead to how subsequent chapters illuminate critical aspects of this issue.

Chapter 8 covers what is most important to get the coaching initiative off on the right foot. The coaching initiative must be grounded in the company culture, integrated with other developmental activities, and directed to achieve organizational goals. A case study is reviewed in which a coaching initiative was launched with little regard for these three important areas. Only after the coaching had been completed did the HR senior VP understand from the chief operating officer (COO) what the COO had expected from coaching. The chapter builds on this experience to highlight the critical success factors for setting the strategic context for coaching. Reviewing these critical success factors shows how the HR senior VP could have done things differently, and as a result, created more value for the business. The chapter concludes by examining how to design a coaching initiative for maximum impact on the organization.

In **Chapter 9**, we go from the worst-case practice of the previous chapter to best-case practice. Four best practices are examined that have proven to increase the value of a coaching initiative. We see how a leader of a coaching initiative establishes and leverages a governance body to sustain the sponsorship for her initiative. Then we explore in some detail how an orientation session for coaches and their prospective leader-clients establishes a firm foundation for the launch and management of the coaching initiative. An innovative approach to setting up signposts is deployed so that the overall progress of the coaching initiative can be tracked and better managed. A balance is struck between allowing each coaching relationship to take its course and ensuring that the coaching initiative drives value to the business. This chapter concludes by showing the value of building evaluation methodology into the coaching initiative.

Chapter 10 shifts gears by looking at coaching from the perspective of a coach. Coaches who wish to work successfully in organizations must be willing to put on a second hat—that of a consultant. It is important for people to know when they need to be a coach and when they need to be a consultant. When a coach dons the consultant hat, he or she becomes engaged in the organization on a broader scale. Value to the business, not just the client being coached, must be considered. Consultants develop strategies to successfully navigate through organizations and to drive the value of coaching to the business. This chapter concludes by examining the role of coaching companies. Coaching companies take on the responsibilities of the consultant, leaving the coaches to concentrate on coaching, and for some, this may be an ideal arrangement.

Section Three: Evaluating Coaching Success

Evaluating coaching success for an organization begins with developing an effective evaluation strategy. The main elements of an evaluation strategy are presented and explored in **Chapter 11**. Coaching goals are established and linked to the business, evaluation objectives that define success for coaching are developed, and techniques to isolate the effects of coaching to improve performance from other potential influencing factors are described. This last issue, isolation, is considered the Holy Grail of ROI evaluation. A case study is referred to throughout the chapter to illustrate these points. This chapter concludes by describing the essential building blocks of an effective evaluation strategy.

Chapter 12 continues the case study that was featured in the previous chapter to get into the nuts and bolts of evaluation. Data collection and analysis procedures are described. Some performance data are converted to monetary benefits, and specific tools are included so that readers may apply the evaluation methodology to their own particular needs. The case study provides an example of how these tools can be used. Because any evaluation is only as good as it is credible, strategies for building credibility are discussed. This chapter is dedicated to ROI and to showing how readers can tackle the ROI issue with a practical, pragmatic, and proven approach.

Chapter 13 takes a different approach from the previous chapter by focusing only on the *application* of what was learned through coaching and not on the monetary ROI. A case study shows how leaders' expectations for coaching were set to better position the evaluation. The four major decision areas for evaluating the application of coaching are reviewed and include the importance of timing for the evaluation, setting performance targets, managing vendors, and selecting the appropriate strategy for evaluation application. The case study reveals how to best plan and conduct the evaluation.

Conclusion

Chapter 14 uses the four-quadrant Leading with Insight model as a guide to show, with empirical data, how coaching creates value. A comprehensive analysis of the data undertaken by the authors reveals six key findings of coaching and value creation. Implications are drawn from these findings that enable the reader to more effectively manage coaching as a strategic initiative. When coaching becomes a strategic initiative, it focuses the insight and power of people to make collective strategic change. This chapter reinforces the notion that the power of coaching can be harnessed in more significant ways to transform organizations and the people who work in them.

Section One

Leading with Insight

2

Defining the Space for Coaching

As coaching has increased in popularity, the number of coaching methodologies and the number of coaches has skyrocketed, making it confusing for consumers of coaching services to discern for themselves which approaches and which coaches to work with. Leading with Insight™ is an empirically derived model forged from the experiences of coaching and the formal evaluation of coaching engagements for large organizations. This model is proven to deliver strategic value for individuals and their organizations. In this section, we look below the surface of successful coaching engagements in order to understand the foundations of the coaching process and the underlying structure that supports the multitude of outcomes that coaching can deliver. The Leading with Insight model demonstrates how the translation of personal insight into action forms the foundation for lasting change.

Characteristics of Successful Coaching Engagements That Deliver Lasting Change

A successful coaching engagement goes beyond just supporting an individual's realization of specific coaching goals. A successful coaching engagement will have a cascading effect, creating positive change beyond the experience of the person receiving the coaching and has the following four characteristics:

1. *The change is targeted to meet the development needs of the individual and the strategic needs of the organization.* Both the coach and the client need to be looking at the big picture when setting the intentions for the coaching engagement. From the client's perspective, the big picture is a willingness to stretch himself in ways that lead to greater personal effectiveness. Shoot too low, and a real opportunity is lost. Shoot too high and the goals do not engage the energy and imagination of the client. From the organization's perspective, the big picture involves aligning the development of the individual with the strategic needs of the organization.

2. *The changes that occur through coaching are lasting.* This is a key point and a true differentiator of coaching that creates personal transformation versus coaching that only scratches the surface. Surface coaching focuses on having the client change the way he or she does something without much regard for changing the client's perspectives that allows the behavior in the first place. The new behavior is "pasted on" to the outside of the client, so that when things are going well it appears that he or she has acquired a new skill or approach. But when the going gets tough—and it will—the person will revert back to the original behavior because it feels safe and familiar. For change to be lasting, coaches have to work on multiple levels with clients, guiding them to gain insight and translating those insights into specific actions. The actions that are taken need to build toward the intended goals. This progressive process of insight guiding outer change delivers significant, lasting results. This inside-out process is the essence of coaching and is discussed in more detail later in this chapter.

3. *The outcomes of a coaching engagement lay the foundation for continued development for the client, with or without the partnership of a coach.* When coaching is done well, the client learns not only new skills and ways of approaching challenges but also *how* to learn. The process of reflecting on experiences to gain meaning and insight enables people to continue to grow

and develop with or without the support of a coach. As a coach, one of the most rewarding moments in a coaching engagement is the time when the client starts to coach himself. With practice, the client becomes accustomed to taking time out periodically to reflect on intentions and performance and finds ways to improve.

4. *The change continues to evolve and add value beyond the individual who experiences the coaching.* Coaching is contagious. As coaching clients make changes in how they interact with others, how they communicate, and how they lead, the people around them are often influenced by the changes. A person who works with a coach long enough to make significant changes will almost always start to coach others. Some people arc purposeful about sharing what they have learned, often taking time to share insights and new approaches with their colleagues and direct reports. Others just naturally pick up on the coaching skills they are exposed to and consciously or unconsciously integrate them into their own leadership style. Although the ripple effect does not generally get picked up on the ROI radar, it is an important source of lasting value for an organization.

Transactional versus Transformational Coaching

Coaching holds the promise of transformational change, but not all coaching delivers on this promise. Coaching that is limited to being transactional, for example, focusing more on surface-level issues such as tactical actions, follow-up, and advice, fails to access the full transformational power of coaching. With transactional coaching, clients often learn technical skills and personal effectiveness techniques but little else. This kind of coaching can be useful in situations where assistance with technical expertise is required, but it is not strategic, and the value derived is minimal. Clients who are engaged in transactional coaching may report making progress initially, often in areas of personal effectiveness, but within a few months they often find that their interest in coaching is waning and they are uncertain about what additional value can be derived.

The transformational power of coaching lies in the ability to transform insight into action. Transformational coaching guides clients to reach into their own treasure trove of inner resources and use those resources to create personal and organizational change. Transactional coaching tends to skim across the surface, whereas transformational coaching creates awareness and delivers results on many levels. Insight—that inner knowing that resides within us all—is the essential ingredient for transformational change. The continuous exchange of insight and action, one fueling the other, forms the core of transformational coaching.

Insight: The Essence of Coaching

Coaching, in its essence, enables clients to gain insight into the underlying dynamics of the challenges that they face, and guides them to apply the insights in the real world to create the desired change. The following case study illustrates how this process of translating insight into action plays out in a coaching conversation. Ted came into a coaching session wanting to work with his coach on ways to improve a difficult but important relationship with a coworker, Frank. His coach asked Ted questions that painted the picture of what was going on in the relationship and also that helped Ted get in touch with aspects of the relationship that were lying below the surface. The coach asked Ted to look at the relationship from Frank's point of view. He also worked with Ted to surface assumptions or judgments that Ted was holding about his coworker. Some of these avenues of questioning surfaced more insights than others. It is the coach's job to guide the coaching conversation in order to find where the richest insights are located. As Ted examined the situation from different angles he realized that he had inadvertently left Frank out of some important communications and that some of the difficulty they were having probably stemmed from Frank's reaction to this perceived slight.

The coach then encouraged Ted to create a plan of action to apply this newfound insight to attempt to improve the situation. Ted decided to address this issue directly with Frank and apologize for his oversight. He also decided to take steps to ensure that Frank was included in important communications in the future. This action alone did not resolve the friction completely, but it was a step in the right direction. Ted understood that he needed to continue to monitor the situation by checking in with Frank and making his own observations about their interactions. As he reflected on what was working and what was not, Ted continued to make adjustments in how he interacted with Frank.

This simple example illustrates the iterative nature of learning from insight. Clients reflect on their experiences, gain insight, and translate their insights into action plans that lead to new experiences. This process continues until clients achieve the desired outcome. In transformational coaching, the coaches guide their clients to establish this pattern of mining experiences for insights. As clients gain more facility at learning from their own experiences, coaches encourage their clients to tap into even deeper levels of insight to support larger and more complex outcomes.

Levels of Insight

Leading with Insight features four levels of insight: reflective, emotional, intuitive, and inspirational.

Reflective Insight

The first source of insight that clients work with is reflective insight: the ability to step back from an experience and notice what went well and what did not. The learning comes through translating insights into logical corrective actions, these actions then improve the outcomes of the next experience.

Nora came to her coaching call complaining that she was getting behind on her work. After some dialogue Nora and her coach identified Nora's difficulty in making decisions in a timely fashion as being a root cause for her situation. Considered a high potential employee, Nora had been moved from finance into an operations role to expand her leadership experience. Nora's coach asked her to reflect upon how she had made decisions in her previous role. Nora noted that she felt comfortable making decisions when she had the numbers in front of her. Nora's coach then asked if it was possible to get that level of detail in her new role and Nora conceded that it was not. There were too many gray areas to achieve that level of certainty. Nora's coach helped her to see that needing to have "all the data" was impeding her ability to manage effectively in a more fluid environment. Through their coaching dialogue Nora concluded that she needed be realistic about the data that she could get in a reasonable time frame and she needed to become more comfortable making decisions without all the detail. Armed with this new awareness, Nora can begin to experiment with making decisions more quickly. She will need to go through several iterations of making decisions and reflecting upon what information is essential versus what information is nice to have before she finds the approach that is right for her.

In order to be able to access reflective insight, clients need to step out of the fast lane and focus long enough to ask and answer questions that surface insight. As clients invest more time in coaching relationships, they naturally integrate the reflective process into their decision making and open the door to the next level of insight.

Emotional Insight

The next source of insight is emotional insight, which comes from the ability to detect and decipher the information received through emotions. Our emotions convey multiple levels of information, yet many people have tuned out this powerful source of insight and require some practice to bring it back online. When we tune into our emotions and the emotional context of our relationships, we start to notice underlying dynamics that greatly impact how we interact. Some people may be uncomfortable with or feel unprepared to deal with their own emotions and the emotional elements of their relationships. As a result, they develop habits of sidestepping or burying feelings rather than acknowledging that their feelings and the feelings of others are valid and play an essential role in forging strong, lasting professional relationships.

For example, in a weekly staff meeting, Joe made an off-hand remark about an idea being proposed by Sandra, another team member. Sandra left the staff meeting steaming about Joe's comment. After the meeting, Sandra spoke with her coach about the experience, and she was clearly still upset about the situation. Sandra's coach asked her what bothered her most about what had transpired. After a moment of reflection, Sandra conceded that it was not so much what Joe said, but the disparaging tone that was used that made her angry. Sandra acknowledged that she cared deeply about the project she was proposing and had been working on it intensively on her own for some time. Her coach asked her to reflect on what might cause Joe to want to derail or diminish the project. Through this conversation, Sandra realized that her project would impact Joe's area in some significant ways, and she had not invested much time or effort in cultivating Joe's support. She had a new perspective on what happened at the meeting and worked with her coach to role-play some different scenarios for conducting conversations to smooth out her relationship with Joe and begin to build support for the project.

By paying attention to her own feelings and reflecting on what transpired in the meeting, Sandra was able to see that she needed to take action. If Sandra had just decided to ignore the remark or lash out at Joe in the next meeting, she would likely have exacerbated the discord and could have jeopardized her project even further. Emotional insight provides valuable clues about underlying issues that can get in the way of realizing our aspirations.

Intuitive Insight

The third level of insight is intuitive. Intuition is the ability to detect dynamics and information that lie just below the surface of a situation. We use our intuition when we follow our hunches, detect patterns, and make decisions without having all of the information that we might like. As the complexity and speed of our world increases, intuition becomes an increasingly important component of our decision making. More and more, leaders are making choices based on an integration of logical, linear information and their best intuitive interpretation of a situation.

For example, on the surface, Linda's leadership team seemed to be moving forward with reorganizing the department. Few overt disagreements took place in team meetings and progress was being made, although it seemed to slow down as some of the bigger decisions needed to be made. Linda had a feeling that something was off, and she decided to talk with her coach about this in their next coaching session.

Linda's coach asked her to describe what she had noticed about how the team was working. Linda recounted that John and Ellen had become quiet, rarely participating fully in the team discussions, even when Linda invited their comments. They were both fairly quiet people, but this was more than just being quiet. Her coach asked her what her intuition suggested about this dynamic. Linda had a hunch that John and Ellen were withdrawing from the team because they felt threatened by the changes being made. Linda decided to have open conversations with all of her team members in their biweekly one-on-one meetings to better understand how her direct reports felt about the changes being made. Through these conversations, Linda learned that Ellen and John felt that they were getting railroaded by Linda and other team members into making changes that they believed were not always in the best interest of their people. As a result of these conversations, Linda was able to construct a more inclusive change management process, and she continued to monitor the team using tangible measures and intuitively observing on several levels how the team was working together.

Linda had some evidence that her team was not operating at top form, but her intuition, her sense that something was off, led her to dig deeper to better understand what was happening with her team.

The more leaders trust their own intuitive knowing, the sooner they are able to take action when situations are just beginning to derail, rather than waiting for a full-blown catastrophe.

Inspirational Insight

Intuition leads naturally to inspiration. Inspirational insight occurs when all the pieces come together and something is seen in an entirely new light. The person who has the inspiration experiences a kind of aha moment when a new possibility is realized. Intuition tends to show up in pieces, such as knowing that an approach isn't likely to work or someone is capable of something, even if they have never done it before. For some people inspirational insight shows up like a seed of an idea of that grows over time, for others it arrives more fully formed. However it happens, inspiration takes the leader in a new direction, expanding the leader and the organization in some material way.

Jeff was an executive with a large health care organization. Several experiences had plunged Jeff somewhat unexpectedly into the world of alternative medicine. His sister had been unable to find satisfactory traditional medical care for a chronic condition and had been successfully working with a homeopathic doctor to manage her health. At first, Jeff was somewhat uncomfortable with his sister's choice; however, as her condition improved, he became convinced of the benefit of this alternative form of care. At his coach's suggestion, Jeff began to practice yoga and meditation as a way of getting back into shape and helping to manage his stress. He was surprised at the benefits he received from these practices. Through conversations with people he met in his yoga class, he became aware of other healing methodologies with which he had no experience.

While taking a walk one day, Jeff was mulling these ideas over in his mind and found himself wondering about the possibility of adding an alternative care clinic to his health care organization. Jeff brought his idea into his coaching sessions and worked with his coach to create a path forward. He began to research different possibilities and began talking with some of his peers about what he was learning. It was a long row to hoe, but eventually Jeff built a coalition of supporters in his organization and the community. With guidance from his coach, Jeff used his experience to hone his leadership and influencing skills and move the project forward.

If someone had told Jeff before all of this happened that he would be championing an alternative health care clinic, he never would have believed them. Inspiration is often the culmination of insights gained from a wide variety of experiences. Inspirational insight creates a real step change for the leaders with the courage to put their ideas into action and the organizations in which they work.

The Action/Insight Connection

- *The key to deepening insight is action.* Action fuels insight. When clients take action, they have real data to learn from. Possibilities go from being hypothetical to real. The things that clients feared most are experienced and most likely found to be far less harrowing than anticipated. By taking action, clients learn what they are made of as they reach deeper into their bench of talents and capabilities to make things happen. Coaches encourage clients to reflect on their experiences, enabling them to see situations from new perspectives, uncover hidden obstacles, and increase their confidence in their abilities to use new capabilities and approaches.

- *Actions that lead to lasting change rest on a foundation of insight.* As clients take on increasingly complex initiatives, they require deeper levels of insight to support those actions. Someone who is focused on improving his productivity will not need to tap into the same depth of insight as someone who is turning a team around or championing a culture change initiative. The more wide-ranging an effort is, the more information needs to be synthesized to guide it to completion. The deeper levels of insight, intuitive, and inspirational, become increasingly important in ever-changing environments.

- *Taking action and evolving insight are inextricably connected.* The relationship between actions and insight is much like the system of roots, trunk, and branches of a tree. Insight is like the ever-deepening roots that nourish and support the tree. As the roots grow deeper into the ground, they create a solid foundation for the tree to grow. In order for the tree to grow in stature, it requires a deeper root system. So it is with action and insight. As clients desire to successfully take on greater challenges, they need to deepen the levels of insight to which they have access. Just as the trunk and the roots are constantly exchanging resources, in transformational coaching, clients are constantly gaining insight from their experiences and translating the insight they gain into more effective and complex actions. This exchange of insight and action forms the cornerstones of the Leading with Insight model of coaching.

- *The development of insight tends to come online in phases.* Continuing our analogy, insight develops in similar ways to the roots of a tree. Just as a tree's roots start out close to the surface and grow deeper and more complex as the demands from the tree above increase, so it is with insight. When clients enter into coaching relationships with coaches who use a transformational model, they initially focus, at least in part, on improving their personal effectiveness. The coaches will encourage their clients to reflect on their experiences in order to gain insight into what is going well and what could be improved, and in doing so, instill in their clients the ability to draw on reflective insight.

  Most clients move quickly into enhancing their interpersonal relationships in some way; perhaps they need to communicate more effectively with their employees or smooth out their relationships with their peers. Whatever the impetus, coaches will encourage clients who are focused on improving interpersonal relationships to expand their insight to include gaining insight from the emotional context of these relationships. Clients who hold responsibilities that include groups, teams, or working with networks of people in some way often find that as they gain facility at tuning into and dealing with the emotional dynamics of situations, they have more intuitive information available to them than they had previously noticed. The demands of these more complex situations provide the fodder for deepening intuitive insight, as clients find that it is not possible to have complete information all of the time and work at the pace that most environments demand. The jump to inspirational insight is often just a matter of having the courage to act on intuitive insights that expand the client and the client's organization in a new direction. As the complexity of experiences increases, the roots of insight grow deeper and wider.

- *Each level of insight supports the next.* Reflection is an integral part of emotional insight, just as emotional insight is an essential component of intuitive insight, and inspiration is a more evolved form of intuition. Each level of insight forms a foundation for the next. As insight deepens, clients will not differentiate between one level and another. Just as a tree uses all of its roots, clients will tend to use all of their insight once they have access to it.

The Leading with Insight Model

The Leading with Insight model is a developmental model of coaching that delivers transformational change for individuals and organizations. It looks at coaching from the perspective of the client's experience and focuses on the personal development that underlies the coaching relationship. The Leading with Insight model is designed to serve as a foundational roadmap for transformational coaching. On the surface, each coaching engagement looks different. One client may be working on transitioning from being a manager to taking on a leadership role, while another is focused on expanding his leadership style to incorporate a more collaborative approach to working with others. The Leading with Insight model shows how personal development is connected to increasingly deeper levels of insight and how together they support increasingly more complex levels of change for clients. The Leading with Insight model illuminates the developmental work that happens below the surface of transformational coaching engagements and, in doing so, helps us to better understand some of the elements that make coaching such a powerful personal development process.

Let's turn our attention to the Leading with Insight model that is presented in Figure 2.1. The Leading with Insight model has four quadrants. Each quadrant explores a deeper level of client development and supports the realization of increasingly complex coaching goals. The four quadrants are:

Quadrant 1: Finding Focus
This first quadrant focuses on personal effectiveness and enabling clients to find their focus and get physically centered.

Quadrant 2: Building Bridges
This quadrant supports clients in enhancing the effectiveness of interpersonal relationships through the development of emotional insight.

Quadrant 3: Creating Alignment
In this quadrant clients focus on achieving goals involving teams, groups and organizations supported by the development of their intuitive insight.

Quadrant 4: Original Action
In this quadrant clients are inspired to achieve goals they may not even have imagined when they first began their coaching work.

Most clients enter coaching through Quadrant 1. The development in each quadrant serves as the foundation for the next. Not all clients will progress through all of the quadrants. The factors that impact how far a client progresses through the four quadrants are discussed at the end of this chapter.

This chapter provides an overview of the Leading with Insight model, illustrated through a case study. The remaining chapters in

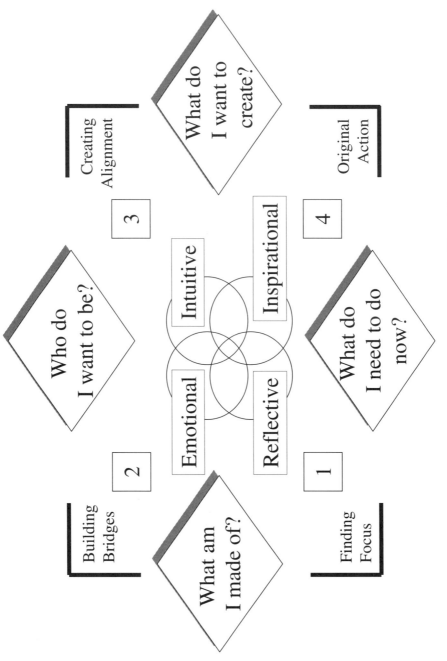

Figure 2.1 The Leading with Insight™ model.

this section explore each of the quadrants of the model in greater detail and provide approaches for working with the concepts that are introduced.

Essential Questions

The coaching process is guided by the questions that clients ask and answer about themselves. While coaching clients are focused on realizing the goals they set for themselves, they are simultaneously exploring their own inner makeup and choosing who and what they want to become. Four essential questions anchor the coaching process from the clients' point of view. Clients enter into the coaching process asking "**What do I need to do now?**" This practical question helps clients identify the gap between where they are right now and where they want or need to be to realize their aspirations. As coaching progresses, clients are challenged to discover and put into action elements of themselves that are not part of their regular lineup of responses. Through their expanding interactions with others, they begin to explore the question "**What am I made of?**" Clients who stick with coaching will eventually be faced with the question "**Who do I want to be?**" as they choose to bring how they work into alignment with their own values. The clients who continue their personal development consider the question "**What do I want to create?**" Answering this question enables the leaders to explore how to leverage their considerable capabilities for value creation.

While the asking and answering of these essential questions may not occur explicitly in all coaching engagements, the exploration of these themes is a strong current that flows beneath the surface of transformational coaching work.

Quadrant 1: Finding Focus

We will explore each of the Leading with Insight quadrants by following the progress of Donna, the director in charge of a 40-person IT services department. Considered a high-potential manager,

Donna was offered the opportunity to work with an executive coach as part of a leadership development initiative within her organization. Her primary goal was to improve the client satisfaction scores for her IT services department, and in the process to begin to make the transition from solid manager to leader.

Donna was a consistent overachiever who drove herself hard to attain her goals and expected her people to do the same. Donna's coach suggested conducting a series of multirater feedback interviews to gain insight into Donna's management style, strengths, and developmental opportunities. Some of the themes that showed up in the feedback interviews were surprising to Donna. She learned that although her people respected her intelligence, integrity, and drive to achieve, many resented the unrealistic expectations Donna set for them and her persistent habit of taking over their work if she felt that it was going to deviate from what she wanted. Many of her colleagues and coworkers stated that Donna could become impatient when the pressure was high. It was clear to Donna and her coach that Donna would need to focus on developing a more collaborative style of leadership to lead her team to the next level.

Donna's coach suggested that a good place to begin their coaching work was to examine some of the patterns in Donna's personal habits that led her to be short or impatient with others. Donna's coach asked her to notice what she did during the day that contributed to her sense of impatience. Upon reflection, Donna noted that she tended to overbook her schedule so that she was constantly running behind. She also noticed that she was a chronic multitasker. As a result, she often felt like her attention was fractured, and small annoyances could cause her to snap.

Armed with this awareness, Donna made some small but significant changes in her personal management, including managing her schedule more tightly so that she could focus on what she was doing and get work done between meetings. She also became more attuned to when she was becoming impatient and started to implement approaches suggested by her coach to calm herself down before she got to the snapping point. Within six weeks of working with her coach, Donna was feeling much more in control of her life.

Key Themes of Quadrant 1

- *Quadrant 1 is the space for enhancing personal effectiveness.* Personal effectiveness is the ability to make and execute good choices regarding the management and focus of one's time and energy. Quadrant 1 lays the foundation for the Leading with Insight model. Donna had set much more aggressive coaching goals for herself than just improving her personal effectiveness, but she needed to create a stronger focus for her time and energy as a foundation for achieving her goals. As long as Donna is racing around at breakneck speed, she will derive little value from coaching and will not be able to progress her coaching work effectively to the other quadrants.

- *Reflective insight is enhanced in Quadrant 1.* As clients enter into coaching, one of the most effective tools for opening the client to both the need for and the possibility of change is awareness. Until Donna's coach asked her to notice the things that contributed to her stress, Donna was unaware of how her habits of multitasking and overscheduling were affecting her and her team. By reflecting on her choices, Donna became motivated to take new approaches to organizing her time and getting her work done. Quadrant 1 illuminates the habits that are not working and works on finding more effective solutions.

- *Physical centeredness opens the door to Quadrant 2.* In order to move to Quadrant 2, clients must be able to calm their minds and bodies from time to time in order to be able to reflect and make choices. Without this fundamental piece of personal development, clients will not find their focus and will not be able to progress their development any further. Let's return to Donna and see how being more focused and physically centered has affected her and her team.

Quadrant 2: Building Bridges

After six weeks of coaching, Donna's direct reports began to comment to Donna that she seemed different. Most could not quite put their fingers on the change, but they used phrases such as "more relaxed" and "less intense." Donna was pleased about this reaction and eager to continue her progress. As an overachiever, she wanted to be a "great coaching client."

As Donna's stress level started to recede, she became more aware of her tendency to take over parts of her staff's projects whenever she felt that a deadline was at risk. Donna recognized that this pattern was causing her to feel overwhelmed at times and it was preventing her people from learning how to deal with the challenges of meeting deadlines. Donna noted that it was easier for her to take over for others than it was to enter into the sometimes emotionally charged conversations that are part and parcel of holding people accountable for their deliverables.

With the help of her coach, Donna began to explore how to read her own emotional reactions and recognize the emotions of others, as she experimented with new ways of negotiating with her staff for deadlines and holding them accountable for the results that were agreed on. Not everything went smoothly, but eventually, Donna's staff started stepping up to the plate and delivering their work more consistently on time. Donna found that the shift from taking over her managers' work to coaching them to successfully take on new challenges had rewards that she had not anticipated for herself and her team. There was less finger pointing and fewer fiery flare ups.

It took about two months and lots of reinforcement for Donna to feel more at ease with stepping into difficult conversations. Over that time, she explored these and other concepts in a variety of settings and was really starting to appreciate that she had evolved an effective and authentic communications style that was truly her own.

Key Themes of Quadrant 2

- *Quadrant 2 is the space for enhancing interpersonal effectiveness.* Clients focus on broadening and deepening their abilities to interact authentically and effectively with others in one-on-one relationships. For some clients, this means addressing difficult interactions with peers, for others it can involve developing stronger ties with key constituents in their network of influence, and still others may need to address their ability to effectively manage others. Donna had to learn to hold her managers accountable for their deliverables instead of taking over their assignments. Although coaching situations are diverse, the central themes are often similar: helping clients become clear on the essence of what they want to communicate, guiding clients to articulate clearly what they want to create through their communications, and working on crafting a unique and effective communications style for the client.

- *Emotional insight is enhanced in Quadrant 2.* The main source of insight for Quadrant 2 is the insight that comes from learning to discern and decipher one's own emotions and the emotional context of situations. At her coach's request, Donna started to tune into her own emotional reactions when dealing with her managers. When she was centered, Donna began to notice the telltale signs that she was becoming anxious about her managers' abilities to meet a deadline. Rather than take her usual step of doing the work for them, Donna began to discuss her concerns with her managers in order to find workable solutions. This led to the team deciding to implement an update system that allowed everyone to know where they were in terms of meeting deadlines. Donna now regularly tunes into her emotions to gain valuable information for guiding her interactions with her team.

- *Emotional centeredness opens the door to Quadrant 3.* Emotional centeredness is the ability to tune into one's own emotions and the emotional context of situations in order to derive valuable information that is used to move the situation forward and deepen relationships. People who are emotionally centered are able to participate in emotionally charged situations without being taken over by their own emotions or the emotions of others. The physical centeredness of Quadrant 1 is the foundation on which emotional centeredness is built. Donna found that by calming down and tuning in, she was able to find successful ways to engage in conversations she had previously avoided. As a result of this change, Donna's leadership style was becoming more collaborative. This was new for Donna, and she was enjoying the change. With this success under her belt, Donna felt ready to tackle some of the bigger challenges she had set for herself.

Quadrant 3: Creating Alignment

Although the IT services department was organized into client service teams, most of the representatives for the various services tended to work independently, rarely interacting with the other representatives on their client team except for updates and reports. Donna believed that if the client facing teams were to work more effectively together to understand and meet the needs of the clients, it would be a win for everyone involved. This would entail a huge shift in outlook as well as in working arrangements for the entire department. Donna was not sure where to start. In the past, Donna more or less presented her ideas to her managers and expected them to toe the line and get it done. Her gut instinct told her that this approach would not work in this case, however, and would erode the gains she had made to become a more collaborative leader.

Donna decided to bring her idea into a coaching conversation. Donna's coach asked her to intuitively think how she wanted to approach this change. After some reflection, Donna noted that her own management team functioned more as a collection of individuals than as a team. Donna engaged her team members in dialogue about what it really meant to be a team and, based on the recommendations that surfaced, the team chartered a new course for itself. The changes that ensued created stronger ties within Donna's management team and was naturally carried by the managers into their own teams.

The change process was not always smooth sailing, but Donna's coach encouraged her to look at the underlying dynamics of team interactions when the team ran into difficulties. With practice, Donna gained confidence in her intuitive ability to detect and surface unspoken concerns for the team to address directly. It was a little unnerving for Donna at times, but she could see that her team was really blossoming with this new approach.

Key Themes of Quadrant 3

- *Quadrant 3 is the space for enhancing group and team effectiveness.* The work in Quadrant 3 revolves around discerning how to interact effectively and assume a leadership role in complex situations, such as groups, teams, or even networks. Clients may focus on launching new initiatives, influencing an organization in some way, or taking a new approach with an existing department, as Donna did. There is often a component of gaining greater clarity regarding the alignment of one's values and the focus of one's work. Leadership styles are expanded, and clients become clearer on what needs to shift or change to create better alignment between who they are and how they work.
- *Intuitive insight is enhanced in Quadrant 3.* Quadrant 3 affords clients the opportunity to tap more deeply into their own intuitive knowing. As the environment in which a client operates becomes more complex, intuition becomes an important navigational instrument. Guided by her coach, Donna gained confidence in her intuitive insights and used these insights to smooth out the path forward for her emerging team. Donna did not rely on intuition alone, but rather, integrated her intuitive insights with her linear observations to make the best choices she could in any given situation.
- *Intuitive centeredness opens the door to Quadrant 4.* A person who is intuitively centered trusts her intuitive insights and easily integrates those insights with concrete, logical information. Leaders who tend to overthink or overanalyze and have

difficulty moving forward have not learned how to use this rich resource to guide their decision making. The fullness of the insight that Donna had already established through her work in Quadrants 1 and 2 served as a solid foundation for her developing intuitive centeredness. When Donna was able to be calm and tuned into her own experience, she noticed things that she previously would have overlooked. The richness of this information helped Donna pick up on dynamics that were impeding the progress of her team. As Donna experienced more success guiding the team in this new way, she found that she was seeing opportunities for the department to develop that she had not previously noticed.

Quadrant 4: Original Action

Donna continued to be delighted and amazed at how her team was finding new ways to learn more about their clients and find innovative solutions to meet the clients' demands. Most of her managers had shown a great deal of initiative infusing their own teams with a new spirit of teamwork. As Donna reflected on the changes that the department had made, it occurred to her that her organization primarily waited for clients to make a request or file a complaint before taking action. Although they had become much more effective and creative in responding to clients' needs, little or no proactive effort was being made to work directly with their clients to prevent issues from occurring in the first place. Reaching out and working directly with the client teams represented a major change in thinking and approach not only for the department, but also for the company as a whole.

Donna had never been one to deliberately stick her neck out too far. She preferred to stay safely inside the box of clearly set expectations and deliver on those as quickly as possible. Donna knew that leadership meant taking risks, and this was one risk that she felt strongly was worth taking. Working with her coach, Donna began to crystallize her thinking around creating proactive service teams.

As she engaged her managers in conversations to explore this idea further, she received a wide range of reactions. She found herself using every level of insight as she listened carefully to her managers' hopes and concerns. Her coach encouraged her to take a much broader organizational view and begin to discern the kind of support that Donna would need to bring her idea to life. Influencing this complex network would put her leadership skills to the test. Although she was not sure how it would turn out, Donna felt ready for the challenge.

Key Themes of Quadrant 4

- *Quadrant 4 is the space of inspired leadership.* The foundation of personal and professional development in the previous three quadrants lays the foundation for the inspirational leadership that occurs in Quadrant 4. In this quadrant leaders experience inspirational insight—a knowing that something new or different is possible. Quadrant 4 is the place of step change, where new possibilities are recognized and attained. Clients typically evolve into this space, drawn forward by an intense curiosity to really experience their own potential and compelled to bring into form the possibilities that are taking shape in their mind's eye. Donna faced many challenges as she worked to create these new teams, and those challenges honed her into the leader she had hoped to be when she started her coaching journey.

- *Inspirational insight is enhanced in Quadrant 4.* Inspiration illuminates this quadrant. While working in this quadrant, clients may identify new markets to serve, imagine new products to produce, or articulate innovative approaches for cultivating leadership in the organization. The outcomes are as varied as the people who originate them. Although inspiration can occur on any scale, this quadrant holds the most potential for affecting entire organizations and systems.

- *Coaching is the path to personal power.* The promise of the Leading with Insight model is personal power. Clients who attain personal power rest easily in their own skin, confident that they possess an incredible depth of capabilities and have the insight to focus their energy to make things happen. There is generally a quiet ease and playful strength about these people that naturally inspires others to expand their own horizons. We need more of these people in our organizations and in the world.

Key Concepts for the Leading with Insight Model

As we walk through the four quadrants of the Leading with Insight model in more detail in the next four chapters, it is important to keep the following key concepts in mind:

- *Relatively few clients engage in the full spectrum of development described by the model.* For several reasons, clients choose to complete their coaching work at different stages in the model. Some coaching engagements are cut off after a set period of time, precluding clients from working their way through the model. Clients may not be interested in developing their insight or taking action beyond a certain level or may meet their coaching goals without the development attained in later quadrants. Other clients may attain a certain level of development and then take a break from coaching to consolidate their gains before returning to coaching at a later date, when they face a new challenge.

    Not all coaches have the capability to coach clients through all four quadrants. In order for a coach to guide a client to realize deeper levels of insight, the coach must have done the personal development work to access his own intuition and inspiration. As a result, some clients experiences are limited by the capabilities of the coaches they are working with.
- *The development that is described by this model is woven into the fabric of coaching relationships.* The coaching that supports the Leading with Insight model is accomplished on multiple

levels simultaneously. A coach who is skilled in transformational coaching will consistently encourage clients to access deeper levels of insight, often without the clients realizing that this is happening. It is not necessary for clients to be aware of this full range of development in order to benefit from it. Coaches earn the right to guide their clients through this developmental process by demonstrating repeatedly that they are individuals of integrity and insight who can be trusted to do this work.

- *Every client experiences the Leading with Insight model differently.* Coaching is, after all, a personalized development process that engages every client in a unique way. Some clients enter into coaching having done a fair amount of personal development already and may breeze through the first quadrant (and sometimes the second). Most clients will be receiving coaching in more than one quadrant at a time, perhaps still working to gain control of their schedules (Quadrant 1) while ironing out roles and responsibilities with coworkers (Quadrant 2). Clients who work in Quadrants 3 and 4 may cycle back through Quadrants 1 and 2 to deepen their learning, especially when they take on new challenges such as a promotion or a new stretch opportunity. They will work to shore up their ability to stay centered and focused when the heat gets turned up to a higher degree than they have experienced before.

3

Quadrant 1: Finding Focus

Quadrant 1 is the place where coaching engagements typically begin. In this space clients focus predominantly on making tactical improvements to enhance their personal effectiveness, and create the foundation for incorporating reflective insight into their lives. For some clients, Quadrant 1 will be the main body of their coaching work. For others, it will provide a solid base that opens the door to the deeper learning of the other quadrants. The following case study illustrates the dynamics of coaching work in the first quadrant.

Case Study: Jane Gets Her Life Back

Jane was an HR manager in a large medical supply company. She had held this role for several years, and generally enjoyed working with her clients to resolve their various HR issues. Lately, though, it seemed that her world was spinning out of control. A recent merger had greatly increased the complexity and urgency of the work that was being demanded of her. Jane's boss was becoming concerned that Jane seemed overwhelmed and generally unhappy. Her boss suggested that Jane consider working with a coach to help her successfully deal with the challenges of the merger environment.

Jane interviewed two coaches and chose to work with Amanda. Initially, Amanda observed that Jane was:

- Chronically overbooking herself, often double-scheduling meetings
- Frequently working late to "get things done" because there was not enough time between all of her meetings to accomplish anything
- Having difficulty saying "no" to any request, and generally perceived her role as one of "making everyone happy," which they rarely were
- Often so stressed that she was having trouble concentrating
- Occasionally short with people who happened to speak with her when she was feeling overwhelmed

When Amanda asked Jane what she wanted to accomplish through coaching, Jane wanted to find a way to serve the needs of her clients without feeling constantly overwhelmed. After an extensive onboarding process, Amanda and Jane outlined coaching goals that included helping Jane better manage her stress levels, focus her work on the top HR priorities of the client, and find more innovative ways to meet her clients' needs.

Initially, Jane found it difficult to find time to even speak with Amanda, but she knew that her boss was expecting to hear about her progress, so she managed to squeeze in some time for her coaching conversations. The first area that Amanda focused on was helping Jane to clear some time in her schedule for her coaching work. Together, they found ways for Jane to carve out some time on her calendar, and Amanda was able to help Jane see that focusing on personal management would provide benefits for her and her clients.

The first coaching conversations focused on helping Jane to get clear on what was most important for her personally and professionally. Through these conversations, Jane became aware of just how much her job had changed with the merger. Jane had responded to the new demands by piling them on top of the old ones, rather than stepping back and reflecting on what was most important to accomplish. Amanda coached Jane to clarify with her boss what his expectations were in this new environment. They agreed that getting her clients through the merger process was the top priority, and they discussed in greater detail what that constituted. Although there was still a tremendous amount of work to do, Jane felt relieved that her boss understood her predicament and would back her up on reducing the level of service that she was providing to some of her clients. Personally, Jane wanted to be able to catch her breath from time to time and to create some separation between work and her family life.

In her coaching conversations, Jane reported that she often felt overwhelmed by the demands of her clients and found herself trying to do several things at once and getting little accomplished. One of the first areas that Jane needed to address was remaining more balanced and composed throughout the day. During a coaching session, Amanda asked Jane to use reflective insight to identify the physical sensations she felt that indicated her stress level was rising. Jane noted, among other things, that she tended to feel more uptight and she had a harder time focusing. Amanda assigned Jane the task of noticing during the week the various things that contributed to Jane's stress level. At her next coaching session, Jane reported back that her schedule was so tightly booked that she was constantly rushing to meetings and rarely took time to eat. Instead, Jane fueled her day with candy and sodas that left her feeling strung out. Through conversation, Amanda and Jane were able to identify a pattern of escalating stress. Amanda coached Jane on establishing practices that allowed Jane more breathing space in her day, such as leaving time between meetings and scheduling a lunch break. She also taught Jane some simple techniques for centering her energy when she noticed that she was becoming increasingly stressed. These changes made a huge difference for Jane, and she began to feel as if she was gaining some control over her life again. Jane found that she was able to get more done in a shorter period and that she was making better decisions because she wasn't as frazzled as she had been before coaching. With this success under her belt, Jane began to look at how she prioritized her time.

Again, practicing reflective insight, Jane noticed that she tended to accept any request that her clients made of her, even if the work was not within her purview. Jane decided that, based on her priorities, she would need to reduce or eliminate her commitments to some activities. Jane was deeply concerned about how others would respond to this change. She worked with Amanda to find diplomatic and direct language to set clear boundaries with her clients. She was pleasantly surprised that, for the most part, her clients understood her need to focus her efforts during this hectic time. Her plate was still very full, but Jane felt as if she could breathe again. Better yet, she could finally see that she was making progress in helping her clients move more smoothly through the merger process, and that achievement gave her a sense of satisfaction that had been missing for some time now.

Answering the "What Do I Need to Do?" Question

Everyone who enters into coaching has to grapple with some variation of the question "What do I need to do?" To become a coaching client, a person has to have the desire to further his or her personal and/or professional development in some way and must have the willingness to make the necessary changes to realize development goals. Asking this question, or some variation of it, initiates the coaching engagement and opens the door into the coaching space.

Sometimes clients answer the "What do I need to do?" question with a list of outcomes designed to alleviate symptoms that are plaguing the person. Joe may feel that he is not getting enough done with his time, so he wants to become more organized, or Patty realizes that her relationship with her team members is a little rocky, and she wants to improve her ability to work effectively in a team environment. In these cases, it is the coaches' role to help clients uncover and address the root causes for these problems. Some clients are uncertain what they need to focus on. They may have a sense that something needs to be changed to improve their effectiveness, address feelings of being overwhelmed, or rekindle their enthusiasm for their work, but they are uncertain as to what that *something* may be. In these cases, the first work of the coaching relationship is often to explore this question "What do I need to do?" in greater depth to gain an understanding of the path coaching will take.

Making Space for Change

Quadrant 1 focuses on personal effectiveness, the ability to make good choices regarding the management and focus of time and energy. The coaching outcomes in this quadrant are most typically tactical improvements in personal management. Clients prioritize their time more effectively, they clean up and clear out old projects and old habits that are getting in their way, and they begin to bring their personal and professional lives back into some kind of dynamic equilibrium.

Examples of Quadrant 1 coaching goals include the following:

- Become more organized
- Prioritize appropriately
- Manage stress
- Set clear personal goals
- Attain goals on time
- Create a stronger professional presence
- Become centered

Clients who will work predominantly in Quadrant 1 tend to enter coaching feeling unorganized, overwhelmed, stressed, and/or unfocused. Regardless of the symptoms they are describing, there is a fundamental need to address some old habits of thinking and getting work done that have probably been successful in the past, but are now impeding the person's abilities to function at the level required to be satisfied and successful in the current position. Both satisfaction and success are important. One of the more common habits that coaches see is the tendency for clients to throw themselves completely into their work until they accomplish their goals. This approach often enables people to be successful, but as their success is rewarded with more and more responsibility, they find themselves working harder and harder, and they eventually burn out; they are increasingly successful but with lower levels of personal satisfaction. The first quadrant is the space where clients bring their personal work habits back into alignment with what matters most to them.

Quadrant 1 Touchstones

Each quadrant has four touchstones, which are areas of development that all clients will need to have a minimum level of facility with in order to move on to the next quadrant. These building blocks open the door to deeper levels of insight. The touchstones in a particular quadrant reflect the core learning that underlies the great variety of tangible outcomes that are achieved in that quadrant. Together, the touchstones in each quadrant serve as a foundation for the development in the next quadrant. Quadrant 1 touchstones are introduced as follows, including references to how these touchstones play out in the case study:

1. Commit to change
2. Cultivate the ability to stay calm
3. Get clear on what matters most
4. Create a positive energy balance

1. *Commit to change.* Making significant personal and professional changes is hard work. A client can't just think about doing things differently, she has to put in the effort to actually make the changes. It isn't always easy. Clients may have to feel a sufficient level of pain to be willing to take the time and energy needed to really look at how they are operating and

choose a new approach. Even after Jane signed up to work with Amanda, she was still so caught up in the relentless rhythm of her work that she found it difficult to find the time to talk with her coach. Amanda had to make the point to Jane several times that by taking time out to reflect on her situation, Jane was empowering herself to work more effectively and efficiently. Jane quickly realized that the changes she was making were significantly improving the quality of her work and helping her reduce some of the stress in her life. This outcome deepened Jane's commitment to continue coaching.

The commitment has to be personal because coaching is personal. To realize the greatest benefit from coaching, clients have to be willing to see the world from new perspectives, let go of old habits, and interact with others in new ways. Jane needed to personally feel value from coaching to commit herself fully to the process.

2. *Cultivate the ability to stay calm.* Many people now live and work at breakneck speed, with little time to stop for even a moment. It is not uncommon for people to fuel their nonstop lifestyles with adrenaline. They get this potent stimulant in many forms, including caffeinated beverages, overscheduling, underestimating time requirements for projects, driving too fast—you name it. People are creative about how they keep their systems pumped up so they can keep going and going. A person who is in this kind of perpetual motion is not available to make meaningful change and will probably not derive much value from a coaching relationship. Clients have to be able to calm down, at least periodically, in order to engage in the personal reflection required for transformational coaching.

One of the first areas on which Amanda worked with Jane was helping her to notice what habits contributed to her high levels of stress. At Amanda's urging, Jane reflected on the choices she made every day that contributed to her feeling overwhelmed. Among other things, Jane noted that she scheduled herself into so many meetings that she did not leave any time in her day to get her work done, she tended to say "yes" to almost every request made of her, and she was consuming a significant amount of caffeine during the day. Once she became aware of this pattern and what it was costing her, she realized that she needed to make some changes.

Amanda guided Jane to experiment with some different tools and approaches that allowed Jane to calm down and find her center, that quiet place within where she is tuned into what is going on around her. Jane found that the combination of taking a walk before work in the morning and some simple breathing techniques she used when she felt her stress levels escalating helped her be much calmer and respond to events with more flexibility and patience. This was a huge change for Jane, which allowed her to make better decisions, communicate more clearly, and focus on important tasks.

3. *Get clear on what matters most.* Clients who work predominantly in Quadrant 1 may have lost touch with or may need to reevaluate what is important for them, both personally and professionally. They may have become so overwhelmed with their responsibilities that they just do not have the time to reflect on their changing priorities or they may know what matters most for them, but they are not sure how to realign their activities to reflect their choices.

   At this point, the coach is not discussing deeply held values or life purpose. Those bigger holistic conversations will come later when clients have sufficient access to their own insight to discern their own inner guideposts. Initially, the client needs to define what success will look like, both personally and professionally, within a time horizon that is typically the length of the expected coaching engagement. These time frames seem tangible for most clients, and thus goals that are set within those time frames will seem plausible. Occasionally, clients enter coaching with a long-range goal established. In that case, the coach will help the client define the steps that need to be taken to achieve that goal in the time frame that is available.

The coach and client will need to spend some time establishing what the client needs to deliver to be successful professionally. This is particularly important for clients who have recently been promoted and need to make some significant shifts in their priorities. Even though coaching takes place in a professional setting, there needs to be a conversation about what is important to the client personally. The work in this first quadrant involves making choices about how to use the precious resources of time and personal energy. A clear articulation of what is important is essential as a guide for making these important decisions.

4. *Create a positive energy balance.* It is amazing how easily we give away our time and energy. We say "yes" to commitments because we think that we *should* do these things or we *have to* without really thinking through whether the effort will be worth the expected return. If we equated our personal energy to money, many of us are in serious energy debt, which takes the form of stress, exhaustion, and illness. In the same way that we learn how to budget money to meet our needs, we also need to learn to expend our energy on initiatives that add value. One of the lessons of Quadrant 1 is accepting responsibility for using time and energy well. Just like a financial balance sheet, there are two sides to this equation. There is the energy creation side, where clients focus on managing their lives so they have energy to expend, and there is the expenditure side, where clients make choices about what to invest their energy in to create the greatest return for themselves and the companies for which they work.

   Jane was feeling overwhelmed as a result of being out of balance energetically. Jane was pouring more time and energy into her work than she had to give. As a result of working such long hours, not taking care of herself, and not feeling like she was accomplishing her goals, Jane was becoming increasingly worn down. It was as if at the end of the day, she had less and less energy left in her personal energy bank account. Most of the things Jane enjoyed in her life or that contributed to her well-being had been eliminated so that she could work longer hours. Jane was not replenishing her energy supply, so she was using adrenaline, in the form of caffeine, overscheduling, and rushing around to make up the difference. Jane was living in energy debt. One of the first areas Amanda focused on with Jane was helping her to see this dynamic of being chronically out of balance and how it was detrimental to Jane's well-being and her ability to meet her goals.

It is important to note that just like a bank account, one's personal energy balance will fluctuate. There are times when a client may "borrow energy" to get a big project done or create a healthy surplus by taking a vacation. The key is not to live in perpetual energy debt. Just like financial debt, energy debt reduces the choices that a client can make, erodes self-confidence, and can lead to serious problems in the client's professional and private life. It takes energy to make change. Clients need to create a positive energy balance to derive significant benefits from coaching.

The Essential Outcome of Quadrant 1: Physical Centeredness

The touchstones in Quadrant 1 work together to form the foundation for experiencing physical centeredness. Physical centeredness is the ability to stay calm and focused even when the world around you is not. As Amanda helped Jane recognize and shift habits and patterns that no longer worked for her, Jane naturally found herself becoming calmer and more focused. This quieter presence paid dividends in many ways, including increasing Jane's ability to get more done in less time, enabling Jane to make clearer choices, and making Jane more approachable for her clients. It is not necessary to be in this centered place all of the time, but it is essential for a client to have cultivated the ability to create this space from time to time in order to progress into Quadrant 2 coaching work.

People who are running around constantly reacting to the latest crisis (and creating more crises as they clash with others) can wreak havoc in a workplace. There is a huge price to be paid in organizations when workers do not take responsibility for how they manage themselves. It is like a basketball game in which none of the players has enough control over his body to keep from knocking the other players. You can't pass and execute a play, or plan a strategy if you can't control the ball. The development in Quadrant 1 is analogous to getting your own game under control so that you can gain access to more of your talent. This is an essential platform for playing a bigger game.

Coaching Tools and Approaches for Quadrant 1

This book is not intended to teach specific coaching skills, but rather, to guide coaches to apply their skills in particular ways that enhance the value delivered to the client and the organization. Every quadrant of the Leading with Insight model holds different challenges for the coach. In Quadrant 1, the main challenges are establishing a solid foundation for coaching, guiding the client to engage fully in the coaching process, and shepherding the client through potential rough spots. The following are strategies for coaches to consider integrating into their Quadrant 1 coaching engagements:

- *Get the whole story.* Every coach has her own way of gathering background information on a client, some more extensively than others. The choices that are made tend to reflect the background and training of the coach. A few things are essential to know about a client in order to coach the person from the strongest vantage point. The coach needs insight into the following areas:
  - *The culture and current business challenges the client's company faces.* Some sources to look at for this information include the company Web site, news articles, annual reports, and asking the client. Before meeting with Jane, Amanda

did a literature search on her company and read some of the latest articles that had been printed about the merger and the challenges that this move was creating for the new organization. She also spoke to Jane's manager to get a feeling for the priorities of the HR department in facilitating the smooth transition to one new company.

- *The role and responsibilities of the client and how that role contributes strategically to the overall organization.* One of the key insights that Amanda made while inquiring about Jane's role and responsibilities was the fact that the merger changed the whole focus of Jane's role in some significant ways, but Jane had not fully recognized how extensively she needed to change the focus of her work in order to fulfill the new expectations.

- *The network of relationships that the client works within and what state those relationships are in.* Amanda had Jane draw a diagram of her most important business relationships and highlight for Amanda which ones were strategically and politically most important. Jane also shared with Amanda her perception of which of those relationships were on solid ground and which ones needed some more care and attention. Given the merger environment, Jane's network of influence had expanded considerably, and Amanda could readily see that Jane could benefit from developing deeper business relationships with several key influencers.

- *The client's work and, possibly, personal history.* The story of the client's life will tell the coach many things about the client, including what is going on in his professional (and possibly personal) life, what he excels at, what frustrates him, what he wants for himself, what bores him, and what he finds challenging—to name a few things. This in-depth understanding of the client enables the coach to see patterns of behavior, gain insight into the client's strengths and development opportunities, and help the client see how coaching can further his development.

- *Current challenges the client faces.* The client's story naturally leads into a discussion of what is currently going well for the client and where he wants to make changes. Clients often describe symptoms of problems, and it is the coach's role to look beyond the presenting symptoms and identify the patterns of behaviors that support them.
- *Set clear, progressive developmental goals.* The written goals for the coaching engagement lay the path that the client will follow as she progresses toward the attainment of her aspirations. The goals need to be clear and sufficiently descriptive that the client will recognize when she has attained the goals and will be able to support the assertion that the goals have been attained with anecdotal evidence, if more tangible results are not appropriate.

Goal setting needs to be done in the context of the stated goals for the coaching initiative. If the overarching organizational goal is to create a pipeline of future leaders, then the coaching goals for individual coaching participants need to reflect the individuals' development needs in terms of the organization's required leadership capabilities. Assessments can be helpful to determine areas in which development is needed. It is important to choose assessment instruments that offer real insight into the development needed by the individual, as well as to reach the organization's stated goals. Coaches should not rely on formal assessments alone to set goals; they should also include their own observations and insights from listening to the client's story and probing the client to gain an understanding of what the client *really* wants to achieve.

The Leading with Insight quadrant model can be used as a guide for breaking down the more global goals of a coaching engagement into clear, actionable, developmental steps that lead to the attainment of the larger goals. The coach will be able to determine in which quadrant the outcomes the client is driving for will reside. For example, a client whose main focus is improving her personal interactions with her colleagues will be focused in Quadrant 2, whereas a client who faces the challenge of building a new corporate university will continue his coaching work into Quadrant 3. The touchstones in each quadrant provide a guide for the coach and the client in terms of discerning the underlying development that will be necessary to attain the desired goals. The following is an example of one of Jane's coaching goals that reflects the development she will focus on in Quadrant 1:

Coaching will enable Jane to focus her efforts on achieving her highest priorities by guiding her to:

- Develop strategies for dealing with stress, including gaining awareness of her own stress levels, and incorporating techniques to maintain her sense of balance when she becomes stressed
- Identify her highest priorities, including expected outcomes
- Manage her time in alignment with her priorities, including reducing or eliminating low-priority commitments, time blocking, and increased delegation

Notice that the touchstones in Quadrant 1 are reflected in the detail of how the goal will be achieved. If Jane found that she was not making satisfactory progress toward achieving her top priorities, she could review the detail of the goal description to see which of the touchstones needs more attention.

- *Recognize patterns of behavior.* In Quadrant 1, clients work on cleaning up old habits and shifting patterns of behavior that no longer serve them. It is the coaches' responsibility to connect the dots and help clients to see how they unconsciously repeat the same pattern or take the same approach, even when it is clearly not working. In the case study, Amanda pointed out to Jane that she tended to say "yes" to almost everything that was asked of her, and as a result, Jane felt constantly overwhelmed and rarely had the time to do anything well. Through discussion, Amanda learned that as an assistant HR representative, Jane had made a name for herself in her department as the go-to person—the person that others could count on to get even the tough assignments done. Jane had developed the pattern in those early years of taking any assignment and throwing herself into her work. This pattern served her well then, but now that Jane had more responsibilities, this way of working was no longer effective. Working with Amanda, Jane could see that she needed to be more discerning about how she focused her time and energy.

Other patterns that coaches may notice include gathering tons of information before making a decision, the need to keep control of every detail of an initiative, or the habit of taking on tasks that belong to others. Some people naturally evolve their working styles as they progress in their careers, whereas others hold on to the old patterns. The latter are most likely to have some significant work to do in Quadrant 1. The coach's role is to illuminate the patterns she sees and help the client name the pattern, understand how the pattern is impacting his work, and choose how to evolve to a more effective way of getting things done.

- *Orchestrate early wins.* The coach typically sets the pace of the coaching relationship at its inception. It is important for the client to make progress immediately and to be aware of the value of that progress. The coach can guide the client to work in areas that will make the most significant difference for the client. Typically, it is most fruitful to look at the pattern of behavior that is creating the greatest havoc or impeding the most progress and find a way to create a shift. In Jane's case, Amanda initially focused on helping her to create the time and space to participate in coaching. She also shared with Jane some strategies for calming down when Jane felt like things were spinning out of control. These small but significant changes made such a difference for Jane that she became increasingly motivated to participate fully in the coaching relationship. Change is difficult, so clients need to have some incentive for going through the process. Creating a space where the client can prove to herself that she can make significant change is essential for cementing commitment to take on bigger challenges.

- *Shine the light ahead on the path.* The work in Quadrant 1 can be a tough slog for some clients. There can be a real roller-coaster of emotions, especially if clients were told to enter into a coaching relationship to improve their performance. As clients start to evaluate the choices they have made in the past in a new light, they may become discouraged or regretful. It is essential that the coach help the client see that change is possible and will bring positive outcomes, if the client sticks with it. By illuminating the path forward, the coach can help the client step into the challenge of changing ingrained patterns of behavior, and this is where the real value lies for the client and the organization.

A couple of months into their coaching engagement, Jane came to the coaching call and somewhat sheepishly admitted to Amanda that she had been abrupt with one of her clients. To her credit, she had recognized her misstep almost immediately and had apologized to the client, who seemed to understand. Still, Jane felt disappointed in herself. Amanda reassured Jane that changing patterns of behavior is an iterative process, and it was expected that some days would be better than others. Amanda explained to Jane that with experience she would become more adept at noticing when she was becoming overly stressed and, with practice, she would be able to keep her cool. She also reassured Jane that this would all get easier over time. Amanda shared with Jane some of the benefits she could expect to derive in the future as she increased her ability to remain centered and focused. Jane found the conversation to be reassuring, and Amanda helped Jane to keep a more positive attitude about her own development.

Quadrant 1: Finding Focus

Insight: Reflective

Focus: Personal effectiveness

Touchstones:

- Commit to change
- Cultivate the ability to stay calm
- Get clear on what matters most
- Create a positive energy balance

Essential Outcome: Physical Centeredness

4

Quadrant 2: Building Bridges

In Quadrant 2, clients focus their attention on building strong, resilient relationships. The foundation for this interpersonal development is emotional insight, the ability to derive valuable information from one's own emotions and the emotional context of situations. The following case study portrays the coaching dynamics found in Quadrant 2 coaching work.

Case Study: Jack Creates Powerful Partnerships

Jack was thrilled when he received his promotion six months ago to become a VP of client relationships for three medium-sized customers of a large benefits services company. In his previous position as the manager of operations for one of the company's larger customers, Jack was the expert who knew the systems inside and out and who could seemingly solve any problem. He was the go-to person, and he loved it, but he was ready for a new challenge. Having supported various VPs of client relationships during his 10 years of operations work, he was certain that he knew what it took to do the job well.

Six months into his new role, Jack felt as if he was drowning, and he regretted that he had ever agreed to take on this new position. It was Jack's job to understand his clients' concerns and then work with the various constituents within the company to create solutions. With no direct reports, Jack had to rely on his ability to influence and persuade others to get his job done. In his previous role, Jack's opinion carried so much weight that most people just followed his lead—not so in the new role. He was deeply frustrated at the time and energy it took to get things done.

Jack's boss could see that he was struggling and suggested that Jack work with a professional coach to find new strategies for dealing with the complexities of his new position. Jack reluctantly agreed. After interviewing three coaches, he chose to work with Anne. Anne initiated the coaching relationship by collecting in-depth information from Jack and his boss about Jack's work situation, current challenges, and desired outcomes from coaching. It was decided that Anne would conduct in-person multirater feedback sessions with some of the key people with whom Jack worked. These are some of the insights that were gained from the feedback review:

- Jack was generally liked and respected, although some of his internal working relationships were strained. Many interview participants noted that Jack tended not to listen, especially when he was under pressure.
- Jack was perceived to have a hard time managing difficult or demanding clients and tended to "beat up" his internal service groups to deliver whatever the client wanted, rather than negotiating the client's demands.
- Jack sometimes had difficulty incorporating the ideas of others into solutions that he proposed. As a result, Jack would try to strong-arm the internal operations people into going along with his plan.

Initially, Anne worked with Jack on the Quadrant 1 touchstones that needed to be addressed, including helping Jack to better control his schedule, integrating some techniques for remaining calm and present when under pressure, and articulating what was most important for Jack to focus on to be successful. One of the key shifts that Jack made was letting go of the notion that he needed to be the expert who served the client. With Anne's help, Jack could see that he needed to change his way of working to become a partner with his clients and the internal service providers. With this fresh perspective, Jack chose to focus his coaching on improving his ability to foster commitment within his internal service providers and expand his relationships with key customers in order to be seen as a partner, rather than an order taker.

Jack and Anne had some in-depth coaching conversations about what it means to be a real partner. One of the shifts that Jack could see he needed to make was moving from being overly directive to engaging others in dialogue to find shared solutions. Initially, this task felt daunting for Jack, who believed that being directive was the only way to move others into action. Jack acknowledged that this approach did not always work and often left others angry with him. Anne pointed out that partnerships are built over time, and the first step was learning how to really listen and engage others in deeper levels of conversation.

In their next coaching call, Anne could tell that Jack was pretty upset about an exchange he had just had with one of the technical support staff. Jack had promised a customer that the customer's benefits Web site would be updated by the end of the week. Jack had just come from a preliminary review of the changes, and they were totally different from what Jack was expecting. It had taken every ounce of control that Jack had not to blow up. He wanted Anne to coach him on how to handle this situation appropriately. Anne asked Jack to recount the conversations that led up to that latest incident. Then she asked Jack at what point he felt there was going to be a problem. Anne prompted Jack to notice how he felt during the previous conversations. He admitted that he had an uneasy feeling when he first gave Stan, the IT person, the assignment that Stan did not really understand what was being asked of him. Later when he asked for an update, Stan had seemed vague about his progress, and Jack recalled feeling a little anxious at that time about Stan's ability to deliver the changes on time, but he had not wanted to upset Stan, so he did not say anything.

Anne asked Jack what he wanted the outcome of the situation to be. After some discussion, Jack stated that he wanted to engage Stan in a conversation that clarified what was expected and moved the process forward as quickly as possible, and in a way that preserved the relationship with Stan. Anne and Jack role-played some different approaches to the conversation, and Jack left the coaching call with some clear next steps to take. Jack and Stan were able to work out an acceptable solution and also made agreements on how they would work together more effectively in the future. Jack continued to practice tuning into how he was feeling during conversations, and he found that he was becoming better at detecting and addressing issues earlier, before they had a chance to get out of hand.

In a later coaching conversation Jack asked Anne to coach him on dealing with a client situation that he needed to address. One of Jack's customers was becoming increasingly demanding, insisting that Jack offer some extended services that were outside of the scope of the contract. In the past, Jack would have given in to please the customer, but Jack knew that was not the right answer. Anne asked Jack several questions to explore the relationship further, including what might be motivating his customer to make such a request. Jack noted that this customer tended to push the limits when he felt he could. Jack added that this customer tended to have temper tantrums when he did not get his way. Anne reflected back to Jack that he unconsciously encouraged this behavior by giving in when the client got angry. This insight enabled Jack to see the situation from a new perspective, and he was determined to set clear limits with his customer in a way that did not jeopardize the relationship. Jack was visiting the customer at the end of the week.

Jack worked with Anne to get clear on the outcome he wanted to create and role-playing the conversation. The toughest aspect for Jack was preparing for the possibility that the customer would become overly emotional. Anne encouraged Jack to practice in advance at remaining calm and focusing on the outcome he wanted to create, rather than the emotions that might be flying. The customer did get a little hot under the collar, but he abandoned that approach when it became clear that Jack was not going to give in as usual. They were able to talk through the request and find a solution that the client could live with.

Jack continued his work with Anne, and with practice and persistence, he was able to create the kind of partnerships with his clients and colleagues that he had hoped for. Jack's boss reported that some of Jack's customers and internal partners had offered unsolicited praise for the changes Jack had made. Most important, Jack began to really enjoy his work.

Creating Relationships That Work

As we can see through the case study, Quadrant 2 coaching is focused on creating solid, authentic relationships that deliver results. The foundation for these strengthened relationships is the ability to engage in dialogue at more than one level. Logically, we believe that a good idea will carry the day, although from our experiences, we realize that the emotional component of our conversations often directs the results. How many times have you seen a good idea dashed because of personality conflicts between the person proposing the idea and others who need to support it? In Quadrant 2, clients use their own experiences to learn how to detect and respond to their own emotions and the emotional context of relationships. There is often a component of redefining one's role, just as Jack needed to rethink his approach to his work and shift from being a directive order taker to a participative partner. Quadrant 2 invites clients to redefine how they work with others, and in doing so, clients get in touch with their own emotional experience.

Examples of Quadrant 2 goals may include the following:

- Increase ability to deal with emotionally charged situations
- Build partnerships with others to attain specific results
- Attain higher sales in one-on-one selling situations
- Communicate ideas to create impact and foster buy-in
- Manage more effectively to deliver results through others

- Transition successfully from an individual contributor to a management position
- Redefine one's role or one's work

Answering the "What Am I Made of?" Question

As Jack became clearer on his need to partner with others effectively, he opened the door to Quadrant 2 work. He began to step through the door as he started to explore new ways of working and being in relationships with others. As he discovered that he was capable of expanding his repertoire of behaviors, he started to explore the question "What am I made of?" Like many people, Jack tended to rely on a few tried-and-true ways of getting things done. His more directive, take-charge way of doing things fit well in the fast-paced operations environment of his previous job. As the acknowledged expert, he commanded the respect of others and was rarely challenged to take a different approach. His management style was effective and he was largely unconscious of it; it was just how he did things.

When we are faced with a new environment or changing requirements, we often need to reinvent how we work by learning to play some new cards in our decks of capabilities. We may not really discover what we are capable of until we are faced with a situation in which our preferred way of getting things done is not going to work. This is where coaches can add great value, because they are trained to see the potential that resides in their clients, even when clients are unable to see this for themselves.

Quadrant 2 Touchstones

Touchstones are areas of development that clients need to have a minimum level of proficiency at in order to move on to the next quadrant. They are not necessarily addressed directly but rather may be woven into the fabric of coaching conversations to create the shifts and changes needed to support lasting change. For Quadrant 2, the touchstones are as follows:

1. Expand your emotional vocabulary
2. Translate emotions into intentions
3. Read the emotional context of situations
4. Speak the language of emotions

1. *Expand your emotional vocabulary.* Clients need to recognize their own emotions in order to respond to them. It is not uncommon for people to ignore or downplay emotional responses, just as Jack did in his conversations with the IT person, often with the misguided hope that if they do not pay any attention to emotions, they will just go away. Emotions that are disregarded usually resurface later more intensely. Jack's anger at Stan for the possibility of missing the deadline is an example of emotions that had built up over time. If Jack had recognized his uneasiness earlier and spoken with Stan then, the later episode might never have happened.

    If we think of our emotions as being like a language our bodies speak to share information with us about what is going on in a situation, then the ability to identify various emotions that we experience is analogous to expanding our vocabulary. The greater the depth and breadth of our vocabulary, the more information we can receive. It takes practice and attention to expand your emotional vocabulary, but it is more than worth the effort.

2. *Translate emotions into intentions.* One of the reasons why people ignore their emotions is because they are sometimes not sure what to do with them. It is uncomfortable when we find ourselves in situations, like Jack, where we are angry with someone and uncertain about what to say or do. It is easier to ignore the situation and/or complain to others about it, than to actually address it appropriately. Emotional situations that are unresolved tend to fester and grow lives of their own. Like monsters under the rug, they can wreak havoc with our professional relationships and cause many sleepless nights.

Coaches can help clients follow the trail of their emotions back to the source of the issue. Questions such as "What is *really* bothering you?" and "How are you feeling about this situation?" can help clients identify their own feelings. Getting at the root cause is usually the hardest part of the equation and the place where a coach can be of great service to the client. Once a client acknowledges the source of his or her feelings, deciding how to deal with the issue effectively is much easier to see. In Jack's case, he needed to address the lack of clear communication between himself and his IT partner. Once he was clear on what he wanted the outcome of his conversation with Stan to be, he felt empowered to take the necessary action. This is how we translate our emotions into intentions. With time and practice, clients become faster and more adept at practicing this essential skill.

3. *Read the emotional context of a situation.* It is a natural extension once we become aware of our own emotions to start tuning into the emotions that are present in our relationships. We can get some valuable clues about how to handle situations when we become aware of what is going on just below the surface. Jack was able to address the demands of his customer by looking more closely at the emotional dynamic that was playing out between the two of them. Previously, Jack had tended to give in to the client when the client became upset. Once Jack saw that he was unwittingly encouraging the client to push the limits of the contract with this behavior, he was able to see how he could change the dynamic by changing how he responded. Through coaching, Anne was able to assist Jack in finding clear and respectful ways to communicate the boundaries of the contract, without losing the customer's respect. In fact, over time, Jack's ability to effectively read the emotional tea leaves in this relationship helped him to more clearly understand what the client valued and to provide stronger service within the bounds of the contract.

4. *Speak the language of emotions.* The ability to speak directly to the emotional subtext of a situation is an essential skill for clients who are building strong, lasting relationships. The unacknowledged feelings that are swirling within a conversation often derail the intended outcome. Jack was not looking forward to his meeting with the demanding customer. He opened his conversation by saying, "Fred, I know that you are upset about this situation. It is my hope that we can work together today to find a path forward." Fred and Jack were able to discuss what Fred was upset about, which gave Jack the opportunity to understand Fred's side of the story. Being able to convey his grievances helped Fred to calm down, and the two men were able to find a workable solution. If Jack had not stated openly that he was aware of Fred's feeling, it is likely that Fred would have demonstrated just how upset he was through his language and his actions, making it more challenging to move forward.

The ability to remain calm that is created from the work in Quadrant 1, coupled with the insight that is derived through the development in Quadrant 2, form a solid foundation for stepping into emotionally charged conversations.

The Essential Outcome of Quadrant 2: Emotional Centeredness

Emotional centeredness is the ability to tune into our emotions and the emotional context of situations and derive valuable information that we use to move things forward constructively. It is the ability to experience emotions without being taken over by them. For example, even though Jack was angry with Stan, he was able to have a meaningful conversation with him that reduced the tension in their situation and resulted in appropriate actions being taken. If Jack had lost his emotional center, he might have gone back and berated Stan to try and get him to deliver on his agreement. Jack might have felt better after venting his anger, but this kind of inter-action erodes the foundations of trust and respect that are essential in highly functional relationships. Emotional centeredness is espe-cially important when there is the need to step into emotionally charged situations and find a solution. This is the real hallmark of personal development in Quadrant 2.

People who tend to vent their emotions or intimidate others with their emotional outbursts can cause huge amounts of disruption and ill will in organizational settings. Equally disruptive, although not always as obvious, are the misunderstandings and roadblocks that arise when people refuse to acknowledge and deal with their emotions and the emotions of others. The ability to find one's center and interact with others from that place of strength creates an envi-ronment where problems get resolved and people feel safe and respected. Just as we need to find our physical center to move into the second quadrant, we need to find our emotional center to progress our development into Quadrant 3. Mastery is not required, but sufficient experience to not fly off the handle or duck and run when emotions heat up is necessary.

Continuing with the basketball analogy from the previous chapter, Quadrant 2 development is like a basketball player who has solid person basketball skills and is now deepening his appreciation of the strengths of the other players on his team. This new level of insight allows him to create plays that take his own skills to a new level and capitalizes on the talents of others.

Coaching Tools and Approaches for Quadrant 2

In Quadrant 2, coaches guide clients to become aware of their own emotional landscape and the emotional context of their environ-ment. These insights are woven into the fabric of the coaching work and are introduced in ways in which the client is comfortable. By helping the client to find effective ways of using his or her own emotional insight to create positive outcomes, the coach role-models how to create clarity in emotionally charged situations. The following are some possible coaching tools and approaches for Quadrant 2:

- *Change perspectives to change behavior.* In order for a client to choose to embrace a new way of working, he must first change his perspective. Jack was not likely to give up his directive, expert way of approaching his role without buying into the idea that becoming a partner with his customers and internal service providers would bring him the kind of success he was looking for. This shift in perspective has to happen at the emotional level; that is, the client cannot just think about something differently, he needs to experience what it feel like to know that it is real. In Jack's case, his first successful interactions that allowed him to experience the power of being in a partnership with others were crucial.

  Coaches guide clients to step successfully into the kinds of experiences that shift perspective. The process is one of engaging the client in dialogue that opens the client to perceive a situation from a different perspective. In Jack's case, Anne helped Jack see that there was a dynamic in his client relationships of Jack taking orders from the clients and then sometimes struggling to carry them out. Jack and Anne explored how those relationships would be different if Jack saw himself more as a partner. He was excited about evolving his client relationships in this new direction. The next step is to anchor the client's new perception with a positive experience. In Jack's case, Anne coached him to enter into conversations with his customers that opened the door to partnership. It took time to make the shift, but with the new perception of being a partner, Jack felt a strong connection to the direction in which he was heading.

- *Build the connection between the body and the emotions.* Emotions need to be experienced. There is little value in thinking about emotions; you have to work with them directly. How many times have you tried to convince yourself not to feel a certain way, only to find that for all of your perfectly rational reasons to the contrary, the emotion still remained? Emotions are experienced in the body, so in order to expand the emotional vocabulary of a client, the coach must guide the client to identify how the client experiences various emotions in his or her body. For example, a client may remember a time when she felt slighted and notice the physical sensations that accompany this emotion; perhaps she experienced heaviness around her heart or tension in the chest. Once clients get the hang of making this connection, they will do it naturally without having to be so deliberate about the process. Noticing the connection between the body and the emotions is essential for developing the first touchstone, expanding your emotional vocabulary.

When Anne was coaching Jack regarding his conversations with Stan, the IT person, she asked him to notice how he felt about the conversations and how he experienced those feelings in his body. This request seemed a bit odd to Jack, but when he remembered the conversations that he had with Stan, he noticed that he felt an uneasy feeling in his solar plexus, like something was off. He realized that if he had tuned into those sensations earlier, he might have spoken with Stan about his concerns before they escalated. Anne encouraged him to check in with his body from time to time to bring his feelings into his awareness.

■ *Work with intentions.* Recognizing and dealing with the emotional level of situations requires opening up to the messy reality of life. Once an emotionally charged conversation is engaged, there is often no telling where it will go. Some clients find this prospect frightening. Jack's greatest fear about setting some clear boundaries with his customer was the possibility that the customer would have a strong negative reaction. Anne worked with him beforehand to clearly identify his intention for the conversation, which was to set clear limits with his customer in a way that did not jeopardize the relationship. Intentions are different than goals; intentions point in a direction, whereas goals tend to focus on a very specific outcome. Setting a clear intention about what the client wants to create allows the client maneuvering room to reach the desired destination without having to take a particular stand. This flexibility fosters the kind of dialogue that is needed for building solid relationships.

- *Uncover assumptions.* We all make assumptions. We assume that people will respond to situations in a certain way; we assume that they know particular information; we assume that they see things the same way that we do because to us, it is obvious. Unfortunately, what is obvious to one person is not obvious to another. Jack assumed that Stan understood the changes that needed to be made to the Web site. Perhaps Jack was so familiar with the material that it was just obvious to him what needed to happen, but it certainly was not obvious to Stan. Unstated and unchecked assumptions cause all kinds of problems in communications. The coach needs to listen for and uncover assumptions that underlie coaching issues, and help the client see how the assumptions that he or she is making may be contributing to a misunderstanding. Eventually, clients begin to recognize their own assumptions as they are making them and check out the ones that need to be confirmed.

  One of the more frequent assumptions made is that others know what is expected of them or that we know what is expected of us. Unmet expectations can cause misunderstandings, which can be avoided by investing some time at the beginning of a new project or new relationship to clearly state how two people will work together and what they can expect from each other.

- *Translate emotions into language.* Some people are uncomfortable in the realm of emotion. Emotions can seem too messy and personal. They don't want to go there. It is the coach's role to listen for and articulate the emotional component of a situation in language that the client finds approachable. Sometimes you have to go in through the back door. Rather than talking about how someone *feels* about something, the coach can inquire about how something "landed" with the client or ask about the client's "reactions." Sometimes the coach will need to fill in the emotional blanks for the client with observations such as "it sounds like you are feeling irritated that this happened," or "I can hear that you are excited about this possibility." The coach might miss the mark with a statement, but as the client clarifies where she is at, she will identify her own emotional state, and there is tremendous value in this realization. It is important that the coach not back away from the emotional aspects of coaching, just because the client is not completely comfortable. As clients become more comfortable with discussing how they are feeling, they integrate the language of emotions into their conversations, creating the context for more meaningful dialogue with others.

- *Getting clear versus getting caught.* It is the coach's role to help a client gain insight from his emotional experience so that he gains insight into what needs to happen next to resolve a situation. The worst thing a coach can do is get caught up with the client in the emotion—like jumping into the pool of anger or pity with the client, there is no one left on the edge to pull either person out.

    Our emotions tell us a story about what is going on below the surface in a situation. If you follow the thread of emotions back through the story, you will come to the heart of the matter and the key for moving it forward. When Anne began asking Jack to recount the conversations he had with Stan and how he felt about them, she was coaching Jack to find the point at which the train left the track, which turned out to be the assumptions that were made about how the Web site changes would be done. If Anne had gotten caught up in Jack's frustration, she might have joined in the chorus of complaining about Stan's incompetence. Instead, she kept her sights focused on helping Jack view the situation from different perspectives and drawing insight from the new awareness that unfolded. From this clearer vantage point, the question "What do you want to have happen?" is much easier to answer, and workable resolutions can be found.

This is the touchstone *translate emotions into intentions* in action. It lies at the heart of building relationships that can weather the emotional storms that blow through our professional lives from time to time. When we get caught in the storm of our own emotions, we sometimes throw away relationships that we need and value because we cannot find our way through to a calmer place. Coaches help clients learn how to navigate in these rough waters so that their clients can build and maintain strong, lasting relationships.

Quadrant 2: Building Bridges

Focus: Interpersonal Relationships

Insight: Emotional

Touchstones:

- Expand your emotional vocabulary
- Translate emotions into intentions
- Read the emotional context of situations
- Speak the language of emotions

Essential outcome: Emotional Centeredness

5

Quadrant 3: Creating Alignment

In Quadrant 3, clients turn their attention to creating alignment between their values and their work. As leaders experience alignment on a personal level between their values and their leadership style, they naturally seek to create a similar sense of alignment between the shared values and goals of the group, team or network with which they are engaged. Intuitive insight is honed and integrated with logical understanding to become a powerful guide in increasingly complex environments. This is the space where the essence of who the client is shines through and becomes an integral part of whatever the client chooses to create. The following case study illuminates the coaching work in Quadrant 3.

Case Study: Mark Takes a Stand

Mark, the director of IT project management in a large pharmaceutical company, was really enjoying the support and development he received as a participant in the company's new leadership development program. He began the program six months ago, along with 80 other managers from within the company, and was inspired by what he was learning and who he was meeting. This was the first leadership development program the company had implemented in many years. The COO and HR VP believed that having leaders adapt change management principles and practices into their leadership responsibilities would reduce bureaucratic sclerosis and propel growth. As part of the program, Mark was able to work with an executive coach to help him apply what he was learning in his own work environment. Other leadership development activities included leadership workshops and action learning teams. At first, Mark had been somewhat skeptical about the value of working with a coach, but he soon found himself looking forward to the insightful conversations he had with Tim, his coach. Tim, meanwhile, familiarized himself with the company, the leadership development program, and the particulars of the change management model.

Mark was facing a particularly tough challenge. When Mark took over his team of IT project managers a year ago, no appropriate standards were in place for designing and delivering projects, and a lot of infighting was occurring throughout the department. The IT project managers had a reputation within their internal client base for missing important deadlines and being a challenge to work with. This was precisely the kind of bureaucratic sclerosis that the COO and HR VP wanted to eliminate. If it wasn't for the company's moratorium on procuring outside IT services, the group would probably have been outsourced long ago.

As part of the leadership program, Mark participated in several assessments, including a leadership assessment and a personality profile. Tim and Mark reviewed the findings and spoke at length about Mark's goals for his participation in the leadership program and his aspirations for being coached. Mark was a technically strong manager who placed high value on developing himself and his team. As a star performer, he was used to leading by example and expected others to follow his lead. His experience with the IT team was the first time that the strength of his character had not been sufficient to propel a team forward. Mark chose to focus his coaching work on expanding his leadership style to include enhancing his ability to inspire others and to manage challenging situations. Mark felt that these new leadership capabilities would enable him to attain his other coaching goal of leading his team to significantly improve their customer service ratings, which were currently well below the acceptable limit of 85 percent satisfaction.

Mark was making good progress in organizing his team and setting up systems to establish accountability when he entered into the coaching relationship with Tim. The challenge was in getting compliance from the team. Initially, Tim focused the coaching in Quadrant 1, engaging Mark in conversations to get clear about what was truly important to focus on to get his team turned around. Tim also helped Mark integrate a few new ways of staying calm and focused under pressure.

Mark could clearly see that instilling discipline around the project management systems was essential, although he was uncertain how to get his team to buy into the ideas, which took him clearly into Quadrant 2 work. With Tim's coaching, Mark began to engage his team members in one-on-one conversations to gain insight about what was working and what was not as they struggled to implement the new standards. Initially, Mark was uncomfortable about conducting these conversations, because he was not sure how his team would respond. Tim encouraged Mark to get to the heart of what was really bothering him about this situation. Through reflection, Mark was able to identify that he was afraid that his team would use the opportunity to blame each other for any problems—a trait they were famous for. Tim was able to coach Mark on how to manage the blame game in these conversations and get at what was really going on. The conversations went well and provided an opportunity for Mark to use some of the coaching skills that he was naturally picking up from his work with Tim.

Moving into Quadrant 3 work, Tim encouraged Mark to spend some quiet time after the interviews were done and reflect on the underlying dynamics that were operating with his team. He suggested that Mark write down the thoughts that came to him, without evaluating them. Mark brought his thoughts to the next coaching session. He noticed that his team really did want to do a good job, and while some of his team members were actively working to implement the new standards, others had given excuses as to why the standards would not work. When Tim asked Mark what he thought was going on, the first thing that came to Mark's mind was that some of his team members were afraid of trying and failing. They were already getting beaten up by their clients, and the new system would give the clients more ammunition with which to attack them. Mark also sensed that they were testing to see if he was really serious about the new standards. He was not the first person to try this approach. It was now clear to Mark that just creating the standards was not enough. He would need to help his team learn the new skills required to be successful, both at delivering their projects on time and using the new system. Mark sensed that the team was ready to rise to this challenge. As the coaching continued, Tim and Mark discussed possible strategies for getting the additional training that the team needed. Mark decided to approach the leadership development program coordinator for guidance on obtaining the necessary training for the team.

Mark's opportunity to demonstrate his resolve came sooner than he expected. In Mark's regular one-on-one meetings with his boss, it was strongly suggested that Mark should fire the bottom two performers of the team. Mark's boss felt that this would provide all of the motivation needed to get the team's client satisfaction numbers up. Mark's boss was getting tired of taking the heat for this team's poor performance. Time was running out. Although Mark's boss acknowledged that overall, the numbers were starting to improve, he wanted them to move faster. Mark asked if he could meet with his boss again at the end of the week to discuss this matter further.

Every participant in the leadership development program was asked to keep a personal journal. They were introduced to the idea of using the journal to reflect on their own experiences and find their own insights and answers. Mark used his journal to sort through his feelings about his boss's request. Mark truly did not want to fire his two team members, but he was uncertain if this was because he was afraid to fire them (it would certainly be a difficult task) or because he felt that it was not the best thing for the team. Mark brought this question to his next coaching session with Tim. Tim allowed Mark to share his thoughts and feelings and then asked him what he intuitively thought the impact of the firings would be on the team. Mark paused and then said with conviction that he felt it would be a huge setback, because the team was really just starting to pull together for the first time in a long time. He believed that with the proper support they could make their numbers. One of the two team members at risk was well liked by the others, and losing him was likely to put the team into a tailspin. Tim asked Mark what he wanted to do. As a result, Mark engaged in two difficult conversations.

The first conversation was with his boss. With Tim's coaching, Mark was able to lay out a plan of action for the next six months for delivering better client satisfaction numbers for the team. Mark shared with his boss the insights he had gained through his conversations with each team member and his conviction that with some supportive training, they had what it took to deliver results. He told his boss that he wanted to keep the team together through that time, but he promised to reevaluate everyone on the team at the end of the six-month time period. Mark's boss was impressed with Mark's plan and agreed to support him in implementing it.

The second conversation was with his team. Mark arranged for a half-day meeting in which Mark shared with the team what he had learned through his one-on-one conversations. He opened the meeting by setting clear expectations that this meeting was about moving into action, and there would be no finger-pointing. He let the team know that he believed they could perform at a much higher level, and he coached them to set some stretch goals. He made it clear that making the changes was not optional, although he allowed the team a fair amount of input into how to achieve their goals.

The team left the meeting energized about moving forward. Mark left the meeting with a satisfied feeling that his words and actions reflected who he was as a manager and leader. He knew that it would be an uphill battle, but it was a battle he believed in and one he thought he could win.

Aligning Who You Are with How You Work

The case study illustrates the essence of Quadrant 3 work—creating alignment between what a client values and how those values are expressed through his leadership style and the focus of his work. By the time a client reaches the third quadrant, he has the ability to reflect on his own experience and draw conclusions about what is important to him on a personal and professional level. These insights are often brought to light by the challenges the client faces and the questions those challenges evoke, just as Mark found himself having to find a way to inspire his team to a new level of performance, whether he felt ready for that task or not. He discovered in the process what was important to him, and he found a way to honor that in his work with his team.

As the problems that need to be unraveled become more complex, our ability to think our way to a solution is rarely sufficient to deliver the needed results in a timely manner. We need to be able to integrate a lot of information and have enough confidence in ourselves and our choices to move into action and adjust our actions as the situations change. This is where intuitive insight plays a part. Mark was able to integrate his logical analysis of his team's situation with his intuitive insight about what was getting in their way to find a way to move forward that felt right to him. This element of finding personal and professional clarity by experiencing complexity is the hallmark of development in Quadrant 3.

Examples of Quadrant 3 goals include the following:

- Expand one's leadership style to include approaches that are less developed
- Accomplish a goal through teamwork
- Gain clarity about the direction or purpose of one's work
- Develop and present an idea to create buy-in from others
- Transition from management to leadership
- Develop a network of influence
- Play a leadership role to forward the action in a complex situation
- Integrate creativity and purpose back into one's work and one's life

Answering the "Who Do I Want to Be?" Question

The leadership development program in which Mark was participating was designed, in part, to direct him toward answering the "Who do I want to be?" question. Through the assessments and personal journals, participants were expected to gain insight into their own makeup and form an intention of how they wanted to develop their potential. The proverbial rubber hit the road for Mark when he had to choose how to respond to his boss's request to fire two team members. This was one moment in which Mark had to decide who he wanted to be. These moments happen over and over again, as we use the grist of our own experiences to reveal our unique composition.

As clients deepen their ability to draw on deeper levels of insight, they achieve greater clarity about what is important for them. This clarity often reveals misalignments between what they come to see as authentic for themselves and how they choose to conduct the business of their lives. "Who do you want to be?" is one of the questions that begins the process of creating alignment between who a person is and how he chooses to conduct himself in the world, and what he creates.

Quadrant 3 Touchstones

As with the previous two quadrants, the touchstones of Quadrant 3 are areas of personal development that are integrated into coaching to support the attainment of Quadrant 3 goals. The touchstones for Quadrant 3 are as follows:

1. Know thyself
2. Learn to work with patterns of dynamics
3. Expand your beliefs
4. Trust yourself

1. *Know thyself.* The central theme for Quadrant 3 is creating alignment, which begs the question, alignment to what? We

realize our greatest potential and tap into our most powerful gifts when we operate in alignment with what we value most. There can be a significant difference between what we believe we should value and the values that have that clear, true ring of authenticity. The work of this quadrant is to discern the difference. Although many exercises can be engaged in to list various values and whittle them down to a neat list, most often the test of our own experiences points us in the direction of our true north.

The work of this touchstone is to readily recognize within yourself the ring of your own truth. Although this statement may sound rather profound, it is actually immensely practical. It is simply the process of synthesizing the available information, both rational and intuitive, and making choices that feel right for you. Mark went through this process when he was faced with the decision of firing his two team members. The development work that he did in the previous two quadrants gave him confidence in his own insights, the ability to clearly express his plan to his boss, and the momentum to take action. With this solid foundation, Mark was able to bring his actions into alignment with his values. It was entirely possible that his boss would not support his idea or that after six months, his team would not make the necessary progress. What was important was that Mark took the initiative to act with integrity.

2. *Learn to work with patterns of dynamics.* Quadrant 3 is also about getting things done in groups, teams, and networks. In these more complex environments, underlying patterns that get in the way of accomplishing goals must be detected. In the case of Mark's team, Mark could see that team members had the habit of blaming others for problems. As long as it remained acceptable for team members to assess blame and pass it along, the team was unable to take responsibility for its own actions and address the core issues that needed to be addressed. Mark could also see that the pattern of blaming served a purpose for the team. As long as no one was ever

completely responsible for an outcome, then no one could be held completely accountable. There was a certain amount of safety in this approach, even if it did not deliver satisfying results. Mark needed to work with this pattern on two levels: (1) to identify the pattern and make the team aware of the consequences of this shared behavior, and (2) to provide training or other support so that the team could create a more functional pattern that delivered the desired results. By guiding the team to take responsibility for the habit of blaming, Mark was able to bring the team closer to being in alignment around their shared goal of increasing client satisfaction.

The ability to see patterns expands with each quadrant. In the first quadrant, clients reflect on their own patterns of habits that get in their way. In Quadrant 2, the focus is on reading patterns that occur in the emotional context of situations, and in Quadrant 3 the scope widens to take in the dynamics of patterns that underlie group behavior. The ability to see these patterns is supported by the deepening levels of insight that occur with each quadrant. The ability to see larger patterns is intuitive and supported by the intuitive insight that is honed in this quadrant.

3. *Expand your beliefs.* There is often a need when working in Quadrant 3 for clients to examine their beliefs about how things ought to be. As clients bring their work into alignment with their values, they often find themselves face-to-face with their own beliefs. In Mark's case, until his boss recommended firing the two team members, Mark may have held the view that a good manager always does what his boss suggests without question. If Mark had decided to hold on to that belief, he would have fired his two team members without putting forward an alternative approach.

At the team level, when Mark first introduced the new standards, he expected the team members to just adopt the new procedures, perhaps because he held the belief that his direct reports should just do what they are told. If he chose to hold on to that belief, he would probably have resorted to telling his team members more emphatically, in e-mails and reminders at their weekly meetings, that they were supposed to be complying with his demands. When he could see that his approach was not getting much traction, he worked with his coach to understand the underlying dynamics of the team and came to see that the team was unlikely to apply the new procedures consistently without some additional support. By flexing his view of the situation, Mark was able to find a workable solution. Whenever clients are stymied, it is important to see if the obstacle is a belief that is out of alignment with current reality.

4. *Trust yourself.* Many ingredients combine to create trust in oneself. The insight and experience that clients gain through their work in the first three quadrants enable them to trust their own judgment. Although Mark was not sure how he was going to inspire his team to realize the stretch goals they had agreed to, Mark trusted that he could do it. He did not have all of the answers, but he did have confidence in his own abilities. It is not uncommon for the choices that clients are presented with in Quadrant 3 to require an element of trust. As the environment in which clients work becomes more complex and the pace at which events unfold quickens, a person who trusts her own intuitive and logical assessments will react with greater speed and agility than someone who doubts himself or needs all of the answers before taking action. A genuine feeling of personal power comes from trusting oneself. This is one of the many gifts clients receive for their efforts.

The Essential Outcome of Quadrant 3: Intuitive Centeredness

When a client is intuitively centered, he is comfortable integrating intuitive information with his rational evaluations of situations and trusts his own assessments of what he sees and senses. It is a deeper form of centering that rests on the foundations of physical and emotional centering from Quadrants 1 and 2. The key to finding your intuitive center is trust. As clients learn to trust their own intuition, they naturally integrate intuitive information more actively into their perceptions. This ability is developed over time, through experience. Clients begin by following their hunches, such as trusting someone or suggesting an idea. As clients notice that their insights have validity, they gain confidence about their abilities to tap into this rich resource of insight. Clients gain the insight and self-confidence needed to work intuitively from a place of strength through the personal development work done in the earlier quadrants. Being able to consistently tap into and trust one's intuition is essential for moving into Quadrant 4.

Quadrant 3 is the space in which coaching clients achieve their goals through work that is done in teams, groups, or networks. In these situations, clear, authentic, and flexible leadership can make the greatest difference. This kind of leadership evolves as clients align their values with their work.

Returning to our basketball analogy, the development in this quadrant is like the translation of team strategy into real-time play on the court. Teams can invest all kinds of time and energy in working out a game plan, but they will only win the game if they can translate that plan into action, responding with fluidity and agility to whatever transpires on the court. Basketball players intuitively see the patterns that are developing in play and instinctively sense the presence of their team members. Quadrant 3 development deepens the ability of businesspeople to tap into more of their own inner resources and connect their talents with others to take their own teams to the next level.

Coaching Tools and Approaches for Quadrant 3

When working in Quadrant 3, coaches are role-modeling integrating structure and intuitive insight in the ways they work with their clients. Coaches listen for values and patterns and guide clients to see these for themselves. Although coaches may offer advice or ideas, it is important for clients to gain confidence in their own abilities to find a path forward that is right for them. In Quadrant 3, coaches act as mirrors for clients, using insights gained through client experiences to enable clients to see their own potential and values more clearly. The following are strategies for coaches to consider integrating into their Quadrant 3 coaching engagements:

- *Listen for values.* Coaches can hear what a client values by listening for the things that the client finds exciting and that make a client angry or upset. One of Mark's roles was to coach his team to a new level of success. When Mark conducted his one-on-one interviews with his team members, he could hear that his team members had values that were aligned with delivering solid results to their clients. Mark asked each of his team members to describe a time when he was most satisfied with his work. As Mark listened to the various stories that were recounted, he could hear that the team desired to be successful, although what success looked like to different team members varied. Much of the team's frustration seemed to stem from their inability to find a way to work that enabled them to find alignment with this desire to do well.

  Values are revealed through our experiences. Values are not about what you want to be; they are the constellation of lights that reveal who you are. They shine clearly in stories we tell about times when we felt whole and successful, and they burn bright when they are thwarted in some way. A coach can hear signs of hidden values that are not finding full expression when he listens for what frustrates the client or what the client longs for. Mark could also hear in the interviews he conducted the refrain of irritation that his team members felt. Some were frustrated that they could not work on more creative projects, some chafed at being pulled off assignments before they were complete, and others wanted new technical challenges. Each complaint revealed something about what the team member valued.

- *Listen for misalignments.* We all have our own notions of a successful version of ourselves. For every role we play, we have some sense of what fulfilling that role well entails. Our perception of success is often inherited—a synthesis of what we feel is expected of us by the organizations we work for, our families, our bosses, our peer groups, and ourselves. As a result, many people are shooting for goals they feel they *should* be working for, even if those goals do not resonate as being meaningful for them.

  As clients gain greater insight into their own values, they may have a vague awareness that something is off in terms of what they are working to achieve. Before Mark entered into the leadership program, one of his own internal barometers of success was to "deliver the goods." He took pride in accomplishing even the most difficult assignments. Challenging his boss's request to fire his two employees forced him to rethink that perception of success. It is the coach's role to help the client illuminate how the client's perception of success may be out of alignment with the client's value system. As a result, a client may shift his coaching goals or his way of working to be in alignment with these new insights.

- *Tell stories.* Quadrant 3 is the space in which clients work with and through larger audiences to get things done. Whether the client is assuming a leadership role, building a network of influence, or pitching a project idea, the ability to capture both the hearts and minds of others is an essential skill. When Mark met with his team to share his observations from the interviews and gain their agreement to set stretch goals, he needed to tell a compelling story. Rather than just parade out the obvious numbers and ask for compliance to the new standards, he conveyed a story that identified some of the challenges the team faced and his belief that the team was capable of making the necessary changes. Too often, clients rely on logic to move people into action. The numbers may get their attention, but the emotion of a story will resonate, as long as the emotion is true. This is one of the real benefits of alignment: your words and actions carry credibility. Encouraging clients to develop the ability to tell credible, authentic stories that capture the imagination of others is an important Quadrant 3 skill.

One of the most effective ways to achieve this goal is for the coach to incorporate storytelling into the coaching process. The coach can encourage the client to tell the story of what she wants to achieve as a coaching technique to help the client get clear on what her intentions are. The coach can also incorporate his own stories to illustrate points that he wants to make for the client. This is particularly effective for helping a client to see a situation from a different perspective or assuring him that he is not the first person to face a particular challenge. Stories are powerful ways of shaping our beliefs about what is possible.

- *Make friends with fear.* The work in Quadrant 3 is much more public and requires change at deeper levels than the previous quadrants. This is where clients put their ideas into action in larger venues and begin to let go of aspects of their lives that are not working. Although these changes typically take place gradually over time, there is still an element of coming face-to-face with one's fears and misgivings. The coach can help the client to deal with these uneasy feelings without being taken over by them or running away from them. Just having the opportunity to discuss feeling nervous or being afraid can be enormously helpful to a client. Using the touchstones from Quadrant 2, the client can get in touch with what he is most concerned about. As Mark prepared for his half-day meeting with his team to set a new course, he harbored some trepidation about his ability to convey his conviction and faith in the team in a way that would inspire them. Tim worked with Mark to get clear on the story that he wanted to tell his team about what he believed was possible, and Tim encouraged Mark to remember what inspired him about the team. These small steps calmed Mark's nerves and raised his comfort level that he could inspire others with his words and actions, which was one of his coaching goals.

■ *Integrate intuition and linear thinking.* Intuition is developed with experience. Like other skills, it is built up through practice and reflection. Coaches working with clients on Quadrant 3 developments will be encouraging clients to trust their own intuitive insights. This change often happens subtly, as a backdrop to accomplishing other goals. Mark's decision to conduct individual interviews with his team members was an intuitive insight that arose during a coaching call with Tim. Mark was expressing his frustration with the team for not using the new project management tools more consistently, and he asked Tim what to do. Rather than list some ideas, Tim turned the question back to Mark and asked him what he felt needed to be done. At first Mark said that he did not know, so Tim suggested that Mark take a guess. Mark reflected for a moment and then noted that something was getting in their way, but he did not know what it was. Tim asked Mark how he might find out what the problem was. The idea to interview each of his team members just popped into Mark's head. He and Tim went on to discuss the best way to conduct the interviews to get the desired results.

Through these kinds of conversations, clients learn to trust their own intuitive insights. By encouraging clients to "take a guess" or "make something up," the coach can help them get past their fears of not knowing or not being right and into the space of intuiting. Like muscles that are built through repeated activities, intuitive insight strengthens with experience. It is part of the coach's role to guide clients to continue to deepen their intuitive abilities.

Quadrant 3: Creating Alignment

Focus: Teams, groups or networks

Insight: Intuitive

Touchstones:

- Know thyself
- Learn to work with patterns of dynamics
- Expand your beliefs
- Trust yourself

Essential outcome: Intuitive Centeredness

6

Quadrant 4: Original Action

Quadrant 4 is the space in which clients find their own innovative ways of doing things and claim their own style of leadership. Not all clients choose to work in Quadrant 4. Clients are propelled into this quadrant by their own ideas and inspirations. There is something that clients can see or sense they want to create, and they require the development embedded in Quadrant 4 to step out and make it happen.

Case Study: Clare Leads the Way

The last two years had been a frustrating ride for Clare, the VP of business development in a medium-sized technology company. She was selected for the VP position, mainly because of her ability to see and cultivate opportunity that others overlooked. At the director level, she had landed some strategically important acquisitions. Since taking the VP role two years ago, almost all of her innovative ideas had been shot down by her colleagues on the leadership team. But now, perhaps, the tide was turning.

The leadership team had been working with an executive coach named Tressa for six months, both as a team and individually. Although there had been some bumpy spots, the coaching had gone well so far, and the team was much more focused and communicating more effectively than ever before. The multirater feedback sessions were a real eye opener for some of the team members.

Coupled with personality profiles, these assessments clearly shone the light on areas that each team member needed to develop. For the most part, team members were making solid strides toward enhancing their abilities as leaders and team members. As a result, they were increasingly able to talk about the kind of challenging issues that previously would have locked the team up in a seemingly irresolvable knot. The team was edging toward taking some greater risks in a bid to turn the tide on their sliding margins.

Clare had focused her coaching work with Tressa on getting her ideas across in ways that others could understand and support. Her multirater feedback revealed that her team members respected her sharp intellect and original thinking, but it was not uncommon for team members to have difficulty understanding what Clare was talking about when she got excited about a new idea. If she perceived that others were not tracking with her, she would just keep talking, piling explanation on top of explanation until even the people who thought they had the concept were not quite sure anymore. As a result, few of Clare's more original proposals were accepted by the team. Clare was deeply frustrated by this outcome, particularly because she felt strongly that the company needed to push into some new areas that she was proposing to spur growth in more lucrative markets.

Clare moved fairly quickly through Quadrant 1. As a former athlete, Clare was familiar with the concept of finding her center, although she had never really thought of applying this kind of focus in a work setting. Tressa helped Clare see how she sometimes derailed her own efforts by getting caught up in her stories about what others were thinking or doing. It was not uncommon for Clare to assume in advance that certain team members were against her proposal even before she presented it. As a result, she often presented her ideas from a defensive posture. Through reflection, Clare learned to discern the difference between stories that she was creating and events that were actually happening. By catching herself in story-telling mode and stopping the story, she was better able to stay centered and focused on what was happening in the moment.

As the coaching work moved into Quadrant 2, Clare became aware that her tendency to become overly enthusiastic about her ideas was getting in the way of getting her proposals accepted. She could see that when she became really excited she tended to tune out the subtle—and sometimes not so subtle—clues that others were sending her about their reactions to her idea. As a result, she did not fully understand why others did not see the value in what she was presenting. Tressa coached Clare on ways to keep her emotional center and really listen to what others had to say. Clare found that if she listened attentively to her colleagues, she became more aware of what their real concerns were. Clare decided to apply this new approach to build support for a proposal she was putting forward. She found that by engaging her team members in one-on-one conversations that addressed their core concerns, Clare could find workable compromises. She started small with some new ways of looking at opportunities that extended the current thinking of the team. It took a lot longer to move her proposals forward, but she was finally getting traction. By the time she presented her idea to the entire team, she had already secured enough support to move the initiative forward. With every success, Clare found her confidence returning.

In team meetings, Clare found herself listening to the dialogue of the team on new levels. As she listened to what was being said—and what wasn't—she started to detect where some of the barriers to change were for the team. She started to see that if several departments worked together, they could offer an integrated solution that Clare knew the market was looking for. She knew where to find the technology that was needed, but there was no point in moving in that direction if the leadership team was not prepared to work together in new ways.

In her previous way of working, Clare would have gone into a leadership meeting and beaten the team over the head with her idea, until the resistance was so great that it was clear the idea was going nowhere. This time, Clare decided to apply some of her insights from her more recent successes. With Tressa's coaching, Clare began to engage some of the key players on the team in dialogues about the integrated solution she envisioned. In the first couple of conversations, Clare found that while there was agreement, and even some excitement, about the idea, the team members with whom she spoke had some deep reservations about the team's ability to implement such a challenging initiative. Clare considered playing it safe and abandoning the idea altogether, but the thought of giving up left her filled with disappointment. She truly believed the team was capable of taking on this new initiative.

In her next coaching session, Tressa asked Clare what she *really* wanted to create. This question, and the dialogue that followed, helped Clare crystallize her thinking and get to the essence of what she saw was possible. With this clarity, she could see several options for moving forward, some that were likely to be more palatable to her team. With this new perspective, Clare resumed her dialogues with team members. Again, Clare found that when she listened carefully to her colleagues, she could detect their concerns, even when they were having difficulty expressing them. For example, the VP of IT services seemed to keep coming back to concerns about "his people." With some careful questioning, Clare was able to uncover the core issue, which was the readiness of his team to take on some of the new client responsibilities the integrated solution would require. With the issue clearly stated, the VP and Clare were able to brainstorm some possible solutions. Although they did not resolve the issue completely, the dialogue increased the VP's comfort level with the proposal, and he became an advocate for exploring the idea further.

Clare knew that her boss, the president of the company, had a difficult time dealing with overt conflict on the team. Although his ability to step into emotionally charged conversations was increasing with the coaching he was receiving, Clare sensed that she would need to have a solid base of support before formally presenting the idea for the team to consider. Clare recruited some of her supportive team members to help her build momentum with the rest of the team.

In the final coaching session before the big meeting, Tressa coached Clare to separate her perception of who she was from the idea she was putting forward. Tressa had noticed that Clare took "losing" personally, and as a result, she would fight to gain acceptance for what she wanted as if she were fighting for her life. This approach left little room for the necessary compromises required to build a consensus. Clare's confidence and insight had grown to the point that she understood what Tressa was saying. She could see how the pattern of being overly attached to outcomes got in her way. She had experienced centered detachment, and she knew that it was a powerful place from which to work.

The meeting went well, and the team committed to work together on crafting an integrated offering. Clare was asked to lead the effort, which both thrilled and frightened her. She knew that through the process of implementing the integrated solution, she would be presented with many new opportunities to deepen her learning and stretch her comfort zone. She looked forward to the challenge.

Creating Step Change

Quadrant 4 is the space in which leaders are inspired to create step change. Drawing upon the solid foundation of development from the previous three quadrants, leaders possess the insight, confidence, and capabilities to make significant change happens. In Quadrant 4, leaders trust their own inner knowing that something new is possible and they learn to draw upon their broad array of capabilities, like symphony conductors, in order to bring their ideas to life. Quadrant 4 is truly transformational. Leaders learn to step into their own power. They take risks. They make mistakes. They sometimes end up traveling in directions that they never expected. They learn to trust themselves. Ultimately, they forge their own unique style of leadership by stepping out into new territory.

Most clients don't set Quadrant 4 goals as they initiate coaching. Quadrant 4 goals are often formed as a natural outgrowth of a client's development and experiences in the earlier quadrants. Clare did not set off to lead her team to create a new integrated solution; she just arrived at that opportunity through her work to become a better leader. As a natural extension of that work, she saw an opportunity that she could not walk away from without feeling as if she had let herself and her team down. When she stepped up to take on that challenge, she advanced clearly into Quadrant 4. Like Clare, most clients find themselves invited into Quadrant 4 through their own desire to create what they perceive to be possible in the world. Whether they are going after a new market or shifting an approach to something that is tried and true, Quadrant 4 is the space for original action. As a result, the goals that clients pursue in Quadrant 4 are often as unique as the person who crafts them. Some examples of Quadrant 4 goals include the following:

- Start a new venture
- Make an innovative change to something that already exists, such as taking a new approach to marketing or client development
- Inspire a team to take on a challenging goal
- Integrate an artform or other creative endeavor into one's work
- Open up a new market opportunity

Whatever the goal, there is an element of transforming something in a unique way and being transformed into a stronger, more confident leader in the process.

Answering the "What Do I Want to Create?" Question

Clare came face-to-face with this question: "What do I want to create?" when she had to decide whether to take the risk and proceed with her idea of convincing the team to support the integrated solution. When Tressa asked Clare what she *really* wanted to create, Clare was able to connect with how important it was for her to have her ideas realized. The alignment between what she saw as possible and what the team needed was so clear that she could not walk away from it. She was convinced that she could make a significant difference, and she needed to at least try to make it happen to be at peace with herself. The coaching that she had received up until that time gave her the confidence that she could find a way to propose and implement the integrated solution. Before the coaching, she had seen similar opportunities, but she lacked the insight and skill to build a strong enough coalition to gain acceptance for her idea.

The root of the "What do I want to create?" question needs to be inspiration in order to tap into the kind of creative energy required to propel an idea forward. When clients answer the "What do I want to create?" question strictly from an intellectual perspective, they end up with goals they think they *should* attain, rather than goals that get their creative juices running. Inspiration cannot be faked or forced, but it can be cultivated. The touchstones of each quadrant build on each other, and in doing so, create an internal infrastructure for accessing creative inspiration.

Quadrant 4 Touchstones

The touchstones for Quadrant 4 revolve around the themes of believing that something more is possible and being in action to create something new. Quadrant 4 is not for everyone, but those who gravitate to working in this space become role models of powerful, creative leadership. The touchstones for Quadrant 4 are as follows:

1. Believe in possibilities
2. Have faith
3. Build connections
4. Demonstrate clear commitment

1. *Believe in possibilities.* It is not possible to work in the fourth quadrant without a willingness to believe that something more or something different is possible. People who habitually argue for the status quo will not enter into this territory.

When Clare reflected on the dynamics of the leadership team, she could see how some team members had become isolated in their own areas and tended to see invitations to collaborate more as threats than opportunities. At the same time, her contact with outside companies allowed Clare to engage in conversation with people who had different perspectives. The insights she gained through these conversations helped her see new possibilities in the marketplace. Clare could see that if the leadership team could find a way to collaborate on an integrated offering, opportunities could be pursued. Without the willingness to see possibilities, Clare would never have noticed these openings for growth.

2. *Have faith.* This touchstone reflects a deeply founded faith that naturally evolves from the work of the previous quadrants. By the time a client reaches Quadrant 4, she has a solid foundation of self-awareness; she knows what is important to her, and she is aware when her work and her life are in alignment with her values. The development that she has undergone as she moved through the earlier quadrants has brought online a full spectrum of capabilities and perspectives that greatly enhance the flexibility and fluidity with which she can respond to a wide variety of situations. Quadrant 4 is the space in which clients focus on integrating what they have learned and putting the learning into action in ways that are uniquely their own. This requires a great deal of faith. For Clare this meant having faith in herself that her insights have merit, faith that she can translate those insights into action, and faith that even though she does not know how events will unfold, she will be able to handle whatever happens.

3. *Build connections.* New ideas often require support systems of some kind to bring them to life. In Clare's case, she needed the support of others on her leadership team in order for the integrated offering to happen. Without the buy-in of others, Clare's idea would be destined to die on the vine, but getting

buy-in was just the first step. Clare's new allies would in turn need to rally support in their own organizations, defend the idea to others who might not understand it, and find new ways of collaborating.

The connections that are created serve like a web of support, allowing an idea to spread into an organization. Without enough support, new ideas can be crushed by the fears, resentments, and misunderstanding of others. For natural creative thinkers such as Clare, the most significant development opportunity is often this touchstone of building connections. This is where the foundation that was built by the previous touchstones really pays off. Inspiring others to expand their perspectives is no small task. It requires the ability to discern subtleties in many levels. Building connections goes well beyond intellectually convincing someone that an idea is worth pursuing. Clare needed to win the hearts of her team mates, as well as their minds. Her conversations about the proposal needed to reach her audience on an emotional level; the team members needed to feel positively about the endeavor to really get behind it. There also needs to be alignment with the values of others.

The size and scope of the support web depends on the impact a new idea will have on the organization. The greater the impact, the more work is needed to pave the way for it. Impact can be calibrated by the extent to which the idea exceeds the general comfort zone of those whose support is needed and also the degree of cooperation and collaboration required from others to get something implemented. The integrated solution that Clare proposed stretched her team in some significant ways, which is why she needed to invest so much time and energy upfront to build the connections to support it.

4. *Demonstrate clear commitment.* It is important for the client to look closely at *what* she is committed to. The focus of the

client's commitment will have a tremendous impact on how she proceeds in getting something implemented. Previously, Clare had become so attached to getting her ideas accepted that she approached the process of gaining approval for them more like soliciting votes than building a support base. This personal focus led Clare to perceive feedback as criticism, and not just criticism of the idea, but criticism of her. Consequently, she defended her ideas more vehemently, which tended to close down avenues of communication, not open them up.

With Tressa's help, Clare was able to discern that her commitment was to finding an integrated solution that the team could embrace and that met the needs of the market, rather than being committed to getting *her* idea accepted. She saw herself more as the person creating the space for this to happen than being the owner of the idea. This broader perspective allowed Clare to be more flexible in how she approached her teammates. She tended to listen for openings for the path forward rather than criticisms that needed to be defended. This also enabled Clare to integrate the suggestions of others into the plan more readily, which cultivated support and enthusiasm for the project.

The Essential Outcome of Quadrant 4: Personal Power

Personal power is the ability to focus the full complement of your personal resources—your creativity, intellect, and spirit—to create what you believe is possible. It is personal because it is not power over or involving anyone else. It's all about you. Sometimes people mistake power for force. Force involves throwing your proverbial weight around to get what you want, whether others want you to have it or not. Force tends to create winners and losers. Power, on the other hand, is about awareness, choice, and focus.

Powerful people are aware that they have a full palette of abilities. They know this because they have stretched themselves through new experiences to discover what they are made of. The wide array of development that occurs as clients move through the four quadrants allows them to experience aspects of themselves with which they are less familiar. Choice is what moves all of their abilities into action. Powerful people take responsibility for choosing who they want to be and what they want to create. Clients who step into their personal power are naturally respected leaders who become role models for others.

Personal power rests solidly on the work of the previous quadrants. The physical, emotional, and intuitive centeredness that evolved through the earlier work forms the foundation of this level of development. Clare was stepping into this space as she took the risk to introduce her ideas to the team. Leading the implementation of the integrated solution will test Clare in many ways. These experiences will hone her leadership style and deepen her base of personal power.

Continuing with our basketball analogy, a leader who is working in Quadrant 4 is like a truly great basketball player whose style of play is uniquely his own and who transforms the performance of the entire team through his inspired approach to the game.

Coaching Tools and Approaches for Quadrant 4

The following are strategies for coaches to consider integrating into their Quadrant 4 coaching engagements:

- *Ask "What if?"* It is the coach's role to ask a client to look beyond perceived limitations and imagine what might be on the other side. Like the elephant that no longer challenges the chains that restrained it as a baby, clients sometimes need to be reminded that they have grown in significant ways and are capable of accomplishing more than they believe.

  Clare first suggested the idea of the integrated solution in a coaching call with Tressa more as a piece of wishful thinking than a viable course of action. Listening carefully, Tressa could hear Clare's belief in the concept hiding under the layer of reasons why it would never work. As Clare's coach, Tressa encouraged Clare to really look at each of the excuses that she was offering for why the idea would not fly to honestly identify which ones were real. Through this process, Tressa was able to help Clare identify the assumptions she was making, both about what others were likely to support and what she was capable of. By untangling the story, Tressa helped Clare see what questions she would need to get answered and what assumptions she would need to test in order to determine if her idea had potential.

Quadrant 4 is the place where clients come face-to-face with the assumptions they make about what is possible. Often the assumptions are ones that help clients feel safe. As long as Clare was certain that no one would support an integrated solution, she felt there was no point in presenting it. If she let go of that assumption, then she would come face-to-face with her fear of stepping out and taking the risk. Coaches must work carefully in this area. It is the coach's responsibility to help the client determine if perceived impediments are real or not, but it is solely the client's responsibility to choose whether to move forward with something. It is the coach's role to hold a space for the client to make these kinds of important decisions.

- *Weave the threads together.* Quadrant 4 is the space in which the various aspects of development that clients have gone through—both inside and outside coaching—come together. Often, the client has some gift or ability that she was not able to give full expression to because she lacked the supporting skills to fully realize that aspect of her potential. Clare had a gift for seeing business opportunities that others missed, yet she was frustrated in her efforts to really experience the impact of her unique perspective because she lacked the interpersonal and leadership skills to enroll others to support her ideas. Through her coaching experience, Clare was able to bring online the skills she needed to champion the team's efforts to develop new technology to take advantage of market opportunities. Tressa helped Clare see that she was ready to play that leadership role. Sometimes the coach has to be the one to say "You're ready! You have everything you need to take this next step."

- *Illuminate the connections.* Building the web of support that is needed to bring new ideas to life requires the ability to see where the support is needed. It is the coach's role to ask the kinds of questions that illuminate the connections that need to be created if the client is not seeing them. At first, Clare felt that she really only needed to bring a few of her team members on board with her idea to get it accepted. When Tressa asked Clare who beyond the immediate team would be affected by what she was proposing, Clare started to see that she would needed the support of IT and other groups to move this idea forward. When Tressa asked Clare who could derail the integrated solution, Clare could see that a few key players were tangentially involved with implementing the idea and could really throw a wrench in the works if they started to actively resist. Clare was not expecting to get complete support from everyone, but she did need to be aware of the dynamics that underlie moving an initiative forward in an organization so that she could cultivate as much support as possible. Tressa guided Clare to see the outlines of the web she needed to build.

  Connections can come in all shapes and forms. Even clients who are implementing much less complicated efforts will need to take a more holistic view of their situation to see what needs to be created to provide necessary support.

- *Ask the courageous questions.* An element of courage is more present in Quadrant 4 than in any of the proceeding quadrants. It takes courage to act on one's inspiration. It takes courage to try something new. It takes courage to choose a direction and pursue it, especially when you are not sure where you are going to end up. Coaches need to be role models of courage, and in the fourth quadrant, that means asking the courageous questions, those that bring the client face-to-face with perceived limitations. Courageous questions need to be asked not as a challenge, but as an invitation to see something from a different perspective. When Clare wanted to wriggle away from introducing the idea of an integrated solution, it would have been easy for Tressa to concur that the idea was too farfetched to consider. Instead, Tressa asked Clare to play with the possibility that it could be done. This led to some big questions for Clare that revolved around who she would need to be in order to step into the role she had described. For Clare, it meant confronting her fear that she would be shot down for having such a bold idea. It also meant that Clare would have to have some difficult conversations.

Courageous questions can also guide clients to acknowledge what they know to be true and have been avoiding in some way, such as the possibility that they are in the wrong position or the fact that the client is participating in something that is not right for the person. Once answered, these questions compel clients to shift or move into action in some way. These questions get at the core of what is going on, the Aha! moments that open new doors of personal and professional growth and sometimes make us all uncomfortable. The discomfort is often fleeting and reveals a profound sense of relief that the essence of a personal or professional challenge is finally revealed, and now action can be taken.

Sometimes this can be a scary place for a coach to be. It is the moment when you see that you have been coaching the symptoms, and the root of what needs to be addressed is coming into focus. Clients need to go through the personal and professional development that the earlier quadrants provide in order to be ready to see and accept the nugget of truth that will open the door to new possibilities. This process occasionally happens as a moment of truth, but it is more likely that clients will come to their own awareness over time, guided by a series of courageous questions that are peppered into coaching conversations. Coaches need to guard against becoming so comfortable in their coaching relationships that they are unable or unwilling to challenge their clients to see the underlying dynamics that limit them from achieving what they want to create.

- *Get out of the way.* By the time a coach and client reach Quadrant 4, they have traveled a long road together. The coach will have played many roles for the client. He may have held her accountable for her commitments in Quadrant 1, guided her through some emotional conversations in Quadrant 2, and been a confidante for her fears in Quadrant 3 as she tried trusting her intuition in a more significant way. It is common for coaches to play a more active role in the earlier quadrants, providing tools, role-modeling new approaches, and offering possible ideas or solutions to consider.

  As the client moves into the fourth quadrant, the coach's touch must become lighter. At times the coach's role may be just to witness the client's success and celebrate his achievements. The questions become more focused and often more profound. So much of what the client needs to know now resides within him, and his real work is to trust this knowledge. The coach needs to recognize when it is time to step out of the picture.

The Leading with Insight Model

Although the Leading with Insight model has been presented in a linear fashion, clients tend to move through the quadrants in a more circuitous manner. They may be working in more than one quadrant at a time, just as Clare had to expand her abilities to engage in meaningful one-on-one conversations with her peers as she worked on her Quadrant 3 goal of getting her team to approve her earlier proposal. Sometimes clients set more challenging goals for themselves and need to shore up their work in earlier quadrants to support this new level of achievement. This often happens when a client is promoted. The new position will most likely create more pressures and may involve having more difficult conversations or working with a much larger network of people. Clients may choose to deepen their facility with the earlier touchstones in order to step successfully into these new challenges.

The Leading with Insight model describes the web of development that underlies the vast array of outcomes that coaching can deliver. The development that is described is sometimes handled overtly in coaching conversations, but it is more often integrated into the context of the coaching work.

It is important to bring this model into our awareness now to ensure that the essence of what makes coaching so powerful is not lost as more structure, focus, and discipline are applied to this complex process. The opportunity before us now is to harness the power of coaching to transform people and organizations in strategically significant ways. The challenge is not to lose the power of coaching in the process.

Quadrant 4: Original Action

Focus: Step change, on any level from personal to system-wide

Insight: Inspirational

Touchstones:

- Belief in possibilities
- Have faith
- Build connections
- Demonstrate clear commitment

Essential Outcome: Personal Power

Section Two
Managing Coaching Initiatives

7

Coaching as a Strategic Initiative

In the preceding four chapters, we have read some wonderful stories about how people grew personally and professionally with the guidance of their coaches. In Chapter 3, Jane was under fire as the HR manager responsible for, among other things, dealing with the challenges of a merger. She felt overwhelmed trying to do all of her responsibilities, was underperforming, and lashed out at her colleagues. Her coach was ultimately able to get Jane focused and performing at a higher level. Jane's relationships with colleagues improved along the way as well.

In Chapter 4, Jack had major issues with relationships, and given his new promotion to client relationship VP, these issues had to be urgently addressed. Jack's coach helped him work more effectively with clients and adopt partnering skills that enabled him and his extended team to deliver what the clients needed.

We learned in Chapter 5 how Mark utilized coaching to expand his repertoire of leadership behaviors, which enhanced his ability to manage those situations that were especially challenging. As a result, his team's on-time performance for project delivery increased, the team was more satisfied with their work, and two team members were brought back from the brink of termination.

In the fourth and final story presented in Chapter 6, Clare hit her stride as a VP. She tempered her enthusiasm, learned how to listen, gained influencing skills, and was able to rally consensus for her business proposals.

The Leading with Insight model demonstrated how coaching created value for people at four different levels. As the coaching relationships evolved, more value was created. The opportunity facing organizations is how to harness that value and drive the value to the business. Coaching taps into a well that is rich in resources. Our challenge now is how organizations can draw from this well to drive tangible results to the business, without losing what makes coaching so powerful in the first place.

The Organization Context for Individual Growth

These stories, as powerful as they were, were played out on a greater stage—that of their respective organizations. At this point, we transition to this greater stage. Let's begin with Jane. Originally, Jane's boss convinced her to work with a coach. At first she was unwilling, because no one else was working with a coach. There were no organizational objectives for coaching, other than to make sure that Jane was at the top of her game to successfully deal with the merger. Jane clearly benefited from the coaching, and we suspect that the organization did as well, although the organizational benefits are intangible. Jane's boss was satisfied with her progress and the outcomes from coaching, but it did not dawn on him that others in the business might benefit from coaching as well. For Jane's boss, coaching was something that "fixed" people, rather than a developmental process with potential business impact.

Jack's situation was similar to Jane's in that both were struggling and both were directed to a coach by their respective bosses. Jack's boss, however, had his eyes set on a bigger prize than just Jack "getting fixed." There were clear business implications for the outcomes of Jack's coaching experience: increased client satisfaction, improved project management, and better teamwork. Jack's boss was satisfied when he heard all of the unsolicited testimonials from clients and team members about the progress Jack had made. So, these benefits, while valued, were intangible and as such did not hit the boss's radar screen. Coaching was not continued in the organization despite Jack's success.

Mark's situation takes us to a bigger stage. He was part of a leadership development program that included 80 other leaders, and coaching was an important element of this program. The company, PharmaQuest (a fictitious name), a large pharmaceutical manufacturer, had a lot riding on this leadership development program. The pipeline of new products was dwindling, and in the COO's words, "the bureaucratic sclerosis was killing us!" Coaching, in contrast to Jane and Jack's experience, was an initiative with an expected business payoff. We will learn in the next chapter just how important it is to set the strategic context for coaching in order for the business payoff to be realized. Without this strategic context, coaching may produce value but not the kind of value expected by senior leadership or most needed by the business.

This begs the question: What makes a coaching initiative strategic? Clare's experience sheds some light on this issue. Clare was a VP who, along with her peers and boss (the company president), was being coached. Coaching was initiated for many reasons. Clare, for example, wanted a coach to help her rally her peers to embrace her ideas for integrated solutions. The company president was most concerned about the eroding product margins and his inability to focus his direct reports on this issue. Everyone had their own issues, and coaching was viewed as the solution to each of these issues. There was no strategic glue to hold all of these coaching relationships together. The glue was structural in nature (e.g., they were all part of the senior leadership team), but just because the coaching was directed at the top of the house does not necessarily mean that the coaching initiative was strategic. Let's now turn to answering the question about what makes a coaching initiative strategic.

Criteria for Coaching as a Strategic Initiative

The missing ingredient in three of these four stories is understanding how coaching created value for the business (the jury is still out with Mark, and we pick up the rest of the PharmaQuest story in the next chapter). In order for coaching to deliver on its value promise to both individuals and organizations, the coaching initiative must be designed and managed as a strategic initiative and, as such, meet the following criteria:

- Sponsorship for coaching must be sustained and unwavering.
- The strategic needs of the business must be articulated and shared.
- Clear goals for the initiative must be set that link to the strategic needs.
- The outcomes of the coaching initiative must be evaluated to determine if the initiative delivered on its value promise.
- The initiative must be actively managed in a way that respects the privacy of the coaching relationships.

Let's examine each of these areas in more detail and look ahead to see how the subsequent chapters illuminate these critical criteria.

Sponsorship for Coaching Must Be Sustained and Unwavering

Sponsoring a coaching initiative may be done at many levels in the organization and requires more than just paying for the coaches. Sponsorship takes on several responsibilities. The sponsor has decided to make an investment of time and money that will have value to the business. These investments must be managed, and the value must be realized. Many people will look to the sponsor for leadership and guidance on how best to manage and participate in the coaching initiative. Business conditions change and sometimes unexpectedly worsen. The sponsor cannot flinch at the continued investment in coaching. Sponsorship must be sustained in order for the value to be realized, and keep in mind that this value may take more than a year to be realized. The mentality of managing quarter to quarter or having all financials neatly tied up in a bow every fiscal year will not work for coaching.

Sponsors are also champions. They must be perceived as active, visible advocates of the coaching initiative and articulate the benefits that will come from coaching. Sponsors must educate themselves about what coaching is (and is not). They have taken on the responsibility, whether they accept it or not, of driving the value of coaching to the business. They must understand the strategic needs of the business and how coaching will address these needs. The next chapter explores the role of the sponsor for the PharmaQuest coaching initiative. We will see how sponsorship was put at risk by not covering some of the bases just discussed.

Sponsorship may be viewed as a capability, rather than as just a person. Spreading sponsorship more broadly in the organization expands the ownership of coaching and spreads the wealth of knowledge about the kind of value coaching can deliver. Governance bodies comprising leaders who are chartered with oversight for coaching can be an effective way to expand sponsorship in an organization. Chapter 9 discusses how to leverage a governance body to sustain sponsorship of a coaching initiative.

The Strategic Needs of the Business Must Be Articulated and Shared

Launching a coaching initiative, or any strategic initiative for that matter, requires leaders to clearly articulate the strategic needs of the business. These needs must be communicated, shared, and widely accepted by others in the organization. These actions cannot be taken lightly; in fact, many leadership teams do not adequately articulate and share the strategic needs of the business. Clare's team is a case in point. Every leader had an important issue to address with his or her respective coach. These issues varied, based on their recent experiences and leadership roles in the organization. The company president's issue struck right to the heart of this point: how to align his leadership team to what he believed was the most critical strategic issue the company faced.

Conducting a needs assessment for the organization is often required to understand the deeper, strategic needs of an organization. The rationale for this assessment is similar to the rationale for conducting needs assessments for individual coaching clients: to get below the surface and get past presenting issues. The next chapter reviews several ways of conducting a needs assessment and explores the consequences of skipping these assessments for gaining value from coaching. We will learn that a lot hangs in the balance. Without a needs assessment, it is difficult to see how coaching is part of a strategic solution for the company. Coaching may not get the traction it needs, and sponsorship may be put at risk.

Clear Goals for the Initiative Must Be Set That Link to the Strategic Needs

A line of sight must be drawn from the coaching initiative to the strategic needs of the business. Realistic and achievable goals for coaching are set that have a direct bearing on addressing these strategic needs. In all likelihood, coaching will be only a part of the solution, but without drawing this line of sight, the potential contribution of coaching becomes opaque. Drawing this link to the strategic needs also provides a firm foundation later on for isolating the effects coaching has on the business from other potential influencing factors.

Goals for coaching that are not linked to the business will have little value as time wears on. Month by month, the investment in coaching builds and the gap between the investment and the expected payoff widens. The chorus of senior leaders questioning the value of coaching gets louder. In the next chapter, we see how linking coaching goals to the business opens new doors to increase the traction of coaching in the organization. A business case formally establishes the value of coaching. Decisions about initiative scope and timing can be better made. It becomes clearer how to best integrate coaching with other HR and business initiatives to maximize the benefit of all initiatives.

Goals that are developed for a coaching initiative must go beyond simply aiming for better learning or leaders having increased insight. From a business perspective, learning and insight are not enough. Applying what is learned and taking action on insights is required in order for the business to benefit. Sights can be set even higher for coaching. Goals can specify business impact areas such as increased productivity or reduced costs. A goal can be set for having coaching provide a satisfactory ROI. Chapter 12 explores how a company articulated a clear strategic need: penetrating the consumer electronics market for point-of-sale optical scanners. Objectives for coaching were set that had a direct bearing on this strategic need. Monetary benefits were documented and the ROI calculated. This chapter explores the mechanics of evaluation and how to build credibility for the analysis.

The Outcomes of the Coaching Initiative Must Be Evaluated to Determine if the Initiative Delivered on Its Value Promise

Hope springs eternal. Without an evaluation architecture in place, it is difficult to know whether coaching delivered on its value promise. Leaders may hope that it did deliver value, but it is difficult to bank on hope alone. Evaluation objectives are developed that flow from the initiative goals. In this way, the line of sight is extended from the overall strategic goals of the business to the evaluation objectives of coaching. The evaluation of coaching then has a direct bearing on achieving business results. Chapter 12 provides an example of how this can be done in a way that shows monetary as well as intangible benefits. ROI was the icing on the cake.

An ROI evaluation has benefits in and of itself: there is an ROI to ROI. This message is brought home in Chapter 11 as the evaluation strategy was developed for a company. The soundness of this strategy sets up the payoff punch for gaining results illustrated in Chapter 12. Evaluation is not an after-market accessory. Rather, evaluation is most effective when it is built into the fabric of the initiative. Interim evaluations are taken as the coaching progresses to nip problems in the bud. Corrective actions can be taken that will increase the overall value of the coaching initiative. Managers of the initiative watch program expenses like a hawk, knowing that a final accounting will be made and that costs will be compared to the return. Consequently, managers will continue to drive down costs, which will ultimately increase the ROI.

Not everyone is looking for monetary benefits or an ROI from coaching. In fact, this is usually the case. Just knowing that leaders successfully applied what they gained from coaching to their work responsibilities may be sufficient. Chapter 13 explores how coaching may be evaluated in terms of application, rather than by monetary terms. The case study shows how to best plan for this type of evaluation and the major decision areas that must be addressed along the way.

The Initiative Must Be Actively Managed in a Way That Respects the Privacy of the Coaching Relationships

Managing a coaching initiative is like doing a high-wire act in the circus. You must have excellent balance between managing the coaching initiative and honoring the privacy of the coaching relationships. One misstep in either direction and you can come crashing to the floor (or hopefully the safety net). If you do not set a strategic context for coaching then you cannot reasonably expect coaching to deliver strategic value. However, if you micromanage coaching relationships the privacy and integrity of the relationships may be compromised. Executive coaching is a high visibility activity—everyone is watching. When the executive coaching initiative has successfully completed and you make it to the other platform at the end of the high wire, there may be cheers, or most likely, quiet recognition that the initiative was effectively managed. How do you as the initiative manager strike this balance? Chapter 9 speaks to those who manage coaching initiatives by presenting the best practices that have been observed during formal evaluations of coaching. In one case, a manager set up signposts for how coaching would progress in the organization. The manager then asked each client and coach to record the date when each signpost was reached. In this way, the manager tracked the progress of each coaching relationship without getting into the private content of their work.

Chapter 9 also introduces the role of coaching companies. Coaching companies work with many different client organizations and can be an excellent source of best practices. These best practices are valuable to the client company in that the overall value of coaching can be improved. Coaching companies also provide a valuable service to the coaches. They perform the consulting services, such as client relationship management, contracting, billing, and gaining extension work, that coaches are unwilling or unable to perform themselves. Chapter 10 is dedicated to helping coaches sort out how to be an effective consultant, if they so desire. Earning more coaching work in an organization requires more—and different—actions than simply providing great coaching. For coaches who do not wish to be consultants, coaching companies are waiting in the wings.

The Cast of Players—and Their Responsibilities

As these stories have unfolded, new players have emerged. We started with the coach and the client. At the close of this section, we find ourselves peaking behind the scenes to see what's next, and new roles have emerged: the sponsor of coaching, governance bodies, the manager of the coaching initiative, providers of coaching services, and the evaluation specialist. Let's look briefly at the top five roles and the responsibilities for each of those who fulfill these roles for a coaching initiative.

The Sponsor of Coaching

- Provides the overall strategic direction for coaching
- Ensures that the coaching initiative will impact a strategic need of the business
- Provides funding and resources for the initiative

- Evaluates progress and makes decisions regarding significant changes to the original deployment plan
- Continues to be an active, visible advocate of coaching
- Organizes, and often leads, a governance body that oversees coaching as a strategic initiative

Governance Body

- Provides direction to the initiative manager
- Performs "blocking and tackling" for the initiative, removing barriers and opening doors
- Makes major decisions about design and deployment
- Ensures that coaching is appropriately integrated with other initiatives
- Oversees the evaluation of the initiative

The Manager of the Coaching Initiative

- Develops the project plan, the evaluation plan, and the deployment plan
- Makes the day-to-day decisions regarding the initiative
- Facilitates the governance body meetings, setting the agenda, cueing up the decisions to be made, and providing periodic updates on progress
- Periodically meets with the coaches, the coaching company, and/or the broker to gain their perspective on progress
- Manages the communications activities so that people are appropriately informed of the coaching initiative, its progress, and accomplishments

Coaching Companies

- Educate potential clients about the value of coaching and the organizational requirements for a coaching initiative
- Contract with the client; agree on the investment, scope, and timing

- Share best practices and thought leadership for designing and managing coaching initiatives
- Qualify coaches and ensure that successful matches are made between coaches and clients
- Partner with the initiative manager to manage the deployment of coaching and, if appropriate, determine how to expand coaching to others in the organization

The Evaluation Specialist

- Provides expertise on setting objectives for coaching and determining how to evaluate success
- Develops an evaluation architecture for the life cycle of the coaching initiative, which includes all data collection instruments and materials
- Conducts interim evaluations and recommends how to improve the deployment of coaching
- Performs the final evaluation that is guided by the evaluation objectives
- Recommends how to improve the impact of coaching and leadership development

This cast of characters must work in unison to deliver on the value promise of coaching. If any of these roles is left out or not successfully performed, the entire ability of coaching to deliver value may be compromised. If sponsorship wanes, then people in the organization will begin to shift their time and resources to other endeavors that enjoy stronger sponsorship. Without a governance body, the coaching initiative will lack the visibility and broad-based ownership required for success. Without a strong manager, the coaching initiative will quickly dissolve into a chaotic collection of coaching conversations. Brokers who do not leverage their expertise deprive organizations of taking advantage of best practices. Not inviting an evaluation specialist to the party leaves the punch line hanging and people asking: "What value did coaching create?"

Managing Value Creation

The stories presented in this section illustrated how coaching initiatives created value for the individual being coached and, consequently, for the organization. In order for coaching to be sustained and to grow as a value-added profession, it must create value in both camps because individuals who do not feel that coaching is valuable will not sign up with a coach, and companies that do not gain value from coaching will no longer sponsor it. It is therefore important to think of coaching as more than just a string of coaching relationships. Coaching is a strategic initiative that expands leadership capability. As a strategic initiative, coaching can be managed in a way that honors the individual coaching relationships and drives value from these relationships to the business. Individual value and organizational value are not mutually exclusive: each is enhanced by the other.

The Leading with Insight model shows that as the coaching relationship evolves, new doors open for individuals. New levels of insight are tapped. Leadership styles expand, and new sources of value are created. These developments produce big dividends for the organization as well. Until now, people sponsoring, managing, or participating in coaching initiatives did not have an effective way of capturing the monetary value of coaching. The subsequent chapters in this book show how to create the strategic context for coaching, to capture the monetary benefits of coaching, to isolate these effects from other potential influencing factors, and to calculate the return on investment. The practical tools, best practices, and methodologies in this book are proven to create bottom-line value from leadership coaching.

8

Creating Context and Purpose for Coaching

Coaching has proven to be effective in developing people to assume greater leadership roles. Section One tells the stories of four such people as they utilized coaching to springboard their careers and self-development. The coach and client deserve all the credit for making such great progress; however, these stories could have taken a different turn if these coaching relationships were not so strongly grounded in the organization. In order for coaching to flourish, many choices have to be made about creating the right context for coaching. As we will learn later with PharmaQuest, rushing in to initiate coaching with several leaders without first setting the strategic context for the initiative can have unforeseen and unwanted consequences.

Choice and Context for Coaching

For most businesses, developing people is a means to an end—not the end itself. Investing in the development of people must return value to the organization. Developing leaders raises the stakes given the higher expectations for how leaders will impact the organization. A lot is riding on how quickly leaders develop to the point at which they can assume greater responsibilities. Coaching adds value by accelerating the development process and focusing development on the most salient and higher impact areas for the leaders.

One way of looking at the organizational context for leadership development is with a supply and demand model. Ideally, an organization wants to achieve a balance between the leaders it needs (demand) and the leaders it has (supply). In a balanced situation, if the demand for leaders increases, then the company has a ready supply of leaders who can meet this demand. In today's turbulent business climate, the demand for leaders can spike or tank with little notice. When either of these situations happens, a lot of stress can be placed on the leader supply process.

When the demand for leaders spikes (i.e., the demand rapidly and unpredictably increases), there may not be enough leaders on hand to meet the demand. People in the organization may be tapped to take on leadership roles they are not quite ready for. In these cases, added support such as coaching must be given to these new leaders so they may succeed. Another source of leaders comes from recruiting leaders from other companies. In these cases, newly hired leaders will need support to readily fit into the new organization. Whether the leader is sourced internally or externally, coaching can be highly effective in providing the support required for these leaders to succeed. Coaches can enable the newly appointed leader to more quickly develop a winning leadership style and gain acceptance from others for the new role. Coaches can work with a newly hired leader to effectively adapt his or her leadership style to the company's culture and business priorities.

When the demand for leaders tanks (i.e., the demand suddenly drops), several leaders may find themselves without a position or underutilized in their positions. CEOs may issue the "abandon ship" order precipitating the exodus of many employees. This situation would seem to eliminate the need for developing leaders, let alone coaching them. In fact, this is what typically happens. The experience of Nortel Networks, however, suggests a different and perhaps better path. In 2001, the markets in which Nortel Networks was a dominant player all took a nosedive. Over the course of a year or so, half of their 100,000 employees were laid off. The business and HR leaders reasoned that during these extremely challenging times, the

Figure 8.1 Leadership Supply Process

need for leadership was even greater. Moreover, these markets would come back at some point, and they knew they had to have the right leaders in place to hit the ground running when the business climate improved. Nortel Networks stayed the course with its coaching initiative during 2001 for more than 70 of its top emerging leaders. This strategy had an immediate payoff in terms of more effectively managing through the tough transition and a longer-term payoff of having a strong bench of leaders ready to seize new market opportunities.

Coaching is but one development activity in the greater leader supply process, and it is important to understand this entire process so that coaching can be placed in an organizational context. A leader supply process has four major components, as illustrated in Figure 8.1: selecting, developing, managing, and transitioning. Organizations may slice and dice these four components in different ways, but all four will be present in any leader supply process.

- *Selecting leaders.* Leaders may be selected internally from within the company or recruited externally from other companies. Generally, internal promotions are favored over recruiting. The track record of hiring leaders, especially senior ones, is not encouraging. These leaders come with a high price tag and often struggle to adapt to the company's culture. Assessment strategies have proven effective in making a better match between a candidate and the culture. Most selection decisions are based on a formal assessment process. The "good old boy" network approach has been largely (but not completely) displaced. Ideally, the assessment tools, such as competency models, are based on the same criteria used for development and performance management. For external candidates, assessment centers are being increasingly used to make successful selection decisions. For internal candidates, rating and ranking systems may be used to identify high-potential leaders, pointing out who is ready immediately and who will be ready soon for promotion. Assessment information based on competencies or behaviors can be extremely valuable to the coach working with the leader. The leader's areas of strength and improvement opportunities can be suggested by assessment data and provide a rich foundation for coaching.

- *Developing leaders.* There are many different approaches to leadership development. Many of the more traditional, classroom-based approaches are being replaced with more experiential activities such as action learning and job rotations. Action learning sessions involve leaders who are drawn from across the business enterprise to work collaboratively for a week or so on a real business issue. Their work is facilitated by someone who works with the client (the person who owns the issue) to set the objectives and then guides the team activities to reach these objectives. Job rotations involve having leaders take on a new position for a limited amount of time, usually less than one year. The intention is for leaders to learn how to quickly assess new situations, set goals, and energize a team to achieve the goals.

  Whatever approaches to development are used, coaching is emerging as an effective way for leaders to reflect on their experiences and to better integrate their learnings from a wide variety of sources. Leaders do not learn only by doing; they also learn by reflecting on what they have done. Coaches can accelerate the reflection process and help leaders focus on the most salient aspects of their experiences, drawing valuable lessons that can shape near-term behavior and long-term leadership style. For example, many organizations are grappling with how to ensure that their leaders see the big picture and work collaboratively across organizational boundaries ("silos"). The big picture here refers to being able to think strategically, decipher major market trends, and see what needs to be done to optimize business opportunities. Leaders must also be silo busters, letting go of their parochial perspectives and doing what is right to optimize the entire business enterprise, not just their own area. Coaches provide an external, more objective perspective that can take the blinders off leaders so they see more of the world around them. Coaches open up possibilities for the client to improve collaboration with other leaders and build effective cross-silo networks.

- *Managing leaders.* Organizations typically have an annual schedule of performance appraisal reviews. This is often the only time people receive feedback on their performance, and even in these cases, the primary purpose of the review is often to make compensation decisions, rather than to open up development opportunities. It is challenging to have an open and frank discussion of performance when this discussion forms the basis for decisions about money and possibly promotion eligibility. It is important to separate feedback for the purpose of development from performance evaluation feedback. Mixing the two in one conversation waters down the impact of the feedback. This leads to performance appraisals becoming safe, relatively comfortable pro forma conversations in which it is easier for managers to sugarcoat performance issues rather than deliver honest feedback. It is little wonder that development planning that is based on these reviews often fails to hit its mark. Managers feel relieved that the annual review has been completed with no ruffled feathers, and the subordinate is left scratching his or her head about what just happened. These data hold little value for a coach to gain insights into a client's development needs. As a result, most coaches will have to conduct their own performance assessments at the beginning of a coaching relationship. Tools such as multirater feedback discussions, leadership style surveys, and others will be used to help the coach and client pinpoint the most critical issues on which to work.

■ *Transitioning leaders.* Transition decisions about leaders are based on individual performance and capability, and organizational need. A formal succession planning process is intended to look into the near future and line up leaders who can potentially be promoted into certain positions. Leaders are often characterized as "ready now" or "ready in one or two years." Positions are ranked according to their criticality to the business. The outcome of succession planning is to ensure that leadership bench strength is queued up to those positions that are most critical to the company. Coaching has proven effective in two ways: (1) accelerating the readiness of leaders to assume new roles and (2) helping leaders hit the ground running when they assume these roles. For example, when Clare became a VP (in Chapter 6), she was faced with many challenges, not the least of which was gaining support from her peers for the business development opportunities she proposed. Her coach provided her with a more structured way to assess people's actions, understand their intentions, and tap into intuition to effectively influence others.

Of course, another transitional path for a leader is to be separated from the company for performance reasons. In some cases, leaders who have performance issues are assigned a coach, even though the decision has pretty much been made to separate the leader from the company. This is when coaching becomes "coach-out," and coaches need to be aware—and beware—of these situations. If the situation is perceived as unsalvageable, the coach must ask the sponsor of the coaching about the true intentions for initiating coaching. If it turns out to be a coach-out situation, then all parties must honestly come to grips with the situation. If this does not happen, then it is best for the coach to disengage from the coaching relationship. This really comes down to a matter of integrity; disengaging from this relationship will avoid a lot of frustration and hurt feelings on the part of all involved.

Case Study: Launching Coaching at PharmaQuest

PharmaQuest (a fictitious name), a large pharmaceutical company, grew rapidly through acquisitions until there was no other company left to buy that would propel its growth. Organic growth was the next challenge. The investment community was interested in how this new global powerhouse would create new drugs. What was in the tank ready to go to market and what was under development? Internally, the company was in near chaos, and the leaders seemed shell-shocked as to what to do next. Some leaders abandoned ship: about 10 percent of the leaders had been recruited out of the company in the last six months to go to other firms. The COO and HR senior VP agreed that they needed to take immediate action: open leadership positions had to be filled, leaders had to be retained, and promising new compounds had to be developed.

Unfortunately, over the past several years, little in the way of leadership development had been undertaken. For the most part, leadership development was viewed as costly, and the business would be better served if the money was deposited in the acquisition war chest. PharmaQuest now seemed to be paying for its past sins of not developing leaders. Now it was time to play catch-up. Executive coaching was viewed as a way to accelerate the development of leaders to take on new challenges and refocus themselves on bringing new products to market. Moreover, this program would be expanded to all support areas, including HR, IT, and finance.

The HR senior VP viewed this as an opportunity to demonstrate the tangible value that his HR team could provide to the business. They identified more than 80 leaders in the organization who were to be assigned coaches. They contracted with an international coaching company to provide the coaching. Their mandate was to get the leaders to build more effective teams and more effectively collaborate across the silos of the business units and functions. Ultimately, it was assumed that these improvements in leadership behaviors would accelerate the pipeline of new pharmaceutical products. The HR team launched other developmental initiatives for the leaders under the umbrella of Leadership Quest. Quarterly leadership workshops featured speeches by thought leaders and time for participants to discuss what they had learned. Cross-functional action learning teams were formed to work on specific problems identified by the COO and other senior leaders.

Twelve coaches began working with the 80 or so clients and agreed to conduct three 1-hour sessions per month for half a year. Given the lack of recent assessment data, each coach conducted a multi-rater feedback assessment for each client. Although gathering and analyzing the data was time consuming, the data suggested development areas that the clients needed to address first. About halfway through the six-month coaching process, the COO asked the HR senior VP for a status update. The HR senior VP was able to report that the coaching was on schedule and on budget and that the feedback from the clients was positive. The coaching initiative was being well managed. The COO, however, was asking a different set of questions. He wanted to know about the *impact* of the coaching, not how well it was being managed: How many more leaders will be ready for promotion? How many more compounds will be ready for first-stage testing? The HR senior VP replied that he did not have data to back up his assertions, but he did feel that the coaching and other leadership activities were contributing to the business. Intuitively, the COO agreed, but given the level of investment in leadership development, he wanted more concrete evidence that business benefits were being realized.

What drove the COO to ask the question about value was that, while the comments of the coaching clients were positive, there were questions about whether the coaching was hitting the mark. Stress seemed to be increasing, and some of the major sources of conflict seemed to be increasing, not decreasing. The coaching, and for that matter Leadership Quest, seemed to be hitting symptoms and not bedrock problems. Feeling better about the problems was not the same as fixing the problems, and fixing the problems was the order of the day if business benefits were to be gained from the investment in coaching.

Business benefits from coaching can be realized if the appropriate context for coaching has been set. The seeds of success for coaching are planted at the planning stage. It is incumbent on both the sponsors of coaching (in this case the COO and HR senior VP), the manager of the coaching initiative, and the deliverers of coaching (in this case the international coaching company) to establish the context for coaching. What could have gone differently at Pharma-Quest to set the context for coaching? This question is answered in terms of the three critical success factors for setting the context for coaching.

Critical Success Factors for Setting the Context for Coaching

There are three critical success factors for setting the context for coaching:

1. A *needs assessment* that shows how coaching is part of the solution
2. *Coaching objectives* that are specifically linked to business goals
3. A *business case* for coaching that includes investment requirements and business benefits of coaching

Each of these critical success factors will be discussed in the context of the case study. We will now turn back the clock in our case study.

A Needs Assessment That Shows How Coaching Is Part of the Solution

The COO and the HR senior VP tacitly assumed that coaching would contribute to achieving their goals. They felt that because there had been so little recent leadership development, just about any development at that point would be appreciated. However, people can appreciate a learning experience without that experience impacting the business or achieving business goals. The real question is: What contributions can the coaching initiative make to achieving business goals?

Answering this question requires an assessment that goes beyond the individual assessments that are typically a part of the coaching process. Table 8.1 summarizes some of the most common assessments for both individuals and organizations. Coaches will routinely conduct intake interviews, conduct or review multisource feedback, and examine standardized test results. Some may have their client's write autobiographies. Coaches begin the coaching relationship on a firm footing of understanding the client's issues. A similar approach to assessment must be done at the organization level in order for coaching—as a strategic initiative—to positively impact the organization and contribute to achieving strategic goals. Several organization-focused assessments are summarized in Table 8.1. Realistically, coaches don't have the time or expertise to conduct an organizational assessment, however, coaches can advocate that such an assessment be conducted if it hasn't already, and certainly coaches can review the data from organization assessments that have been done.

Let's return to PharmaQuest and see how expanding the needs assessment to explore organizational issues helped to hone the objectives for coaching. Table 8.2 presents two of PharmaQuest's business goals, summarizes the needs assessments, and describes the coaching goals. The first business goal, increasing the number of leaders ready for promotion, was further explored with a series of focus groups and day-in-the-life studies. These assessments revealed

Table 8.1 Needs Assessment Activities

Assessment Activity	Description
Individual Intake Interview	The initial interview conducted by the coach with the client. This interview, which can last several hours, delves into the client's life history, professional background, perceived strengths and development opportunities, and charts an initial course of action. Actions typically include additional data collection.
Multisource, multirater	Data about a client's behaviors and performance are collected from his or her manager, peers, and subordinates to provide a variety of perspectives. Data are summarized to focus on themes, observed strengths, and development opportunities.
Standardized Tests	Standardized tests enable comparisons between the client and others who have taken the same test. Tests can be differentiated from surveys in that tests have been statistically calibrated (e.g., validity and reliability) so that norms can be established. The Myers-Briggs Type Indicator, for example, can provide insights into a client's personal styles and preferences.
Autobiography	The client writes his or her life history, beginning with early childhood and continuing to the present day. Data are reviewed to discover patterns in the client's life that continue to play out in his or her current professional situation. These patterns, if dysfunctional, may offer insights into more root cause issues of performance.
Organization Focus Groups	Several people, typically 10 to 12, are organized into a group to review and discuss a specific topic or issue. A facilitator follows a protocol of questions to guide the group's inquiry into the organizational topic or issue. Focus group members are drawn from a diversity of backgrounds to provide a wide variety of perspectives and create "out-of-the-box" thinking.
Day-in-the-Life Studies	The consultant will spend the entire day as the employee's "shadow," observing everything the person does that day. The consultant will be as unobtrusive as possible and collect data on how the client interacts

Table 8.1 *Continued*

Assessment Activity	Description
	with others, conducts meetings, makes decisions, and so forth. Observing call centers or customer care centers can be especially revealing about operational problems.
Process Mapping	The consultant will construct a "box-and-wire" diagram that describes the leader's process for doing business. This enables the coach to better understand the business context for the leader's issues and the leader's role in the business.
Organization Structure Analysis	The consultant reviews organization charts and documents the major responsibilities for the key people who interact with the client. These data can be reviewed for span-of-control, diagramming power structures, planning for data collection, and many other uses.
Customized Surveys and Interviews	Customized surveys and interviews are used to explore key themes and issues that are specific to the organization. Interviewing selected leaders, for example, may be useful to follow-up on issues uncovered during process mapping.
Six Sigma or Quality Improvement Projects	Most organizations have an institutionalized quality or continuous improvement program. Six Sigma methodology is the latest in a long line of such programs. Quality projects are an excellent source of information about a company's operational issues and how these issues have been addressed. This information can be reviewed as part of an overall effort to learn more about the company and its key performance issues.

that the leaders were struggling to manage change in their respective organizations. Their employee's weren't sure what was going to happen next and the overall level of communications was quite low. The leaders were perceived as bottlenecks that kept employees distant from the more senior leaders of the organization and from fully understanding the business strategy. As a result of the assessment, it was decided that leaders would participate in change

Table 8.2 Setting Coaching Objectives at PharmaQuest

Business Goals	Needs Assessment	Coaching Objectives
1. Increase the number of leaders ready for promotion to open leadership positions	Leaders lack the requisite change management skills to embrace challenging new opportunities, diagnose organization needs, and engage others to meet these needs. • Focus groups • Day-in-the-life studies	Each client successfully adapts the change management principles and practices to his or her specific situation.
2. Increase the number of products ready for the first stage of testing	Leaders lack role clarity, which limits their ability to work collaboratively with other leaders and compromises their ability to provide direction for their direct reports. • Organization structure analysis	Each client enacts his or her new responsibilities quickly and collaboratively with other leaders.

management workshops to gain the requisite skills. As part of the follow-up to these workshops, the leaders would work with their respective coaches to adapt the change management principles and practices to their work environment.

The second business goal was to increase the number of products ready for first-stage testing. A series of "turf battles" had broken out amongst the leaders as they jockeyed for position in the leadership hierarchy. No one was being well served while these battles continued. An organization structure analysis revealed flaws in the design of the organization that muddied the waters about who was supposed to be responsible for what. As a result of the assessment, roles and responsibilities were remapped and more closely aligned with the product-to-market business process. Leaders then looked to their coaches to help them hit the ground running with their new responsibilities, and in some cases, to rebuild some bridges to other leaders.

Coaching Objectives That Are Specifically Linked to Business Goals

We just learned how expanding the assessment process to include more organizational issues can open the door to developing coaching objectives that are specifically linked to business goals. Coaching clients in change management will accelerate their readiness for promotion opportunities (Goal #1) and coaching clients in enacting their new roles will enable them to work more effectively together to develop new compounds more quickly (Goal #2). This is not to say that the *only* objectives for coaching are those that can be linked to business goals. Indeed, clients will have personal and professional objectives for coaching that do not have an immediate bearing on a business goal. The point here is that business goals and individual objectives are not mutually exclusive, and in fact, are two sides of the same development coin. The first section of this book provides some wonderful examples:

- In Chapter 3 Jane utilized coaching to get more focused on top priorities and work more effectively with her colleagues. As a result she was more effective dealing with the challenges of the merger and made the merger more successful (business goal).
- In Chapter 4 Jack struggled with his new promotion and utilized coaching to improve his partnering and collaboration skills. As a result he was better able to meet customer needs, improve customer satisfaction and increase revenue (business goal).
- In Chapter 5 Mark developed a new set of more effective leadership behaviors that were adapted to specific situations. As a result his team's on-time performance metric improved (business goal) and employee retention increased (another business goal).
- In Chapter 6 Clare utilized coaching to improve communication and influencing skills. As a result she more readily gained approval for her business proposals, which in turn improved the financial results of the business (business goal).

These stories illustrate the two-way street nature of a successful coaching initiative. Value propositions for both the individuals and the organization must be met. Ultimately, it is the business that is making the investment and this investment must have an acceptable return. All of which brings us to the business case.

A Business Case for Coaching That Includes Investment Requirements and Business Benefits of Coaching

A business case is a document that captures all of the relevant information for deciding whether to invest in a coaching initiative. This information includes how coaching will contribute to achieving business goals, the scope, the expected benefits, and required investments. The business case provides a foundation and direction for the design of the initiative and consists of five major sections: executive summary, contribution to business goals, scope of the coaching initiative, business impact and investment, and recommendations.

- *Executive summary.* Senior leaders in organizations who make investment decisions rarely have time to read voluminous reports and documents. Executive summaries express in one or two pages only the information necessary for leaders to make a decision about whether to proceed with the coaching initiative. Preparing the executive summary is also a useful exercise for the learning and development practitioner in that it forces the practitioner to distill all of the material in the business case down to its essence. This mental exercise will produce the few key messages that have to be delivered to the business leader to make the right decision.
- *Contribution to business goals.* The leader's decision to invest in the coaching initiative will be strongly swayed by how the initiative will contribute to achieving business goals. In this section, these goals are presented, and the specific ways in which the coaching initiative will help achieve these goals are

detailed. Achieving business goals at PharmaQuest, for example, was constrained by leadership. The HR senior VP presented coaching as a way to accelerate putting capable leaders in key product development positions. As a result, new products would be developed more quickly, which the COO identified as a top business goal.

- *Scope of the coaching initiative.* The scope represents the boundary conditions of the initiative and answers the who, what, when questions: How many executives will be coached from which business units or geographies, to address which kinds of issues, and over what time frame. Given how new coaching is a leadership development tool, it is often a good idea to describe what coaching is to the reader. This will dispel any misconceptions readers may have about coaching. Describing scope conditions in the business case may help inoculate the organization from "scope creep," which sets in as more people who were not originally intended to be coached end up being coached. Or the coaching reveals additional needs for team building, and the coaching company is authorized to launch a series of team-building workshops. These extensions of the original initiative design may all be good ideas, but having proscribed boundaries in the business case makes it clear when these boundaries are being crossed and supports making the right kinds of decisions during the authorization process.

- *Business impact and investment.* This section clarifies the why of conducting the coaching initiative: the benefits to the business. These benefits may be intangible or monetary. Intangible benefits are important, and their value to the business cannot be underestimated. Increasingly, however, business leaders want to know about the potential monetary benefits of development and HR initiatives. The evaluation methodology contained in this book clearly shows how the monetary benefits of coaching can be isolated from other potential influencing factors. Presenting monetary benefits, however, inevitably raises the question about how much it cost to produce the benefits. The projected cost of the coaching initiative must also be presented. The projected cost is fully loaded and includes items such as facilities cost, opportunity cost (the time of people to participate in coaching), vendor costs, telecommunications cost, and all other cost factors. ROI can be forecast based on projected benefits and cost, noting key assumptions.

- *Recommendations.* This section gets to the crux of the matter: making the decision to proceed with the coaching initiative. These recommendations outline the decision areas. In the case of PharmaQuest, for example, recommendations could have been made about the scope (80 clients) and key activities (multirater assessments). Given that coaching, or even leadership development for that matter, was new to the company, a pilot coaching project could have been recommended. The coaching pilot would have involved fewer people (say five to ten) and limited the initial risk to the company. The pilot project could have been evaluated, lessons learned, and then a larger initiative could have been deployed more effectively.

Of course, all of these good ideas were bypassed by the HR senior VP at PharmaQuest. The COO and HR senior VP had already agreed on proceeding with the coaching, so why bother with projecting the business impact, offering different options, or for that matter, why do the business case at all? For the simple reason that completing the business case helps create the organizational context for coaching to be successful. When the COO asked the question about the value coaching was creating, the HR senior VP was not prepared to answer the question. Moreover, if the HR senior VP had completed the business case, it would have been clear for everyone how this value was to be created. Preparations could have been made, evaluations planned, and impact on the business goals described. The business case is also the cornerstone for the design of the initiative. Preparing the business case precipitates critical deliberations about the scope and impact of the coaching initiative, which must be taken into account in order to successfully design the coaching initiative.

Designing a Coaching Initiative for Impact

Designing a coaching initiative is more than just stringing together a series of coaching relationships. The whole is different from the sum of its parts. The successful initiative design will secure strong sponsorship for the initiative, set clear boundaries in determining the scope of the initiative, integrate coaching with other developmental and/or HR processes, and define criteria to evaluate the success of the initiative.

Sponsorship

Sponsorship boils down to sustained commitment. A coaching initiative, or any development initiative for that matter, must have a sponsor who is willing and able to see the initiative through to completion. Together, the sponsor, who is often a senior business leader, and the learning leader commit to successfully designing and deploying coaching. This commitment is a two-way street. The sponsor is committing to invest in coaching, and the learning leader is committing to maximize the value of this investment. The business case (previously discussed) formalizes these commitments and provides a foundation for designing a coaching initiative with impact.

Sponsorship from a business leader must be earned. The key for a learning leader to earn sponsorship is for the learning leader to demonstrate that he or she cares about the success of the business. Learning leaders must be students of the business, learning what they can about business strategy, competitive position, markets, products, services, and solutions. Increasingly, learning leaders are business savvy and are able to articulate how the learning solution will benefit the business. The days of simply taking the order for "20 pounds of training" are over. Learning leaders must position coaching as a strategic solution required for achieving business goals.

Whether it's creating a need for change, identifying the "burning platform," or highlighting the performance gap, the needs assessment data can be leveraged to increase the level of sponsorship for the coaching initiative. The quality of sponsorship is only as good as the knowledge of the sponsor about the underlying needs for the initiative. As we saw from the PharmaQuest situation, the COO's continued sponsorship of the initiative was on thin ice, partly because the needs analysis did not dig deeply enough or in the right places.

Scope

Scope was defined in the previous section as outlining the boundaries of the coaching initiative: the who, what, and when factors of the initiative. The scope of a coaching initiative must address people, places, and processes.

Integration

Coaching is not done in a vacuum. In the case of PharmaQuest, coaching was one developmental initiative as part of an overall leadership development effort. The more all of the developmental activities can be integrated into one cohesive effort, the greater the value is likely to be from these activities. Integration optimizes the value for the whole effort. What does this mean for coaching? For starters, the coaching conversations can serve as a way for clients to reflect on and deepen their learning from other developmental activities. The coach, for example, can help a client reflect on how well he or she led the action learning team to solve a product development problem. Together, the coach and client can explore how effectively leadership and communication skills were applied and what could have been done differently.

Coaching conversations can also bring into sharper focus the specific developmental needs of each client. The client is then better able to seek those developmental activities that best address these needs. Coaching conversations are a journey that may end up in some unexpected places. The starting place for a client may be, for example, setting clearer goals for a team. As the coaching conversations dig deeper into the root causes for the lack of focus, what emerges is not goal setting but rather the need for the client to facilitate stronger partnerships between team members, fostered deeper appreciation for how the various disciplines represented on the team can work more effectively together. The real solution and development need for the client becomes deepening his insight into the underlying dynamics of the team and learning how to influence them more effectively. The client may seek additional developmental opportunities outside of the coaching sessions to address this need.

Integrating coaching with other developmental activities is accomplished through two major avenues: competencies and curricula. Many organizations have developed and validated a set of competencies that define success behaviors for people in the organization. Leaders are assessed according to these competencies, and then developmental activities, such as coaching, are offered to address the competency gaps. For example, cross-business unit collaboration and business acumen are two commonly revealed competency gaps. Organizations, especially larger ones, are under a great deal of pressure to have business units that are aligned, integrated, and focused on doing the greatest good for the entire business enterprise. Business units that act as a lone wolf—even if successful—are no longer tolerated by the rest of the pack. Business unit leaders must do more than run their own show; they must reach out to their peers to collectively run the business enterprise, even if it means suboptimizing the performance of their particular business unit. Understanding the big picture of the business taxes the business acumen of leaders. Someone who has spent his entire career in manufacturing now has to also understand inventory and distribution and appreciate the special challenges facing inventory management and the logistics of product distribution.

The learning curve for many leaders is steep, which brings us to the curriculum. Developmental activities are meant to accelerate the learning curve and speed a leader's time to develop required competencies. Coaching is an important piece of the curriculum, but not the only piece. Action learning, job rotations, job shadowing, leadership workshops, university courses, and other activities all make up the curriculum for leadership development. Coaching may be used to help leaders integrate all of their experiences, draw essential learnings, and apply these learnings to their leadership responsibilities. For example, a leader may be coached to build more effective collaboration skills while she participates in an action learning team. Coaching is most effective when it is integrated with other developmental activities and grounded in a validated competency model.

Success Criteria

A central question for the design of a coaching initiative is: What will success look like? Success can be broadly measured in two ways: intangible and monetary benefits. Intangible benefits are those that are not, or cannot, be translated into monetary terms. Just because benefits are intangible does not mean that they are not important. In fact, the opposite is true. Intangible benefits are often the most important benefits to the business. Benefits such as employee engagement, customer satisfaction, and improved teamwork deliver real value to the organization. Coaching initiatives must compete with other business initiatives for investment, and these other business initiatives offer intangibles along with a monetary return on investment. In order to be considered successful, coaching initiatives must deliver well defined benefits.

9

Best Practices for Managing a Successful Coaching Initiative

For two years, Wendy had advocated executive coaching for the top 100 leaders of this global large equipment manufacturer. When Wendy finally got the green light from the new CEO, she found new meaning in the old adage: "Be careful what you wish for because you may get it." Wendy was challenged to provide coaching to 100 leaders in eight countries around the world and was soon confronted with the reality that very few companies were capable of providing globally distributed coaching services.

Wendy turned to a global coaching services provider. This coaching company had qualified more than 150 coaches according to criteria including business experience, coaching experience, education, and other credentials. These coaches, although mostly U.S.-based, were drawn from other regions around the world as well and covered most of the countries (and all of the languages) that Wendy required. One big advantage that the broker provided to Wendy was giving her a single point of contact to manage the delivery of all the coaching. This was especially important, given that more than 20 coaches would be utilized over an eight-month period. Another advantage of using this company was tapping the company's expertise in designing and managing a coaching initiative. In fact, a big selling point for Wendy came when she reviewed the coaching company Web site and saw how they had drawn from their practical experiences to describe four best practices for managing a successful coaching initiative. In the months that followed the launch of the coaching initiative, Wendy worked with the coaching company to implement these ideas, which have application to all coaching initiatives. These four best practices are as follows:

1. Leverage a governance body to sustain sponsorship
2. Conduct an orientation session to improve deployment
3. Set up signposts to gauge how coaching is progressing
4. Build performance evaluation into the coaching process

Leverage a Governance Body to Sustain Sponsorship

As we learned in the previous chapter, sponsorship for a coaching initiative, like any strategic initiative, must be earned every day. Senior leaders who sponsor coaching have so many competing interests that it is often difficult for them to sustain interest and focus on coaching. Sponsors of coaching are footing the bill, and they typically expect a return on this investment, whether monetary or intangible. Sponsorship begins to wane when leaders become skeptical that the coaching initiative will deliver the value it is supposed to deliver. The loss of sponsorship will likely stop any plans to expand coaching in the organization. When leaders begin asking "What value is coaching providing the business?" it is a sign that sponsorship may be at risk. If leaders see the value, they will not feel the need to ask this question. If this question is not answered quickly, the leaders will fill in the blanks and assume that coaching is providing no discernible value. Sponsorship should never be taken for granted.

Some strategies for sustaining sponsorship are as follows:

- *Decentralize sponsorship to a governance body.* Given the global nature and scope of the coaching initiative, Wendy reasoned that a cross-business unit governance body was required to spread the wealth of knowledge about the value of coaching at a high and broad level in the organization. As the coaching initiative progressed, leaders on this board, and other leaders that they interacted with, more readily developed a sense of ownership for coaching. This governance board also proved to be a valuable resource to capture leaders' expectations for the coaching initiative. As the deployment of coaching progressed, the board was helpful in resolving problems and overcoming barriers.

- *Develop and share a business case for coaching with the sponsor or governance body.* The business case states the objectives for the coaching initiative, how coaching will address critical business issues, the expected intangible and monetary benefits, and the required investment. The business case can be used as the guiding light for the coaching initiative. Wendy and the project manager from the coaching company collaborated early in their relationship to develop a sound business case for the coaching. For Wendy, this meant casting coaching as a business initiative, not just an HR initiative. For the coaching company, the coaching initiative would begin on solid footing that was rooted in the business and, as such, was at less risk to be scaled back or limited in scope by business leaders.

  Wendy kept this business case front and center in the discussion the governance board had about the coaching initiative. In part, this was done to refresh their memory about why coaching was launched in the first place. Wendy and the governance board shared the business case with other leaders in the organization, which created good buzz for coaching and added to the momentum for positive change. Coaches and those being coached were viewed in a more positive light as the expected business outcomes for coaching became clearer to people. Key messages from the business case were used as the basis for articles in the company's newsletter about coaching. Wendy developed talking points for leaders so they could include information about coaching in their presentations and conversations with employees.

- *Communicate success stories.* The business case is just one source of information to more broadly share in the organization. Another powerful source of information is the collection of individual coaching success stories (with permission of the individuals, of course). Communicating these success stories increases the understanding of how coaching is adding value and casts coaching in a positive light. For Wendy, this was an especially important issue because coaching previously had a negative connotation in her organization. For years employees were "coached out" of organizations. Being coached became viewed as a polite way of firing people. Although the actions of being coached out had no bearing whatsoever on the executive coaching initiative, the fact that the word *coaching* is used in both contexts was confusing to some people. Communicating the success stories helped clear the air and cast coaching in a positive light. Consequently, the support for coaching was expanded, and a broader base of support for coaching was created, which also facilitated greater ownership and sponsorship for coaching.

Conduct an Orientation Session to Improve Deployment

Wendy fully understood how challenging it would be to get the coaching initiative off the ground. For the most part, leaders did not understand what executive coaching was all about, and for many people, coaching still had a negative connotation. Leaders were concerned about the privacy of their coaching conversations and the kind of relationship they would enter into with someone who was a stranger and not an employee of the company. After all, how much did these coaches really know about the company, its strategies, and its competitive challenges?

One of the first decisions of the governance board was to proceed with a one-day orientation session for the coaches and for the leaders who were selected to be coached. This decision was not taken lightly, given that most leaders would have to travel to the meeting, and some of whom would be traveling from other countries. Expenses would also have to be incurred for the coaches' travel and compensation for their time. The purpose of this session was twofold: (1) to set the strategic context for coaching and (2) to successfully launch the coaching initiative. Prereading materials were e-mailed to the participants, which included company background information for the coaches and biographies of the coaches and published articles explaining executive coaching for the leaders. Each leader was also asked in advance to select three coaches to talk with during the orientation regarding a potential coaching relationship. Wendy received this information in advance from most of the leaders, which enabled her to better organize and facilitate the matchmaking portion of the session. A presession conference call was conducted with the coaches to better prepare them for the meeting and to explain their facilitation role.

Table 9.1 summarizes the agenda for the orientation session. This session accomplished four key objectives:

1. *Coaches were grounded in the company's strategy and culture.* Wendy distributed prereading to each coach about the company. This information included the company's history, its organization, descriptions of products and services, major markets, and industry analysts' assessments. During the session, coaches learned directly from the CEO and two top business unit leaders about the strategic direction for the company and how coaching fits into the picture. They also had the opportunity to ask questions and at least get an idea of what the company culture was about. Having the coaches facilitate break-out discussions contributed to their learning about the organization and how the leaders behaved with peers.

2. *Clients were prepared to begin coaching.* This session was designed as a two-way street: the leaders also had some learning to do about coaching. The prereading assignment helped frame what executive coaching looks like and how it is being utilized by many companies in many industries (including theirs). The presentations by the CEO and leaders helped clarify how coaching fits into the business and the leaders' personal development. There was ample question-and-answer

Table 9.1 Agenda for an Orientation Session to Launch a Coaching Initiative

Timing	Activity	Resources
6:30 p.m.	Evening reception, networking, and dinner CEO Welcome presentation: 1. Fast-track leadership development will lead to fast-track business results 2. CEO's expectations for leaders and the business 3. Q & A	Members of the governance board; Welcome presentation
9:00	Adjourn	
Main Session 8:00 a.m.	Opening, introductions, review of agenda and objectives	Opening presentation; talking points for HR SVP
8:30	Presentation: The strategic challenges facing the company 1. Profitable growth in selected emerging markets 2. Closing the leadership gap 3. Expected contribution from each leader and how coaching is a key enabler 4. Q & A Table discussions: Coaches facilitate each of 10 tables: 1. Key messages from the presentations by the CEO (last evening) and the two BU leaders 2. Implications for what the leaders must do differently to rise to the strategic challenges General discussion: Some tables report out to the general session what they discussed. Leaders were asked to write down, on 3-by-5-inch cards, questions they may have about coaching.	Two business unit leaders; coaches who acted as cofacilitators for each table (10 pairs of coaches
10:15	BREAK	

Table 9.1 *Continued*

Timing	Activity	Resources
10:45	Presentation: Executive coaching—what it is and isn't (Question cards were collected by coaches and then organized.) After a brief presentation, the panel of coaches addressed the questions on the cards as well as questions from the general audience.	Wendy and four coaches present and conduct a panel; 3-by-5-inch cards; Coach/leader meeting schedule posted on wall
12:00	LUNCH	
1:00	Coach/leader round-robin meetings Explanation of the meeting schedule and the round-robin format Each coach spent 20 minutes with a group of up to five leaders to get acquainted, talk about backgrounds, coaching expectations, and experience. Then, after 20 minutes, the leaders walked to their next meeting with a coach.	Break-out areas for each coach (20)
2:30	BREAK	
3:00	Expectations exchange: What will maximize the success of coaching? Five break-out sessions were each conducted with about 18 to 20 leaders and 4 coaches: 1. What do we collectively need to do to make coaching as successful as possible? 2. What do we need from the organization to make coaching successful? 3. What ground rules for coaching can we all agree on? (Facilitators quickly organize discussion summaries to share with the general audience.) General discussion: Facilitators share summaries and seek consensus on operating ground rules.	Five break-out rooms; facilitators for four groups that came from the HR leadership development function

Table 9.1 *Continued*

Timing	Activity	Resources
4:30	Review of next steps 1. Each leader e-mails to Wendy his or her priority of coaches to work with. 2. Wendy finalizes and distributes the list of coaching assignments. 3. Session notes, including operating ground rules for coaching, are distributed. Wendy fields final Q & A and adds next steps as needed.	List of next steps
5:00	ADJOURN	

time to address any issues the leaders had. The bridge activity was when the leaders identified what they must do differently to support the business strategy. Having the coaches facilitate these break-out sessions enabled them to see firsthand how the leaders viewed their role and challenges to achieve the strategy.

3. *Clients were given the opportunity to select a coach.* Getting the chemistry right between the coach and client is one of the most important determinants of a successful coaching relationship. There really is no way to know in advance how well the coach and client will hit it off. The round-robin approach enabled each leader to spend 20 minutes with a coach that he or she preselected. Although not a lot of time, it was sufficient to get acquainted and get some hints as to whether the chemistry may be right. As a next step after the session, leaders sent in their first, second, and third choices for a coach. Wendy later honored as many of these choices as possible, while evening out the workload for each individual coach.

4. *Coaches and clients shared ground rules for coaching.* One of the biggest derailers for a successful coaching relationship is a kind of creeping passive resistance on the part of the client. Clients are late to their coaching calls or repeatedly reschedule

coaching sessions. The length of time between coaching sessions stretches out as clients take longer and longer to implement action items from the coaching sessions. Establishing operating ground rules can be an effective way to inoculate a coaching relationship from losing steam. Examples of ground rules include being punctual on coaching calls, completing action items in a timely way, and investing the time and energy required to make substantial behavior changes.

The afternoon of the orientation session featured an activity that allowed all participants to identify and then agree to the operating ground rules to make coaching successful. This agreement became the commitment that each participant agreed to bring to coaching. If the coach, or client, begins to sense that the commitment to these ground rules is wavering, then he or she can raise this issue in the context of what has been previously agreed to. There are, of course, times when coaching may legitimately have to take a back seat, but this decision should be mutual by both client and coach. Referring to the ground rules can be a way to discuss this issue in a non-defensive atmosphere.

Set Up Signposts to Gauge How Coaching Is Progressing

Successfully managing a coaching initiative means striking a balance between making sure coaching is valuable for the client and for the organization. If you tip too far in the direction of value delivery for the individual client, then you run the risk of generating little value to the company. Tip too far in the other direction and you may compromise the integrity and privacy of the coaching relationship. Wendy developed a unique and successful approach to strike the appropriate balance. She asked each leader and coach to achieve a series of signposts as the coaching relationship progressed. These signposts included the following:

- First coaching session conducted
- Assessments completed, including multirater interviews
- Objectives set for the coaching relationship
- Each objective achieved by the client (there was usually more than one objective)

The coach and client would mutually agree that each signpost was completed and then forward the dates to Wendy. Wendy did not need to know the content of each signpost (thus maintaining the integrity and privacy of the relationship), only the date that it had been completed (thus managing the coaching to ensure value for the organization). Wendy kept a master chart showing the progress of each coaching relationship. One of her key learnings was that the assessments were often not completed until after coaching had progressed for two or more months. This meant that the objectives were often modified in the middle of the coaching process to respond to the feedback. Coaching often began with a presenting problem and previous assessment data. Coaches often had their own surveys they administered early in the relationship, which offered further insight into behavioral issues. As a result, the process of setting objectives and achieving them was more fluid and dynamic than Wendy expected. Still, the signpost process was valuable in tracking these developments and taking appropriate remedial actions. For example, Wendy explored why the multisource assessments were taking so long and discovered that some of the people who were asked to provide assessment data (e.g., peers and supervisors) knew little about the coaching initiative. Consequently, they were reluctant to provide data until they learned more about the intentions and scope of the coaching and data collection. Wendy responded by communicating directly with people who were asked (or going to be asked) to provide data.

The role of the company's competency model came up as well. Competencies were descriptions of behaviors, and these behaviors were viewed as outcomes of deeper issues that had to be addressed by coaching. These deeper issues, like those discussed in the first section of this book, dealt with managing (or repairing) relationships, gaining alignment with personal values, and risk taking. Soon after embarking on this deeper journey, clients were off the charts of competency models. Competencies were viewed as a great place to start, but the deeper work took the client and coach to address other issues. Each coaching relationship required the freedom to go down its own path.

Build Performance Evaluation into the Coaching Process

In the previous chapter, we followed the travails of the HR senior VP at PharmaQuest. He initially viewed evaluation in terms of schedule attainment and budget performance. The unsolicited and positive comments by coaching clients were icing on the cake; however, the COO had other ideas. What the COO was looking for was evidence of the impact of coaching on the business. The question of impact is answered through an evaluation process, and the earlier this process is started, the greater the benefit to managing the coaching initiative.

Wendy's initial discussions with the coaching company centered around the results that were expected. When Wendy got her marching orders from senior leadership, she was also given clear expectations for what the coaching initiative was to accomplish: accelerate the development of leaders so they could more quickly assume added leadership responsibilities. In consultation with the coaching company project manager and agreement by the governance board, she decided on conducting a pre/postassessment of all leaders according to the competency model. Of the 100 leaders initially identified for the coaching initiative, about 20 were not able to participate at that time. This opened up the possibility of using this group of 20 as a comparison group for the 80 or so who could participate in coaching (statisticians might cringe here, given the unequal size of the two groups and the nonrandom assignment of leaders to one of two groups, but in the real world we make due). Arrangements were made to conduct pre/postassessments and compare those who received coaching with those who did not. If the evaluation issue had not been addressed at the beginning of the initiative, the preassessments would not have been conducted with the 20 people in the comparison group. The earlier evaluation is considered, the greater the options are for conducting a meaningful evaluation.

There are two other upsides to building evaluation methodology into the coaching initiative early: (1) gaining greater discipline in how the coaching initiative is managed and (2) reinforcing accountability for results. Greater discipline comes from how evaluation makes sure that all bases are covered. So many coaching initiatives are launched like the one at PharmaQuest with little initial thought given to leadership expectations, specific objectives that are tied to business goals, and an acknowledgment of what success will look like at the end. Evaluation cannot be done without answering these questions.

Few people working in organizations today, especially large organizations, feel they have the time to conduct these evaluation activities. There is a time investment; however, there is also a payback including time savings. How much time would the HR senior VP at PharmaQuest have saved if he had made the effort to understand the COO's expectations upfront and taken the appropriate actions? More to the point, how much more valuable to the business would coaching (and other developmental activities) have been if the HR senior VP had conducted the appropriate activities?

People cannot fairly be held accountable for outcomes for which they are unaware. Following the evaluation methodology clarifies expected outcomes and makes sure that everyone understands what is expected of them. Wendy learned early that she was going to be held accountable for reducing the time to develop leaders' competencies. As a result, she put in place a series of signposts to help manage the initiative and developed an evaluation architecture to demonstrate results. Not only was Wendy accountable, she had the means to deliver on her accountabilities. Business leaders expect no less from leadership development professionals and, therefore, leadership development professionals should expect no less from themselves.

10

How Coaches Navigate Turbulent Organizations

Let's start with an all-too-familiar story. Sarah had done a spectacular job coaching three insurance company executives. In the six months she had been working with them, each had made a shift to a more authentic and powerful leadership style that was more compatible with the culture of their company than their previous styles. Each client was complimentary to Sarah and deeply appreciated her contributions to their development. Sarah debriefed the HR VP on these successes and was looking forward to building on this success to coach more executives with the company. The HR VP said that he would call when an opportunity arose. The call never came. Sarah was a great coach, but she was not a consultant. Let's explore what it means to be a coach *and* a consultant and what Sarah could have done differently to leverage both roles and expand her business opportunities.

Being a Coach, Being a Consultant

Being a coach and being a consultant are very different roles, and both are required in order for a coaching initiative to be successful. *Initiative* is the operative word here. A person who is in the role of a coach works on an individual level with a client or series of clients. For this person to also wear the hat of a consultant takes the focus to an organization level (Table 10.1). Working at the organization level opens up new opportunities and responsibilities. The

Table 10.1 Contrasts Between Coach and Consultant

Coach	Consultant
Individual	Organization
Client	Sponsor
Competencies	Capabilities
Development Needs	Company Strategy
Personality	Culture
Motivation	Power
Personal Values	Stated Values
Content	Context

consultant must ensure that there is strong senior leader sponsorship for the coaching initiative. Very often, and especially initially, sponsors need to be educated about what coaching can offer and how it must be supported. Sponsors and other senior leaders must have a firm grasp on how coaching will ultimately contribute to achieving the company strategy. Coaching may be the "right thing to do," but few leaders will sign up for sponsoring a coaching initiative unless this initiative is anchored in achieving business results.

Another important focus of consulting with business leaders to deploy a successful coaching initiative is the organizational context in which coaching operates. How well is coaching integrated with the competency model in use in the organization? The coaching initiative must be perceived as a natural outgrowth of the company's learning strategy or HR strategy. Chapter 8 explored how to make sure that coaching is integrated with other people-related strategies. The consultant then partners with the leaders of learning, leadership, HR, and others to shape their perceptions of how coaching contributes to achieving these people-related strategies.

Ultimately, the value of a coaching initiative is viewed by how it closes a performance gap. What performance levels are required in the future? What is the current level of performance? and How will coaching close this gap? It isn't enough that coaching be viewed as a more effective or less costly alternative to other leadership development efforts. Whereas the coach is concerned with how coaching will improve the individual client's leadership skills, the consultant is concerned with building the business case for how coaching is an indispensable tool for building strategic capability and closing performance gaps. Let's rewind our story with Sarah to see what she could have done differently.

What Sarah Could Have Done Differently

- *Understood business strategy and how coaching fits.* In her six months coaching the three clients, Sarah had learned little about the business. Her updates with the HR VP were limited to generalized descriptions of the progress the clients were making. Each of these updates was a golden opportunity to educate the HR VP on the business value of coaching, and more to the point, the potential positive impact on the business that would be gained by expanding the coaching initiative. Most HR VPs have a lot on their plate, and it is a mistake to assume that they will automatically understand how coaching will relate to achieving business strategy.

  First and foremost, the person wearing the consulting hat must be a student of the business. He or she must access Web sites, annual reports, investor reports, magazine articles, and other sources of information to quickly come up to speed on the organization and the industry. Effective consultants develop a point of view. Do not just regurgitate information: translate the information into insights about how to achieve strategy. Educate the business leaders about how a coaching initiative can make a meaningful and strategic contribution. Open up possibilities. Coaches often leave their consultant hat on the table and are content to be a business tourist. As Sarah learned, the time of being only a tourist can be short-lived and ultimately less satisfying than a longer-term relationship with a client organization.

- *Diagnosed the performance gap and how coaching can close the gap.* Why coach? Unfortunately, the answer is often: "Why not?" Everyone is doing coaching, so it must be good. Coaching books have proliferated. Coaching gurus are sprouting up like daisies. Get on the bandwagon early so you're not left out! This bandwagon mentality may be viewed as good for the burgeoning coaching industry in the short term; however, this mentality is good for no one in the longer term, especially client organizations.

When people put on their consulting hat, they begin to ask business leaders and potential sponsors some tough questions. If Sarah had put on her consulting hat, she could have asked questions such as the following:

- What do you view as the top performance issues your business faces?
- How do you feel your strategy has raised the bar for leadership?
- What are you *not* getting from leadership that you most need?
- How does your people strategy support leadership development?
- What are your expectations for how coaching will improve performance?
- What objectives have you set for the coaching initiative?

Sarah would ask these questions within a backdrop of her own research, and based on this research, she would have her own ideas about the answers to these questions. This is where developing a point of view comes into play. Let's look at a specific example of how Sarah could have worked with the HR VP in a different way.

Prologue. Sarah had read the company's people strategy, and it had all the right words about the importance of people and commitment to learning. What was conspicuous in its absence (at least to Sarah) was that the strategy and tangible business outcomes were not closely linked. This was, to Sarah, a serious strategic disconnect. She could see why HR initiatives were viewed as fluffy by business leaders. She developed a point of view: the coaching initiative must be linked to a business outcome, and the HR leader must own not only the coaching initiative but also part of the business outcome.

Act One. Sarah decided to devote her third monthly progress review session with the HR VP to mutually exploring potential business outcomes. Well-armed with a point of view, she began the following conversation:

Sarah:	I have really enjoyed coaching these three leaders, and I believe we are making real progress.
HRVP:	Yes, I agree. I am hearing some good early buzz from these sessions.
Sarah:	We have talked about what you generally expect from each individual I am coaching. What I would like to explore with you now is what you expect from coaching as an intervention or initiative for your company.
HRVP:	What do you mean exactly?
Sarah:	Well, for starters, how do you think coaching fits within the people strategy?
HRVP:	I think that it's pretty straightforward. Coaching is a developmental tool, and people development is one of the central pillars of our people strategy. Is this what you're driving at?
Sarah:	We're driving in the right direction. Specifically, when I read your people strategy, I could see how coaching fits as a development tool, but to what end? I guess my question is how you think leadership development will impact the business?
HRVP:	Hmm, that's a good question. I would say that it would surface in many ways, such as better decision making, improved problem solving, increased effectiveness as a leader . . .

Sarah: Yes, I would agree with these outcomes, and let me go one step further.

HRVP: All right.

Sarah: You mentioned increased effectiveness as a leader. Given your business growth strategy, it seems like you will need many more leaders than you have now.

HRVP: Yes, our business will grow 40 percent in the next three years.

Sarah: Is it fair to say that the business outcome of leadership development will be to accelerate building the bench strength of leaders?

HRVP: Most definitely.

Sarah: So, by accelerating the supply of available leaders, it seems that you are producing a tangible business outcome.

HRVP: Yes, it's very tangible and one that we measure. Every year leaders are rated as "ready now, ready in one year, ready in two years" to assume greater leadership roles in the company. Come to think of it, given our three-year growth strategy, we should probably do this every six months, not annually. At any rate, coaching could play a key role in accelerating this leadership supply process.

Sarah: It may be time to think about how to leverage coaching across a bigger base than just three leaders.

HRVP: Yes, that's a good point. There are at least forty other leaders who would benefit from coaching, and more to the point, the business requires this for achieving the strategy.

Sarah: I'm prepared to help in any way I can. What do you see as our next steps?

This conversation served as a platform for Sarah and the HR VP to design a coaching initiative with a tangible and strategic business outcome. She knew that the HR VP would need help in moving this initiative forward, so she got the green light from him to meet with more leaders and key influencers in the decision to move forward with a broader coaching initiative. Which brings us to the next thing she could have done.

- *Increased networking within the company.* First, networking does not mean selling. A big hot button for most leaders is having coaches stealthily network throughout their organizations looking for more coaching clients. The intention of networking is to open up possibilities for new relationships and to add value along the way. The one-act play opened the opportunity for Sarah to meet new leaders with a specific purpose and mandate from her sponsor: Position coaching as a business initiative with a tangible outcome and seek the support of key business leaders and influencers to proceed with coaching. Of course, if Sarah is successful, she will have a lot more coaching work to do. The point is that she is approaching these meetings from the vantage point of how to achieve the business strategy, not how to feather her own nest.

- *Focused on building relationships.* These initial meetings are openings and, if appropriate, can lead to building stronger relationships with a broader group of leaders. For example, Sarah could debrief the HR VP on her leader conversations and identify a critical set of leaders who will need to continue to be engaged in the coaching initiative. Sarah can work with the HR VP to develop an agenda and a set of outcomes for these conversations, and in so doing, can define how these relationships can grow and blossom.

- *Asked for the business.* Sarah concluded the one-act play with the right punchline: "I'm prepared to help in any way I can. What do you see as our next steps?" She asked for the order. So often, as consultants we do all of the legwork, work hard, get right to the altar, and then fail to pop the question. Don't be shy about asking for the work. By wearing the consulting hat, you are offering a new set of valuable services. Work with your sponsors to understand their needs, performance issues, and business requirements. Educate your sponsors on how your solutions will meet their needs. And when you get their attention, be sure to ask for the work.

Sorting Out the Cast of Characters

Our one-act play had two characters: Sarah and the HR VP who was sponsoring the coaching of three leaders. In reality, consultants have to deal with a whole cast of characters, including the following:

- *Sponsors.* These people (or person) own the performance issue and the outcome of the coaching initiative. The HR VP was the coaching sponsor in our vignette.
- *Buyers.* Sponsors may or may not have the budget to pay for the entire coaching initiative. The budget to pay for coaching often comes from many sources, especially in larger organizations and those that are decentralized. So, in the previous example, the HR VP is sponsoring coaching, but the budget money for the delivery of coaching comes from the individual business units whose leaders are being coached.
- *Key influencers.* Sponsors and buyers have a lot of influence in the course and direction of coaching, but there may be others as well who, by virtue of their stature in the organization, can exercise considerable influence on a coaching initiative. A couple of examples include a leader who "has the ear" of the CEO or someone who is widely viewed as a thought leader in the area of leadership development. Each may hold considerable sway over decisions regarding coaching.
- *Pathfinders.* These people are often initial contacts in an organization and help consultants learn the ropes. In the case of the vignette, this could have been a direct report of the HR VP, perhaps the director of leadership development. The director could have helped Sarah understand the company culture, sort out the cast of characters, provide introductions to others in the HR organization, answer questions about people, and performed other kinds of orientations.

- *Dragons.* Not everyone is enamored of coaching or, for that matter, consultants. These people will likely oppose coaching, perhaps have had a bad experience with coaching, or have some misconceptions about coaching. Some leaders have an axe to grind that, although not directly related to coaching, will surface during decision making about a coaching initiative. A VP of manufacturing, for example, who had a key initiative shot down by the HR VP will oppose the HR VP's proposal for coaching as payback. Pathfinders, by the way, can be helpful in flushing out these dragons so the dragons can be dealt with as effectively as possible.

- *Running buddies.* Over a period of time, a consultant may work closely with a particular person and develop a strong relationship. Running buddies are those people with whom the consultant can let down some of his or her guard and privately share concerns or problems regarding the coaching engagement. There is certainly an element of risk in doing this, but this sharing is also a reflection of trust in the relationship. As long as the intention is to always work in the client's best interest, and the trust is established, then the risk is well worth taking.

Develop a Navigation Strategy

Now that we have sorted out the cast of characters, how can coaching consultants best carve out a winning role for themselves by navigating these potentially turbulent organizations? The following represents some tips for developing a strategy for working within a client system. It is important to keep in mind that an organization is a complex system in which any action can have unintended consequences. Although no one can predict what these consequences may be, successful consultants prepare for what may come. This underscores the need to become a student of the business, quickly identify the key players, set your sights on the prize, and develop a winning business proposal.

Tip 1: Become a Student of the Business

Really good consultants have an insatiable curiosity about how business works: how things get made, transactions get processed, and services get delivered. Learn as much as you can about the client company and the client's industry. The Internet offers a treasure trove of information and easy access to client information, annual reports, investor analysis, magazine articles, and so forth; however, being a good student means more than doing the homework. When going on-site to the client location, take the opportunity to tour the facilities. Come to the tour with a set of questions about how business gets done. Learn about how the company units are connected (or disconnected!); see product move through the system; see how customers are dealt with; take in the company culture and begin to understand the organizational context in which people work.

Demonstrating an active and visible interest in the business can also be a differentiator from other coaches who may not don the consulting hat. Conversations with several senior leaders and coaching clients revealed one of their hot buttons in this regard: they have trouble relating to coaches who do not understand the company culture or the organizational context in which they work. This concern or frustration can continue to build as coaching sessions are delivered exclusively over the telephone. Clients who say they prefer coaching sessions to be in person are often expressing a wish for the coach to understand the extent to which the client's behavior is adapting to the organization's norms and cultural context. Beginning the coaching relationship with an on-site onboarding and orientation process can alleviate these concerns early in the relationship. Occasional follow-up on-site visits can be undertaken to continue the process of understanding the client's behavior in the broader organizational context. These on-site visits also provide a platform for spending time with the sponsor of coaching, meeting other client people, and better understanding the cast of characters.

Tip 2: Quickly Identify the Key Players

The previous section of this chapter identified some key roles. The coach/consultant's job is to find out who is playing these key roles, and in some cases, to convert people to either play an additional role or change roles during the course of the coaching initiative. This exploration typically begins with the pathfinder or sponsor. The pathfinder could be the initial contact within the organization, perhaps someone who contacted the coach at a conference. This person, although not the decision maker, can put the coach in contact with the decision maker. Gaining this entrée often puts the coach in contact with the person who is the sponsor of coaching. Early conversations with the sponsor will reveal the potential buyers of the coaching services. Follow the money. Whoever is paying for the coaching will have to be reckoned with at some point. If at all possible, arrange to meet these buyers to better understand what they expect from the coaching and to begin to educate them about the coaching process and possibilities. Shape the expectations of buyers for what coaching can do for their business.

All buyers have influence on the course and direction of the coaching initiative. In fact, they are often less interested in coaching as an initiative and more interested in how coaching will positively (and quickly) impact their business. Decentralized organizations often create decentralized buying networks. This arrangement can greatly complicate the consultant's job to cobble together the buyers to fund a coaching initiative. This also increases the risk factors for the consultant. The consultant will need to invest considerable resources to secure initiative funding and, for larger initiatives, line up additional coaches to handle the potential demand. Key influencers can accelerate this process by encouraging buyers to make the decision to proceed with the coaching initiative more quickly.

Tip 3: Set Your Sights on the Prize

A coaching initiative is a business investment, and it must be perceived as value added to the business by the senior leaders. In charting the cast of characters, we followed the money to see where the investment in coaching was going to come from. These investors need to see value, as does the sponsor. It is important, therefore, to articulate the value proposition to each of these leaders in order for them to buy into the coaching initiative. For example, in the vignette, Sarah was able to draw from the HR VP, who was the sponsor, what he would view as of value to the business: increasing the supply of leaders who are ready for promotion. Had Sarah gone deeper, she would have continued to spin this idea until she discovered a personal value need of the HR VP. Perhaps he felt that he needed to be seen by his peers as an effective and capable leader of the leadership supply process. Or perhaps he felt that he needed to be viewed by the CEO to be more of a strategic business partner and not just a supplier of HR services and transactions. Coaches have the intuitive powers to readily get to these deeper value needs, and by putting on the consulting hat, they must step up and ensure that the coaching initiative addresses these needs for each of the major decision makers.

Let's not forget the needs of the coach either. The coach must examine what he or she needs from the coaching initiative following a similar process that was used with the HR VP and other leaders. For starters, Sarah wants to expand her coaching business in the client organization. She will develop some revenue and client goals to reflect her expectations for business growth. Upon further reflection, Sarah may also recognize deeper value needs (especially if she has her own coach!). For example, she may need to be seen as a business peer by the HR VP or the CEO, or perhaps she feels that she needs to position herself as someone who builds strategic capability in organizations and not only as a coach of individuals. Whatever these needs are, she must perceive that the coaching initiative is meeting her higher value and developmental needs.

One outcome that all people value is the impact on the business. At this point in the process, we are on the verge of writing a work proposal (which is covered in the next section of this chapter). We cannot say for certain how coaching will impact the business and the potential monetary value that may be produced. We can, however, unlock this potential value with two simple words: "so that." Case in point: Sarah got the HR VP to see how coaching will accelerate the supply of available leaders. Both agreed that business impact would occur, but they did not explore this issue any further. How could this have been done? Sarah could amend the statement with "so that" and have the HR VP fill in the blanks. Coaching will accelerate the supply of available leaders *so that*:

- Critical leadership positions will be filled more quickly.
- The company will rely less on external recruiters.
- New business opportunities can be explored.

Sarah can continue to explore with the HR VP (and others) the potential chain of business impact using the "so that" process. For example: Critical leadership positions will be filled more quickly *so that*:

- Sales targets in existing markets will continue to be met.
- Employee focus and morale are maintained.
- Customer relationships will not be interrupted or compromised.

Sarah can continue this "so that" process until all major avenues of potential value creation are identified. Some of these sources of value will be formally explored in the evaluation process, converted to monetary value, and factored into the ROI equation. At this point in the initiative, these "so that" probes heighten leaders' awareness of the potential for value creation. The prize begins to take shape in people's minds, and coaching becomes viewed as a *business* initiative, not just a developmental initiative.

Tip 4: Write a Winning Proposal

The next chapter delves into developing an evaluation strategy for a coaching initiative. The work proposal provides a bridge from the value propositions and the groundwork that has been laid to the design and evaluation of the coaching initiative. Winning proposals are short and sweet and present just enough information in order for the senior leaders to make the right decision about moving forward with coaching. Less is more. If information is not needed for leaders to make a decision, then leave this information out. Work proposals must highlight value to the business and respond to the value propositions of the key players. The requirements for coaching must be outlined so that leaders know what they are getting themselves into. Including an evaluation strategy will show the leaders how they will know if and when the value is delivered. A final section on investment will help the leaders appropriately budget for the initiative.

- *Highlight value to the business.* This is the headliner in any work proposal and represents the culmination of the "so that" series of probes. In fact, if this section is not hard hitting and business focused, many leaders will not read much further. Paint a picture of how the organization will be improved as a result of the coaching initiative. Earlier in this chapter, we talked about describing the performance gap and how coaching will close this gap. Connect the dots for the reader of the proposal. Do not rely on the reader's imagination to make the conceptual leap of how coaching will create value and close the performance gap. Make sure the proposal reflects the value the decision makers expect.
- *Outline the requirements for coaching.* Present the broad strokes of the coaching initiative: how many people, over what time period will receive coaching. Show what the coaching will entail. Describe the initial orientation session. Present the coaching initiative in a way that demonstrates how the initiative is

integrated with other HR and developmental efforts. For example, the individual assessment phase may be based on the company's leadership competency model. A multisource interview process will be incorporated into the assessment phase. Coaching will be formally inducted into the company's leadership supply process. Position coaching as a strategic integrator of the elements making up the company's people strategy. All of these efforts show how critical the coaching initiative will be to meet the needs of the people and the business.

- *Show how the coaching initiative will be evaluated.* Accountability is a precious commodity. Initiatives are often launched in organizations with big promises of a payoff, but as the initiative drags on, these promises become a distant memory. For hard asset initiatives, such as redesigning a manufacturing plant layout, business leaders are sanguine about cutting the initiative sponsor some slack. When it comes to the softer side of business, like leadership development, business leaders are more hard-nosed. In part this is because of the skepticism many leaders harbor about the value of people development. It's a bigger conceptual leap to think in terms of people development contributing to business value. It's turning an intangible (learning) into a tangible (ROI) that takes longer to understand than how a tangible (plant relayout) turns into an ROI.

  This is where the evaluation plan comes into play. The next chapter goes into considerable detail about how to design and execute an evaluation strategy. At this point in the proposal process, what is needed is to commit that this evaluation will be done and that the promises made will be kept. The evaluation plan also provides leaders with some signposts about what is working and not working. By monitoring these signposts, leaders have leverage over some risk factors in their investment. Leaders have some early warnings about the progress of their investment and can take some corrective actions. The ability to manage risk lowers the resistance to proceeding with the proposed initiative.

- *State the required investment.* At this point in reading the proposal, it is hoped that the business leaders are so enthusiastic that any level of investment will seem modest, in our dreams. Business leaders will invest in a coaching initiative that promises to meet their needs, but they may look for options and choices for moving forward. One of the most frequent options is to begin with a pilot program. The pilot represents a subset of the greater population that may ultimately receive coaching. The risk is less, because fewer people are involved and the investment is less than full deployment. Another option is for the client to rely on existing assessments and not pay for the coach to conduct additional assessments. This option can be less viable than the first, depending on the quality of the assessments. Some company assessments that are institutionalized can become pro forma and do not reveal someone's true strengths and improvement opportunities. It is usually best to give the coach free reign to collect and analyze assessment data on which to base the coaching.

One popular option is for companies to have coaches train employees to be coaches and to avoid most of the expense of hiring outside coaches. These employees can belong to an HR organization or be line managers in a business unit. Although there is merit to building the coaching skills of staff and managers, it should be recognized that these employees will provide substantially different services than what a professional executive coach will provide. There is coaching, and then there is *coaching*. Like any profession, coaching requires commitment, education, practice, and achieving certification levels. The International Coach Federation (ICF), for example, provides certification and educational accreditation for the coaching profession. If a company decides to launch an internal coaching group, then the professional standards of the ICF should be adopted. The worst-case scenario, which unfortunately is played out all too often, is that leaders think a weeklong training class in coaching will get them the same value that an experienced professional coach provides. In these situations, the experience with coaching is mixed, and leaders become disenfranchised with coaching, not recognizing the quality difference between a low-budget, homegrown affair and professional executive coaching.

Finally, clients may wish to exercise some choices about how best to finance the coaching initiative. Clients may decide, for example, to handle the administrative aspects of the initiative and factor out of the proposal any fees related to administration. Coaching via the telephone as opposed to in-person may also reduce the total investment. The point is that clients appreciate having choices about how to maximize their investment. Coaches should be flexible as long as the coaching process is not compromised.

To Be or Not To Be a Consultant—and the Role of Coaching Companies

No one said that consulting would be easy. What is outlined in this chapter is really the barebones approach to moving from coaching a few leaders to gaining the go-ahead for a coaching initiative. This chapter represents the standard operating procedure for consultants, but let's face it: not all coaches are willing or able to be consultants. So what do they do? This is where coaching companies come into play. Coaching companies are responsible for developing business, managing the client relationship, presenting proposals, and managing the coaching initiative. Coaches coach. Clients value coaching companies because they offer a single point of contact to manage the coaching initiative. These companies scan the marketplace for coaches, qualify the coaches to a level of standards, bring the coaches onboard, and manage their performance. Coaches will pay a premium for this service, typically receiving less than their usual coaching fee. The brokers assume most of the risk of the coaching initiative, while the coaches—who are freed up from managing the relationship with the client organization—can concentrate on their coaching.

Many coaches have aligned themselves with coaching companies for this very reason. This represents a choice for coaches: to be or not to be a consultant. Given how coaching as a profession is evolving, not crossing over to embrace the consulting aspects of building coaching capability may be a career-limiting move for a coach. Coaches are increasingly expected to be well-rounded businesspeople, providing real value to organizations and openly accepting accountability to deliver this value.

Section Three
Evaluating Coaching Success

11

Developing an Evaluation Strategy

Evaluations are performed against a set of criteria. In a business setting, these criteria relate to business impact and achieving business goals. For coaching to count it must be focused on business impact and directed at achieving business goals. The evaluation strategy ties together all of the pieces and ensures that a clear line of sight is established from the business goals to the coaching initiative objectives to the evaluation objectives. Moreover, developing the evaluation strategy has value as a litmus test to ensure that coaching is positioned to produce business value. Specifically, there are five practices of an effective evaluation strategy, each of which must be in place for a coaching initiative to be evaluated, and even more important, for coaching to have the intended impact on the business. This lesson was learned the hard way at OptiCom (a fictitious name).

The Five Practices of an Effective Evaluation Strategy

By all accounts, the five-month coaching pilot project at OptiCom was viewed as a success: Comments and feedback from participants were positive, and the Leadership Advisory Board seemed impressed. So, given this outcome, Jacqui was a bit puzzled by the advisory board's request to formally evaluate the business impact of the pilot before they authorized full deployment of the coaching initiative. At stake here was deploying coaching to the top 80 leaders at this telecommunications company. The pilot had been completed for almost two months now, and while several of the 10 pilot participants had chosen to continue their coaching, Jacqui was concerned about losing momentum for coaching the remaining 80 leaders. She felt a strong sense of urgency to do the evaluation the Leadership Advisory Board had requested and get it over quickly so full deployment of the coaching initiative could get underway. Analysis paralysis could jeopardize full deployment of coaching.

In her role as the director of leadership development, Jacqui decided to hire an outside evaluator, thinking that the evaluator could quickly focus on the salient impact areas of the coaching and produce a report that was credible in the board's eyes. Michael, the evaluator, sat down with Jacqui to map out the evaluation. Jacqui presented the objectives and outcomes that were part of the proposal for the coaching initiative (Table 11.1). It soon became apparent to Michael that the coaching pilot could have been better positioned in the organization. Reading between the lines, he could understand the board's uneasiness with moving the initiative to full deployment. The immediate question before Michael was how to share his critique with Jacqui in a way that would not make her feel defensive.

At first, Michael complimented Jacqui on completing the pilot and shared with her how the board's request for a business impact evaluation was a good sign. It showed that they were keenly interested in coaching and were looking for ways to leverage coaching in the organization. Besides, Michael reasoned, pilots are conducted to learn about how best to move to full deployment, and this is really what the board's request boiled down to. Michael then shared five practices of an effective evaluation strategy:

1. Link coaching to achieving business goals
2. Set objectives that include the *application* of coaching to the workplace
3. Develop evaluation objectives that directly tie to coaching objectives

Table 11.1 The Purpose and Outcomes of Coaching Document at OptiCom

Executive Coaching Pilot **OptiCom Leadership Development** **Presentation to the Leadership Advisory Board** **July 10, 2003**	
Overview	It is proposed to provide all ninety Leadership Forum members with five months of executive coaching. Given the level of investment to implement this coaching, a pilot will be conducted to determine if coaching would be an effective development approach for OptiCom.
Objectives	The objectives of the coaching are: 1. To provide executives with a personalized five-month development experience. 2. To incorporate the leadership competency model into the coaching. 3. To provide each executive with internal and external feedback so they gain greater perspectives on their leadership style.
Outcomes	The expected outcomes of the coaching initiative are: 1. Ninety executives (ten in the pilot) will have each received five months of coaching. 2. Participants will have learned how to be more effective leaders. 3. Participants will have embraced the leadership competency model as their guide for leading people.

4. Decide how to demonstrate the contribution that coaching makes on performance apart from other potential influencing factors (e.g., isolating the effects)
5. Describe expected areas of performance improvement

Jacqui was getting fidgety as Michael took her systematically though each of these five practices based on the document she shared with him. He positioned his critique as a requirement for the evaluation and also a way to better sell full deployment of the initiative to the board. "Let's talk their language" Michael intoned.

Link Coaching to Achieving Business Goals

In all of the material Jacqui prepared to position and launch coaching, there was nary a word about how coaching would advance business objectives. Coaching objectives pointed to developmental experiences that would enable executives to gain a "greater perspective." There are a whole host of experiences and perspectives to gain that have nothing to do with achieving business goals. Just because an executive develops in some way does not mean that his or her leadership style becomes more effective. Gaining a new perspective and acting on this new perspective to improve the business are two different things.

The third objective related to how coaching would incorporate the leadership competency model. Although integration of development-related initiatives is appropriate, even necessary, it is rarely sufficient to sustain or justify the investment in coaching. Linking coaching to competencies, which are linked to other developmental processes, is critical to ensure that all activities are appropriately integrated. However, integration by itself does not guarantee that these activities will deliver strategic value. Only by linking coaching to achieving business goals can the promise of strategic value be realized.

Set Coaching Objectives That Include the Application of Coaching to the Workplace

Learning is one thing, but applying learning to the workplace is another. In the case of OptiCom, the coaching objectives were directed to "gaining perspectives," which says nothing about applying these new perspectives in a meaningful way in the workplace. The stated outcome for the coaching of "learning how to be a more effective leader" says nothing about applying this learning to the workplace. Setting these objectives is not trivial; and as we will see later in this chapter, these objectives guide the design of the entire initiative. A coaching initiative focused on application of learning to the workplace, for example, may set expectations for both participants and coaches of realizing tangible application of learning from the coaching conversations to the workplace. HR managers may, halfway through the coaching process, talk privately with the executives about their experiences in applying new leadership behaviors in their work settings. Midcourse follow-up sessions can be conducted in which executives discuss what they are doing differently as a result of their coaching and share success stories. These open forums provide recognition to those who are experiencing success and encourage others to take the plunge and apply their learnings.

Develop Evaluation Objectives That Directly Tie to Coaching Objectives

One of the first questions business leaders ask when reviewing objectives for a coaching initiative is: "How will we know if you have achieved these objectives?" The first step in answering this question is to develop evaluation objectives that flow from the initiative objectives. For example, when coaching objectives specify how the coaching will be applied in the organization, then evaluation objectives must address the application of coaching. If business leaders expect the evaluation to determine monetary benefits, then the initiative objectives should be calibrated accordingly. The danger arises when the coaching initiative sets its sights too low (e.g., leaders gaining new knowledge—but not necessarily applying the knowledge) for evaluation to meet the business leaders' expectation of value. This is precisely what happened with OptiCom: Jacqui positioned coaching as a learning initiative, whereas the advisory board was looking for tangible business impact. Jacqui's learning objectives were met, but a large gulf existed between the learning objectives and the advisory board's expectation for business impact. As the evaluator, Michael performed a valuable service for Jacqui by highlighting this discrepancy and quickly moving to a solution. Later in this chapter, we will delve into this issue in more detail and review the five levels of evaluating coaching.

Decide How to Isolate the Effects of Coaching on Performance from Other Potential Influencing Factors

Isolating the effects of coaching on performance from other potential influencing factors is the heart of the evaluation strategy. Failing to credibly isolate the effects will doom the evaluation. What do we mean when we say "isolating the effects?" We mean that we have identified monetary benefits that we can directly attribute to the effects coaching had on the performance of those being coached. In other words, coaching led to behavior changes, these behavior changes had an impact on business performance, and this impact was translated to monetary benefits.

Generally speaking, the earlier the evaluation is planned, the more options are opened up to isolate the effects of coaching. There are three main methods to isolate the effects: (1) conducting a pre/postanalysis of performance, (2) using comparison (control) groups, and (3) using expert estimation.[1] Isolating the effects is strengthened when all three of these methods are used. A later section in this chapter delves more deeply into the issue of isolation; however, suffice it to say at this point that an effective evaluation strategy works out all of the details of isolation before coaching is formally evaluated. The deployment of coaching can often be designed to take advantage of natural comparison groups and collecting pre/postdata. If, for example, coaching is to be deployed across several sales regions, the deployment can be staged so that the performance of the first regional sales managers to be coached can be compared with those regional sales managers who receive coaching later.

Describe Expected Areas of Performance Improvement

When coaching is treated as a strategic initiative, the outcomes of coaching are expected to impact business results. Coaching becomes an investment with an expected return on this investment. An

[1]Anderson (2003); Campbell and Stanley (1963); Phillips (1997).

important aspect of this return is monetary in nature. A key contribution of the evaluation strategy is to specifically show how coaching will be expected to impact organization performance. By presenting expectations for performance improvement in the evaluation strategy, it becomes clear to everyone involved in the coaching initiative what outcomes are expected. Sponsors of coaching also gain early buy-in to coaching and understand better what to expect from it. The original coaching proposal at OptiCom was devoid of these considerations. Performance improvement was not even on Jacqui's radar screen. It's no wonder, then, that the sponsors and leaders of the coaching initiative were left scratching their heads about what business value was gained from the coaching pilot—and what future gains would come from full deployment.

Developing an Evaluation Strategy at OptiCom

With these five practices firmly in mind, let's revisit OptiCom and see how they developed a winning evaluation strategy for coaching, and along the way, put the full deployment of coaching on much stronger footing. The first order of business was to respond to the advisory board's request to evaluate the business impact of the pilot. Given how the pilot was positioned (vis à vis the five practices) and the fact that only 10 participants were being coached, Jacqui decided to take a risk and push back on the board's request to evaluate the pilot.

Jacqui arranged a meeting with the board's leader and shared her concerns about the evaluation. Then she asked the leader the question that turned the tide of the conversation: What are your business issues, and how can coaching help? The advisory board leader was the executive VP of the point-of-sale business unit (BU). They were planning a major foray into the consumer electronics market. He said that what kept him up at night was that "we couldn't make the mistakes of the past and keep hiding in our own silos." He went on to explain that he was concerned that his direct reports—each a VP of a division—were not collaborating quickly enough or

Table 11.2 Evaluation Strategy for Full Deployment of Coaching at OptiCom: Example of One Business Unit

Business Goal: Point-of-Sale Business Unit	
Penetrate the consumer electronics market for point-of-sale optical scanners	
Coaching Initiative Objectives	**Evaluation Objectives**
Business Unit leaders effectively collaborate across functions to develop market penetration plan.	Increased collaboration among leaders as a result of coaching
Leaders quickly engage their respective teams to implement penetration plan.	Increased productivity of leader's teams
Isolating the Effects of Coaching	
Expert estimation of impact resulting from coaching by the clients; estimations discounted by error factor.	
Expected Areas of Improvement	
More effective planning	Faster revenue stream
Higher leader productivity	Increased customer satisfaction
Higher team productivity	Reduced market penetration cost

effectively enough to penetrate the new market. Moreover, he said, several of the VPs seemed slow to engage their respective divisional leadership teams on achieving project goals. Jacqui replied by saying that full deployment of the coaching initiative could successfully address these issues. They agreed that the focus of the pilot evaluation would be limited to lessons learned and point out ways to maximize the success of full deployment. Jacqui had her work cut out for her, and she turned to Michael to develop the evaluation strategy.

A good evaluation strategy is really a good business strategy. Going through the discipline of developing the evaluation strategy often brings added clarity to accomplishing the business strategy. Evaluation represents the ultimate "so what?" question. Implicit within this question is having business and learning leaders being held accountable for results. Table 11.2 summarizes the fruits of Jacqui and Michael's labors to develop an evaluation strategy that responded to the business leaders' issues. This document chronicles the journey they took to hardwire the coaching initiative into the business. Let's do a quick sanity check of this document in terms of the five practices, and then we'll explore some critical issues that the OptiCom story raised regarding evaluation strategies.

Sanity Check of the Evaluation Strategy for Full Deployment of Coaching

- *Was coaching linked to achieving business goals?* Yes. When Jacqui shifted the conversation with the BU leader from talking about coaching to talking about the *business*, she opened the door for coaching to contribute to the business. She shifted the leader's mindset from thinking about coaching as just a cost to creating coaching that counts. The BU was planning to penetrate a new market, and the BU leader felt that the behavior of the leaders would have to change in order for the BU to be successful. Coaching was positioned as a key enabler for the divisional VPs to develop more collaborative behavior and increase team productivity. Coaching is now on the critical path to business success.

  One hot-button issue for many coaches is having company groups, such as HR, or company people, such as Jacqui, impose restrictions on the coaching relationship. Many coaches bristle at the thought of having someone tell them what the coaching conversations should be about. On the other hand, coaching as a business initiative must show value to the business as well as to the person being coached. The good news is that these two areas of value—the person and the organization—are not mutually exclusive. In fact, these two areas of value go hand in hand. In the case of OptiCom, the two objectives were set for the coaching *initiative*, not for the coaching relationship. Will each coaching relationship deal with these two issues? Clearly, yes. Will the coaching relationships deal with other issues? Yes, and it's likely that these two issues will serve as jump-off points to address more root cause issues unique to each client. For example, one coaching client at OptiCom might focus his coaching work on finding a stronger personal focus (Quadrant 1), and expanding his ability to engage his team (Quadrant 2) in order to lay the path for capitalizing on synergies between his division and others (Quadrant 3) and in the process create a more integrated approach for the overall initiative (Quadrant 4). While another client might work on keeping his cool (Quadrant 1), and successfully conducting emotionally charged conversations (Quadrant 2) enabling him to lead his team to deliver an essential element for the new market entry (Quadrant 3).

- *Did the evaluation objectives tie directly to the coaching objectives?* Yes. The two evaluation objectives—increased collaboration and increased team productivity—relate directly to the coaching objectives. Deciding which evaluation objectives to include in the evaluation strategy defines the scope of this strategy: what will be measured and what will not be measured. An effective evaluation strategy focuses on those few areas that are the most salient. Many important aspects of the value the coaching initiative provides to the business are left out. For example, employee engagement and customer satisfaction are clearly potential outcomes of the coaching initiative and may in fact be the most important outcomes. According to the evaluation strategy, however, these outcomes, while important, will be viewed as intangible benefits. Later on in this chapter, we look at valuing intangible benefits in more detail. Suffice it to say at this point that an evaluation strategy reflects choices. Choose what areas to evaluate based on the coaching initiative objectives.

- *Did the coaching objectives include application of coaching?* Yes. Check out the verbs: *collaborate, develop* market penetration plan, *engage* their respective teams, and *implement* penetration plan. These are all observable, actionable items that can be measured. Taking these actions can reasonably lead to positive impacts in the workplace.

- *Did the evaluation plan show how to isolate the effects of coaching?* Yes. Many potential factors will influence how well the leaders collaborate with one another. The coaching initiative is but one of these factors. The challenge is how to isolate the effects of coaching on performance from these other potential influencing factors. Jacqui and Michael decided that the best way to meet this challenge was to rely on the ability of the leaders to estimate the impact coaching would have on the business. Because no estimation is perfect, the error of this estimation would also be taken into account. Third-party validation would also be conducted when appropriate. Later on in this chapter, we delve into the issue of estimation and isolation in more detail.

- *Were areas of performance improvement described?* Yes. Six potential areas of performance improvement were identified. Two of these areas (i.e., planning and customer satisfaction) will likely be cited later as intangible benefits of the coaching. Leader and team productivity will be expressed as monetary benefits. The other two areas (i.e., revenue and cost) may be converted to monetary benefits or left as intangible benefits. Some wiggle room is left here about how best to decide on which areas to convert to monetary benefits. For example, if the market penetration plan is executed ahead of schedule, then revenue will accrue more quickly. The margins of this incremental revenue may be converted to monetary benefits. If this plan is executed below budget, then cost benefits may be identified as well.

The Building Blocks of Evaluation Strategies

The OptiCom story taught us about how to craft a winning evaluation strategy. Three major issues emerged as this strategy was developed that we will now explore in more detail:

1. The ingredients of a good evaluation objective
2. The five levels of evaluating coaching

3. How to isolate the effects of coaching on performance from other potential influencing factors

The Ingredients of a Good Evaluation Objective

Given the key role that the evaluation objectives play in setting the tone and scope for the evaluation strategy, it is important to examine what makes a good objective. A good evaluation objective must address three elements: attribution, direction, and relevance.[2]

- *Attribution.* The evaluation objective must relate to changes that can be brought about by the coaching. In other words, we evaluate that which changed as a result of the coaching. We can attribute the changes to the coaching. For example, the objective: "Increased collaboration among leaders" specifically includes the attribution of "resulting from coaching."
- *Direction.* The evaluation objective states what will increase (sales) or decrease (costs). If specific targets are set, then include these targets in the objective as well. For example, the objective just cited includes the word *increased*, which shows direction.
- *Relevance.* The objective must relate to a strategic business goal. The evaluation objective draws a clear line of sight with the business goal, as illustrated in Table 11.2. In this example, increased collaboration among leaders will lead to a more effective market plan (initiative objective) and ultimately to deeper market penetration (business goal).

The set of evaluation objectives does not need to be comprehensive. That is, not everything should be measured. Rather, focus these objectives on the most salient outcomes with the greatest likelihood of producing monetary benefits. In the OptiCom example, the evaluation objectives focused on collaboration and teamwork. Left out were areas such as customer satisfaction. Achieving high levels of

[2]Anderson (2003).

customer satisfaction may be the greatest, albeit intangible, benefit of all. It was left out in part because it is difficult to express in strictly monetary terms. Following this example, let's say that collaboration and team productivity did not generate the expected monetary benefits. Then it is possible to go back to some of the other potential outcomes, such as a faster revenue stream, and evaluate these outcomes and convert them to monetary terms. This refers again to the flexibility and judgment required in documenting monetary benefits. Additional benefit areas can be explored until a sufficient quantity of monetary benefits has been documented.

The Five Levels of Evaluating Coaching

During the course of the OptiCom story, we learned that coaching objectives should include the application of coaching in the workplace. We want our leaders to learn from the coaching and gain insights into their behavior; however, we also want them to apply these insights to their workplace. As Table 11.3 shows, learning and application are but two of a total of five formal evaluation levels. This leveling scheme has been in operation in training and development for more than 30 years and is a natural fit for evaluating coaching.[3]

Level 1 looks at the initial reaction of the coaching client to the first two or three coaching sessions. Specific areas to look at include the following:

- How well the foundation for the coaching relationship was set
- How much rapport has been established
- How clear the intentions for the coaching initiative were understood
- How effectively the coach and client agreed on behavioral objectives
- How effective coaching is being delivered (e.g., via telephone or in-person), session length, and frequency

[3]Kirkpatrick (1998); Phillips (1997).

Table 11.3　The Five Levels of Evaluating Coaching Initiatives

Level	Description
Level 1: Reaction	This level looks at the initial reaction of the coaching clients to the coaching they received. Reaction data are typically captured after the first two or three sessions.
Level 2: Learning	This level captures what the clients have learned from their coaching sessions.
Level 3: Application	This level evaluates how well clients have applied what they have learned (and committed to) during the coaching to their workplace. All evaluation strategies for coaching initiatives should include assessments at this level.
Level 4: Business Impact	This level documents the business impact from the coaching initiative. Impact areas include output, cost, quality, and time.
Level 5: ROI	This level tabulates all monetary benefits from the coaching initiative, factors in the fully loaded cost of the initiative, and calculates the return on investment.

- How well the assessment data were explored and explained
- The pacing of the initial sessions (e.g., too fast or too slow)

The purpose of gathering these data early is to take stock of how the coaching relationship has gotten off the ground and, if there are issues, to deal with them early. The last thing anyone wants is for issues to be left unattended so they can fester and impede the progress of coaching. If, for example, after three sessions the client is still not clear about the behavioral objectives he or she must address, then this issue must be dealt with quickly in order for the coaching to have focus and direction. If the client still has lingering questions about his or her personal assessment data, then the client and the coach need to explore these questions and incorporate the learnings into the coaching conversations.

Data that capture the initial reaction of people to coaching are grouped and summarized from all coaching participants. These data are important for the sponsors and managers of the coaching initiative to review. There may be issues common to the participants that must be dealt with in order for the initiative to be successful. For example, if after three sessions most clients have not developed objectives for their coaching, then some additional support would have to be provided to the clients. Or if many clients are struggling with the available assessment data, then perhaps the appropriate data were not adequately collected during the initial stages of the coaching process. Additional multisource feedback data could be collected or an entirely new assessment process could be implemented. The point here is that it is better to hear about these issues after three sessions rather than during a debriefing at the end of the six-month coaching initiative. The more that is learned at the beginning about how to make coaching more effective, the fewer the number of lessons learned that will be recorded at the end of the coaching.

Level 2 explores what the clients are learning from their coaching experiences. Every client will have a unique learning experience, but themes may emerge and topic areas common to many clients may become evident. Examples of learning areas include discovering new ways to do the following:

- Be a more effective leader
- Gain insights into personal changes required to grow and develop
- Better understand how personal actions affect others
- Work more effectively with peers to accomplish business goals
- Improve communication skills
- Improve the ability to collaborate with other leaders
- Increase teamwork
- Embrace a big picture view of the organization
- Think more systemically about finding solutions to problems

Each of these learning areas can be a stepping stone to accomplishing a business objective. For those who sponsor or manage a coaching initiative, it is not so important which stepping stones are being touched, as it is to know that at least some stepping stones are being touched. If halfway through a six-month coaching initiative little of significance has been learned by many of the clients, then something is not working. If people are not making significant strides in learning how to be more effective leaders, then it is unlikely they will do anything differently. One cannot apply what one has not learned.

Level 3 is where the rubber meets the road. Evaluation at this level looks at how well people have applied to the workplace what they have learned from their coaching experiences. Of course, not all of what people learn from coaching can be immediately applied, but coaching conversations conducted in business settings will at some point turn to what the client will do differently. These changes in behavior are the subject matter for the evaluation of application. For example, in Chapter 3, Jane was able to accomplish her top priorities by focusing her time and energy more effectively. The actions she took were tangible expressions of what she learned about herself from the coaching sessions. Here are some other examples of taking actions based on coaching:

- More clearly setting priorities for major initiatives
- Making decisions based on a greater diversity of input
- Using vision and passion to motivate others
- Recasting roles and responsibilities to smooth out working relationships
- Expressing appreciation for the contributions of others to increase retention
- Articulating problem statements in a way that engages people to take action

In each of these examples, a client did something differently as a result of coaching. These behaviors can be observed and recorded, which begs the question: What data are required to conduct an evaluation of application?

The answer to this question lies in how best to tell a story about the growth and development of the coaching client. Virtually all clients will apply at least something they learned to the workplace. Recording percentages and rates of application while important, don't come close to telling the whole story. What is of interest is how coaching stimulated the client to take bold and successful actions. Each of the four stories of clients in Section One of this book chronicle successful actions that were taken. These stories, while qualitative in nature, pack an emotional punch. Sharing these stories (with the client's permission of course) can have a powerful impact on initiative sponsors and business leaders about the value of coaching. In a successful coaching initiative, almost every client will have a compelling story to tell.

The stories and experiences of coaching clients can be summarized to show areas of application.

Level 4 examines the success stories of the coaching clients to determine the potential impact on the business. Taking action is one thing, but having this action translate to business results is quite another. There are four types of business impact: output, quality, cost, and time. Output measures include such areas as productivity and sales revenue. Quality measures include such areas as increased product reliability and reduced manufacturing defects. Cost measures refer to reducing costs in operations; sales, general, and administrative (SG&A) expenses; manufacturing; and other areas. Time measures include reduced cycle time and product-to-market time. A coaching client may affect one or more of these areas, based on his or her work responsibilities. A leader in research and development may take actions that reduce the product development cycle (time), whereas a sales leader may work in a new way with sales representatives that leads to increases in revenue.

The impact on the business can be both monetary and intangible. In a sense, all benefits are intangible until we make the decision to convert these benefits to monetary value. Making this decision is not to be taken lightly. A considerable amount of effort may be required to convert benefits to monetary value. There are two major avenues for converting coaching benefits to monetary value: expert estimation and performance indicator tracking. Keep in mind that at this point we are developing the evaluation strategy, so all that is required is to plan which benefits will likely be converted to monetary value and how this conversion will take place. The first approach, expert estimation, means that the coaching clients, and perhaps others, will give their best estimate of how their actions created monetary value to the business. So, for example, a leader who, as a direct result of the coaching she received, reduced the product development cycle time by 15 percent would estimate the annual monetary value of this improvement to be $250,000. She would then state her confidence in this estimate to be 50 percent. The benefit would be discounted by this amount to result in a value of $125,000. As an option, additional steps may be taken to validate the monetary benefit. For example, the leader's coworkers could be interviewed to see if they would agree with the 15 percent cycle time reduction.

The second approach, which may be combined with estimation, is to track established performance indicators. An important aspect of determining business results is to isolate the effects of coaching from other potential influencing factors (which is dealt with in more detail later in this chapter). Briefly, these effects are isolated by looking at performance indicators according to a base period and then a treatment period. The base period refers to performance before coaching, and the treatment period refers to coaching. So, in this product development example, the performance of the product development team could be examined after coaching and compared to the performance before coaching. Changes in performance could be attributed to coaching, all other factors being equal.

At this point of developing the evaluation strategy, it is important to think through how business results will be measured. In all likelihood, both estimation and metrics tracking will be used. The advantage of building these measurement activities into the evaluation strategy is that plans can be made to obtain the required data. Also, sponsors of coaching and other business leaders can understand and buy into how business impact will be measured. Gaining this buy-in early will save a lot of headaches later. In situations where the required data are not being tracked, having this early warning allows people to put the appropriate measurement tracking in place. Coming to this realization at the end of the coaching initiative may be too late to collect the required data.

Level 5 looks at ROI. A coaching initiative may have produced monetary benefits, but did these benefits outweigh the cost of the initiative? This evaluation level factors in the cost of the coaching initiative and, when compared to the monetary benefits, the ROI can be calculated. The formula for ROI is as follows:

$$ROI = ((Benefits - Cost) \div Cost) \times 100$$

The ROI formula can be contrasted with the benefits-cost ratio (BCR) in that ROI deals with net benefits whereas the BCR deals with total benefits. ROI is expressed as a percentage whereas the BCR is expressed as a ratio:

$$BCR = Benefits \div Cost$$

So, for example, a coaching initiative that produced $400,000 in value and cost $200,000 to execute would produce the following calculations:

$$ROI = (($400,000 - $200,000) \div $200,000) \times 100 = 100\%$$
$$BCR = $400,000 \div $200,000 = 2:1$$

It is important to include both the ROI and the BCR given that people often confuse the two. Some people, for example, will report a "3 to 1 return on investment." Upon closer inspection it's clear that they did not follow the standard formula and use net benefits. There is no quicker way to lose credibility than to appear confused about the standard formulas for showing monetary value for the investment.

Structuring an Evaluation Strategy Based on the Five Levels

At first, structuring an evaluation strategy that addresses all five levels may seem to be a daunting task. How do these five levels fit into an evaluation strategy? It really boils down to two options: evaluate at level 3 application or evaluate at level 5 ROI. A central tenet of this book is that every coaching initiative should be evaluated at either of these levels. Which level is best? Let's contrast these two strategies and look at the reasons for conducting a level 5 evaluation.

Table 11.4 contrasts level 3 (application) and level 5 (ROI) evaluations. Although both kinds of evaluations collect data on intangible benefits, these benefits are the primary stated benefits of a level 3 analysis, whereas with a level 5 analysis, intangibles supplement monetary benefits. Monetary benefits are central to a level 5 analysis and are not included in a level 3 analysis. As such, isolating the effects of coaching is critical to a level 5 analysis and not required for level 3. Likewise, initiative cost data are not required for a level 3 analysis, although they are required with a level 5 analysis. The

Table 11.4   Contrasting Level 3 Evaluation with Level 5 Evaluation

Differentiator	Level 3 Evaluation: Application	Level 5 Evaluation: ROI
Intangible benefits	Intangibles included as primary benefit	Intangibles included as a secondary or supplementary benefit
Monetary benefits	Not included, although incidental cost savings may be cited	Included as a central benefit
Isolating the effects	Not needed, given that no monetary benefits are cited	Central to establishing monetary benefits resulting directly from coaching
Initiative cost	Cost data are not collected for the purposes of the evaluation	Cost data are collected and, when compared to benefits, the ROI is calculated
The punchline of the story	How what was learned from the coaching was applied in the workplace	How what was applied in the workplace created monetary value for the business

punchline of the level 3 story is how what was learned from the coaching was applied in the workplace. For level 5, the punch line is how what was applied in the workplace created monetary value for the business.

Given that at least a level 3 evaluation is recommended for every coaching initiative and is also conducted for every level 5 evaluation; the real question becomes whether or not to evaluate at level 5. Let's examine the reasons to conduct a level 5 evaluation for coaching:

- *The business leader or initiative sponsor asks for it.* This was the case with OptiCom, and although Jacqui pushed back on the request, she did construct an evaluation strategy for the full deployment of coaching.
- *The coaching initiative has especially high visibility.* If a lot is riding on the outcome of the initiative, it is probably worth the investment of time and money to ensure that the organization gets the most out of the initiative.
- *The initiative (or pilot) is the first of many deployments of coaching throughout the organization.* Evaluating the first of many deployments will enable the learnings from the evaluation to be leveraged across subsequent deployments. For example, at OptiCom, coaching will be deployed to 80 leaders. Still in the offing is potential deployment to an additional 250 leaders, who represent the next lower level of management. Leveraging the learnings from the 80 to improve the deployment and coaching experiences of the 250 represents an excellent investment.
- *You, as a learning or change leader, need to learn as much as you can about how coaching created value.* A level 5 evaluation provides a deeper understanding of the sources of value for coaching, the areas in the organization that were impacted, and how a monetary ROI was realized overall.

Any one of these four reasons is sufficient to launch a level 5 evaluation. If none of these reasons is met, then a level 3 evaluation may be best. Evaluating application provides insights into how the coaching clients utilized their learning to create value for the organization. This value, while intangible, may nonetheless represent a substantial benefit to the business.

Conducting an evaluation is a more formal way of telling a story. Every coaching client has a story to tell. Each level of evaluation represents, in effect, chapters in these stories. It is important not to leave any chapters out. So, when evaluating at level 3, consider beginning the story with the initial reaction (level 1) of the client to the coaching, the foundation that was set, and the rapport that was built. This foundation supported the client in gaining insights into his or her behavior and discovering ways to grow and develop (level 2). These insights and discoveries led to taking bold new actions and directions to impact the organization (level 3). Filling in these three chapters tells a great story. When evaluating at level 5, the story continues by showing how these actions and directions created value for the business (level 4) in such a way that the coaching initiative more than paid for itself (level 5).

Isolating the Effects of Coaching

A coaching initiative can certainly have a major impact on the business, and yet it is just one of many potential influencing factors on business performance. Isolating the effects of coaching on business performance from all other factors is critical for the evaluation. This can also be one of the most contentious issues in the evaluation process.

In the case of OptiCom, coaching was expected to increase collaboration and increase productivity. However, a major reorganizing project was also underway and salespeople were getting refresher training in relationship selling techniques. If collaboration and productivity go up, who should get the credit—coaches, reengineers, or the sales trainers? This is the essence of the isolation issue.

The effects of coaching can be isolated in the following three main ways:

1. Pre/postanalysis
2. Control group analysis
3. Expert estimation[4]

Each of these isolation techniques is now discussed, although we will see that estimation is usually the only viable alternative.

1. *Pre/postanalysis.* This technique involves assessing performance before and after the coaching and then comparing the change in performance (if any). In the case of OptiCom, levels of collaboration before the coaching would be compared with levels of collaboration after the coaching initiative. Ditto with changes in productivity. In order for increased levels of collaboration or productivity to be attributed to coaching, all other potential factors that might influence collaboration and productivity would have to be held constant. In looking at productivity, for example, the major reengineering effort that occurred contemporaneously with the coaching would have to be taken into account when deciding how coaching contributed to productivity gains. Likewise for sales training. The challenge then becomes how to separate, or isolate, the effects of these three initiatives (reengineering, sales training, and coaching) on productivity. Pre/postanalysis alone can't do it. This is where other isolation techniques come into play.

2. *Control group analysis.* Control groups, or comparison groups, are two groups that are identical in all major respects except for participation in coaching. One group, the treatment group, was coached, and the other, the control group, was not. Returning to the productivity example, gains of productivity would be observed from precoaching to postcoaching. However, this group also experienced reengineering and sales training. So another group would have to be selected that was also part of the reengineering and training efforts, but that did not receive coaching. This second group, or control group,

[4]Anderson (2003); Campbell and Stanley (1963); Phillips (1997).

would be compared to the coaching group. The only major difference between the two groups was the coaching, so comparing productivity between these groups would further isolate the effects of coaching on productivity. The challenge is that, in real life, parsing out treatment and control groups is extremely difficult to do. Reengineering, sales training, and other business initiatives are undertaken to make money, and business leaders are not going to delay or reschedule development of these initiatives just to suit the needs of the evaluation. This brings us to expert estimation, which can be a very powerful and credible tool to isolate the effects of coaching.

3. *Expert estimation.* This technique represents the third evaluation method and is the most widely used for evaluating coaching. Experts here refer to those who were coached; the superiors, peers, and subordinates of the coaching clients; the coaches; and others who could provide credible data about the impact that coaching had on an outcome. Let's say that in the productivity example, initiative sponsors were still skeptical that coaching produced the productivity gains. The coaching clients could be interviewed about how *they* attributed their productivity gains to coaching, reengineering, sales training, or other factors. The subordinates of these clients, or a randomly selected subset of the clients, could also be interviewed to validate the claims made by the clients. Adding expert estimation to the evaluation strategy provides a credible set of data to isolate the effects of coaching.

   Given the complexity of organizations and the plethora of business initiatives intended to improve business performance, expert estimation is typically the only method available to isolate the effects of coaching from other potential influencing factors.

Developing the Isolation Strategy

When it comes to deciding which of the three isolation techniques to use, the more the merrier. Ideally, all three techniques will be used.

Practically, this is often not possible. It is recommended that expert estimation always be included in the evaluation strategy. In the case of OptiCom, this was the only technique used (e.g., Table 11.2), and expert estimation can be a powerful stand-alone isolation technique. Coaching does present three unique challenges for evaluation in contrast to more traditional leadership development activities:

1. *Each coaching experience is unique.* More traditional learning programs practice "sheep dipping," where all leaders go through the same experiences.
2. *Coaching initiatives may lack a "quorum for impact."* When coaching participants are drawn from across the organization, it is not reasonable for coaching to impact business measures.
3. *The benefits of coaching may require a gestation period.* The higher up the leader is in the organization, the longer it may take for the benefits of his or her actions to be realized.

Despite these challenges, initiative managers and evaluators can think creatively about how to include pre/post and comparison groups techniques in an evaluation strategy. For example, coaching deployment can be phased in over a period of time so that natural comparison groups are created. The productivity of those groups that experience coaching early in the deployment can be compared to those who have yet to experience coaching. Preexisting performance data collection and reporting procedures can be utilized to provide high-quality data at little additional cost. In the case of productivity, the output measures of groups that experience coaching can be compared to those who have not experienced coaching. Measures such as units produced or units sold can be included in the evaluation.

In this chapter we covered a lot of ground. As we set the stage for the postprogram ROI evaluation: important decisions were made about setting objectives in the context of an evaluation strategy. In the next chapter we'll see how such a strategy came to life in the evaluation of coaching at OptiCom.

12

Demonstrating the ROI of Coaching

In Chapter 11 we learned how to develop a strategy for evaluating coaching. In particular, we learned how best to isolate the effects of coaching on performance from other potential influencing factors on performance. This chapter deals with how to collect and analyze the data so that the effects of coaching on performance can be converted to monetary benefits. Given these benefits, then, tabulating the cost of the coaching initiative completes the ROI equation and enables us to calculate the ROI. The Data Collection and Analysis Plan pulls all of these activities together.

The Data Collection and Analysis Plan

When it comes to determining the ROI for coaching, we certainly have our work cut out for us: converting benefits to monetary value, isolating the effects, tabulating program costs, and calculating the ROI. The intention of this chapter is to make this evaluation as simple and painless as possible. An evaluation process will be presented that has been battle-tested and proven to work with coaching time and time again. Consequently, not every possible angle for the evaluation will be explored. Readers who wish to further explore alternative approaches to evaluation are encouraged to review the References and Further Reading section at the end of this book. Many excellent resources are available to help build knowledge and skills in the art and science of evaluation.

This chapter cuts to the quick: how to plan the data collection and analysis and quickly select those data collection tools that will creditably show the ROI. The sponsors and leaders of coaching initiatives, evaluators, HR professionals, coaches, and others will have, in this chapter, all they need to conduct an ROI evaluation of coaching. The next chapter presents a slimmed-down version of evaluating only the application of coaching.

The first step is to develop the Data Collection and Analysis Plan. This plan is the link from the evaluation strategy to conducting the evaluation. The Data Analysis Plan has six major elements:

1. The *evaluation objective*, which comes directly from the evaluation strategy
2. The *isolation strategy*, which again comes from the evaluation strategy
3. The *sources of data*, which are required to execute the isolation strategy
4. *Data collection tools*, which will be used to gather all relevant data from the identified sources
5. The *analysis approach*, which summarizes how the data will be collected and analyzed
6. The *key events schedule*, which includes the major activities required to execute the data collection plan

Let's return to OptiCom to see how they utilized this format and created an effective plan to analyze the evaluation objectives. In this example, we look only at how they planned the Data Collection and Analysis Plan for the first objective: increased collaboration among leaders resulting from coaching. Table 12.1 presents this plan. Let's break it down as follows:

- *Isolation strategy.* The isolation strategy was taken directly from the evaluation strategy document (Table 11.2). Expert estimation is planned as the only isolation technique. Neither a pre/post nor a comparison group analysis were planned to be used. This means, of course, that the credibility of the entire

Table 12.1   Data Collection and Analysis Plan for One Evaluation
Objective at OptiCom

Evaluation Objective 1: Increased collaboration among leaders resulting from coaching		
Isolation Strategy	**Sources of Data**	**Data Collection Tools**
Expert estimation of impact resulting from coaching by the clients and validated by selected peers; estimations discounted by error factor	Coaching clients who estimate increased collaboration Validation of monetary benefits by peers	Questionnaire A: Reaction and learning Interview Guide B: Application and impact

Analysis Approach: Questionnaire A will be administered to every coaching client via e-mail immediately after the client completes his or her fourth coaching session. This questionnaire will assess the reaction of clients to the coaching and document some initial learning experiences. Interview Guide B will be conducted with clients about two months after the coaching has been completed to assess how they have applied what they have learned and to document the business impact.

Data Collection and Analysis Key Events Schedule		
What must be done?	**Who will do the activity?**	**When is the activity due?**
Develop evaluation communications packet	Senior Communications Specialist	2 weeks before kick-off of the coaching initiative
Gain approval for all evaluation tools and timing	Initiative Manager (Jacqui)	2 weeks before kick-off of the coaching initiative
Administer Questionnaire A	Evaluator (Michael)	6 weeks after coaching initiated
Analyze Questionnaire A data; prepare report with recommendations	Evaluator (Michael)	8 weeks after coaching initiated
Share report with recommendations to the initiative sponsor and Leadership Advisory Board	Initiative manager (Jacqui)	9 weeks after coaching initiated
Etc.		

evaluation rests on one method of evaluation. Credibility of the evaluation is a critical issue that is dealt with in more detail in the last section of this chapter.

- *Sources of data.* Coaching clients were to be interviewed to produce the main body of data. These data include the clients' initial reaction to their coaching experience, what they learned from their coaching, how they applied what they learned to their workplace, and how these actions produced value for the business.

- *Data collection tools.* Two data collection tools were required for the evaluation. Questionnaire A (Figure 12.1 located in the Evaluation Toolkit section of this chapter) is intended to capture reaction and learning data from the coaching clients. Interview Guide B (Figure 12.2 and also in this next section) captures application and business impact data. The questionnaire and interview guide, when combined, collect all of the data required for an ROI analysis. This interview guide offers a step-by-step process to successfully demonstrate ROI. Readers are encouraged to review these documents and the specifications that follow in the Evaluation Toolkit section. Later we will see how these data collection tools were utilized at OptiCom.

- *Analysis approach.* Jacqui and Michael planned to administer Questionnaire A via e-mail to each coaching client after his or her fourth coaching session, which occurred about six weeks into the coaching initiative. Clients were to receive the e-mail message, complete the questionnaire, and then e-mail it back to the evaluator. These data represent the early returns of the coaching initiative: Are the clients responding well to their coaching? Is rapport being established? Is the coaching being conducted effectively? The answers to these questions are critical to understand if any corrective actions are needed. Later on we will see how OptiCom used this survey to spot and fix a potential trouble point. This questionnaire also sheds light on the initial learning experiences of the coaching clients: understanding how to be more effective as a leader, engaging work teams more effectively, and improving communication skills. These and subsequent learning experiences form the foundation for making significant personal and professional changes.

Interview Guide B was planned to be administered by the evaluator, Michael, with each coaching client in a personal interview setting about two months after completion of the coaching. The external evaluator brings objectivity and privacy to the data collection with a certain measure of credibility. Coaching clients are naturally sensitive about their coaching experience and the changes they would like to make, both personally and professionally. Clients more readily open up to a third-party evaluator who ensures that their individual data will not be revealed to the sponsoring company. Only grouped data were presented.

The two-month time lag for administering Interview Guide B is important. An appropriate gestation time is needed for the impact of coaching to be felt in the organization. Later on we will look at a specific example of this kind of impact. Suffice it to say at this point that leaders who make significant changes in their behavior will likely have significant impact in the organization. This impact takes time to manifest in the form of monetary benefits. Generally, the higher up the leader is in the organization, the longer this time frame becomes. In other words, those leaders who are higher in the organization will take actions that have greater strategic value and it is the strategic nature of these actions that take longer to have impact on the business. There are no hard-and-fast rules for timing the data collection. Common sense is the best guide. Just ask yourself: Has a reasonable amount of time elapsed for the leader's behavior changes to have impacted the organization?

- *Key events schedule.* The last piece of the Data Collection and Analysis Plan is the key events schedule. These key events refer to everything that must be done to successfully execute the plan: communicating the purpose for the evaluation, gaining approval for the evaluation tools and approach, conducting the data collection, preparing reports, and other activities. Table

12.1 presents a few of these activities. Each activity is described in terms of what must be done, who will do it and when the activity must be done. Ideally, these evaluation activities are integrated into the overall plan for the coaching initiative and not kept as a stand-alone plan. Having one, integrated project plan enables the manager of the coaching initiative to more easily make the connections of coaching activities and evaluation activities.

The next section of this chapter presents the two evaluation tools with detailed specifications. In the subsequent section, we learn how OptiCom used these tools to evaluate the coaching initiative.

ROI Evaluation Toolkit

Questionnaire A: Reaction and Learning

Questionnaire A: Reaction and Learning: Specifications

Reaction: Your Initial Coaching Sessions

- *Questions 1–8.* These closed-ended questions enable the respondents to quickly rate their initial experiences with coaching. The seven items included in the scale were determined by the client and the evaluator to be the most important areas for which to collect data on the coaching initiative. These items may change based on the particulars of a coaching initiative.

  A four-point scale is used to force a choice between agreement and disagreement with each of the seven statements. It is recommended not to include a response category for "uncertain" because these responses do not provide any clarity about what respondents are thinking about a particular item.

  Items 2 and 4 are called reversal questions, in that these items state a negative situation in contrast to the positive cast of the other items. Reversal questions are included to counter "response set," or the tendency of some respondents to quickly

Leadership Coaching Survey
Initial Reaction and Learning

Introduction: Thank you for participating in this important survey! The intention of this survey is to better understand the value and business impact of the coaching provided so far to the leadership program participants. The results from this survey will enable OptiCom to best utilizecoaching in the context of the business.

Survey results will be anonymous—the data will be presented in group form only and individual names will not be reported. A third party, MetrixGlobal LLC, will analyze all data and a summary report will be provided to the sponsors of OptiCom. You will also receive a summary report.

Thank you so much for your participation!

Your Initial Coaching Sessions

Please provide your initial impressions of coaching based upon your first four sessions. Place an "X" in the appropriate category for each item.

	1	2	3	4
	Strongly Disagree	Disagree	Agree	Strongly Agree
1. My coach and I set objectives for coaching.				
2. The expectations from the senior leaders for the coaching initiative are not clear.				
3. My coach and I connected and established rapport.				
4. I was skeptical that coaching was going to work for me.				
5. I was satisfied that the first three or four sessions provided a strong foundation for our coaching conversations.				
6. Conducting coaching over the telephone is very effective for me.				
7. The pacing of the coaching sessions is about right; not too fast or too slow.				
8. The personal assessment data were effectively explained to me.				

9. What suggestions do you have for improving the introduction and initiation of coaching?

(Write your response here.)

Figure 12.1   Questionnaire A: Reaction and Learning.

Initial Learning Gained from Coaching

Please reflect upon your initial experience with coaching and respond to the following items. Place an "X" in the appropriate category for each item.

	1	2	3	4
	Strongly Disagree	Disagree	Agree	Strongly Agree
10. I understand how to be more effective as a leader.				
11. I am gaining insights into personal changes that I needed to make to be more collaborative with peers.				
12. I am learning about the impact my actions have on others.				
13. Coaching is opening up new ways for me to look at business situations.				
14. I understand how to work more effectively with my peers to accomplish business objectives.				
15. I am learning how to engage my work team more effectively to achieve goals.				
16. Coaching is enabling me to explore new ways to increase teamwork.				
17. I have begun to improve my communication skills.				

18. How has your experience with coaching increased your knowledge about how to be more effective?

(Write your response here.)

Figure 12.1 *Continued*

run down the list of items and select the same response category without actually reading the questions. The values of these questions are reversed during data analysis so that all responses can be grouped.

- *Question 9.* This open-ended question is the opportunity to hear from the respondent in his or her own words how the coaching initiative could be improved. The preceding closed-ended questions often act as brain ticklers to help the respondents think of additional improvements. The qualitative data from this item are important because, no matter how well written the preceding closed-ended questions are, you cannot include everything that might be important to the respondents. Open-ended questions enable the respondents to speak with their own voices.

Initial Learning Gained from Coaching

- *Questions 10–17.* These items use the same scale as the reaction items (e.g., items 1–8). The content is specifically tailored to the initiative objectives so items dealing with collaboration, working with peers, engaging work teams, and so on are included in the survey.
- *Question 18.* This open-ended question is included to capture key learnings that were not necessarily addressed in the previous set of closed-ended questions.

Interview Guide B: Application and Impact

Interview Guide B: Application and Impact: Specifications

- *Question 1.* This open-ended question is designed to have the respondent reflect on how coaching has contributed to improved performance. The data will be qualitative and will provide some written comments that will complement the monetary data. The answers to this question will also yield intangible benefits.
- *Question 2.* This question is intended to capture all of the major ways in which improved performance management will impact business results. Given the diverse nature of coaching clients (e.g., sales, production, human resources), six response categories are provided. The first three categories (e.g., A, B, and C) are output measures. Cost (D), quality (E), and time (F) are also included. Respondents will rarely check more than three or four categories.
- *Question 3.* This item comprises five elements and two sets of calculations. Each of the five elements is answered by the

---

Capturing the ROI of Coaching Worksheet

Instructions: This worksheet is designed to serve as an interview guide for evaluators to assist coaching clients in evaluating the monetary impact of coaching. While not an exact science, this worksheet follows a well-established, conservative, and credible approach to evaluation. Estimation is a necessary and accepted part of the ROI process.

1. Describe the performance improvements that you have realized as a result of coaching.

   _____

   _____

   _____

2. Identify the potential sources of impact of these improvements. (Please check all that apply.):

   a. Increasing your personal productivity   _____

   b. Increasing the productivity of your work group   _____

   c. Increasing sales   _____

   d. Reducing cost   _____

   e. Increasing product quality   _____

   f. Reducing cycle time   _____

3. For *each* item checked above, please complete one of the benefits calculations on the following page. Use one letter code for each response. Identify currency used in the analysis: _____

   Determine/use the standard values of the client organization. If these are not known or available, use the following values in calculating the monetary benefits. If the benefits are not in $US, then convert the values to the appropriate currency. All benefits must be recorded in annualized numbers (i.e., a benefit that is recorded in monthly terms will be multiplied by 10.5 months to get to the annualized number).

Compensation rate	= $75 USD
Hours per week	= 40 hours
Weeks per year	= 46 weeks
Months per year	= 10.5 months
Sales margins	= 20%
Cost of money	= 10%

Figure 12.2   Interview Guide B: Application and Impact.

---

respondent for each letter code checked in question 2. The calculations are done by the evaluator (or coach) either during the discussion with the respondent or after the discussion. The entire response series is repeated for each letter code selected by the respondent.

The five response elements for Question 3 are as follows:

1. *Letter code.* The participant enters a letter code from Question 2. Only one letter code is entered for each set of responses. If two letter codes are checked in Question 2, then

Benefit Calculations: Please describe the benefit in the left margin.

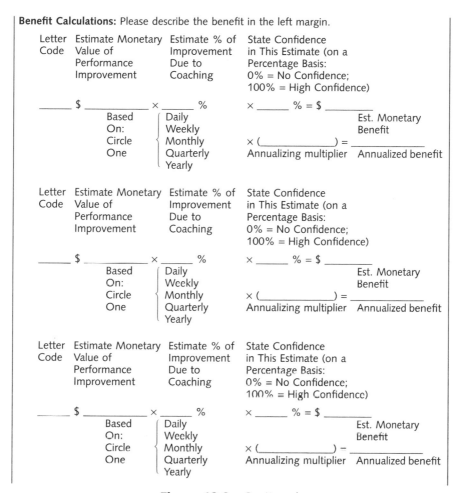

Figure 12.2 *Continued*

the entire set of responses illustrated in Question 3 is completed twice, once for each letter code.

2. *Estimate monetary value of performance improvement.* The participant estimates a monetary value, expressed in U.S. dollars or another currency, of the improvement in performance for the letter code category that was checked.

3. *Select the appropriate time frame.* The respondent then selects the appropriate time frame (e.g., daily, weekly) for the monetary benefits.

4. Determine the cost of the coaching.

_____ Professional fees

_____ Cost of client's time to participate in coaching (hours × $75 or standard value)

_____ Materials

_____ Travel expenses

_____ Telecommunications

_____ Administration costs (includes cost of evaluation)

=   _____ TOTAL

5. Calculate the ROI

Tally the annualized benefits (A through F) =   _____

Enter the values into the formula:

ROI = ((Benefits − Cost) / Cost) × 100

ROI = ((−   ) /   ) × 100   =   _____

6. Identify the intangible benefits.

A. _____

B. _____

C. _____

D. _____

E. _____

Figure 12.2 *Continued*

4. *Estimate percentage of improvement resulting from coaching.*
The participant estimates, on a percentage basis, how much of
the monetary value can be attributed to performance
improvements that were made as a direct result of coaching.
This item is intended to isolate the effects of improvements
realized through coaching. This approach to isolation has
proven to be both effective and credible (e.g., Phillips, 1997).

5. *State confidence in this estimate.* The participant expresses,
on a percentage basis, his or her confidence in the previous
estimate of how much of the monetary value was attributed
to coaching. This item is intended to determine the error
factor for the estimate of benefits.

The two sets of calculations are as follows:

1. *Calculate the estimated monetary value.* Multiply the first
three values in the equation to produce the estimated

monetary value of the benefit (e.g., multiply estimate of monetary value × % attribution × % confidence).

2. *Calculate annualized monetary benefit.* Record the appropriate annualizing multiplier provided by the respondent. For example, if the respondent said that coaching reduced costs by $5000 per month, then the interviewer would select 10.5 months to annualize the benefits ($5000 × 10.5 = $52,500). Note that 10.5 is used rather than 12 months per year to account for time away from work (e.g., holidays). Multiply the estimated monetary benefit by the annualizing multiplier to produce the annualized benefit. These calculations are based on what are called *standard values*. Standard values may be estimated and/or supplied by the organization's HR department or finance group. These values are posted on the first page of the interview guide:

> Compensation rate = $75 USD (fully loaded)
> Hours per week   = 40 hours
> Weeks per year   = 46 weeks
> Months per year   = 10.5 months
> Sales margins   = 20%
> Cost of money   = 10%

It is important to apply these values consistently throughout the analysis to avoid comparing apples and oranges. For example, if the compensation rate is higher for the numerator (benefits) than the denominator (cost) of the ROI equation, then the results of the ROI can be viewed as tainted or biased. Note too that the compensation rate is fully loaded with salary, benefits, and other employment costs.

- *Question 4.* The cost of the coaching initiative is then tallied according to the listed categories. The cost for coaching all clients is included in the cost total, *whether or not these clients produced any monetary benefits* or whether they responded to the survey. In other words, if a total of 10 people were coached and only three of the seven people who responded to the survey were able to document benefits, then the benefits of these three people would have to cover the costs of the 10 people who were coached.

- *Question 5.* If you are calculating the benefits of more than one coaching client, the qualified benefits of all participants are tallied. The values are entered into the ROI formula and calculated.
- *Question 6.* Qualitative data are captured in the form of written comments by the participants. These comments add insights into how participants perceive that coaching created value for the business.

Evaluating Coaching at OptiCom

As the coaching initiative got underway at OptiCom, the initial and informal feedback from the participants was very favorable. As the initiative manager, however, Jacqui had been down this road before with the pilot. The first blush of positive feedback from participants fell short of sustaining the commitment of senior sponsors for the coaching initiative. The evaluation plan, therefore, represented a two-pronged approach to collect credible data that will tell the whole story of how the coaching initiative created value for the organization. Jacqui soon learned that this approach to evaluation represented more than just a measuring stick: it represented a structured approach to increase the value of coaching for the clients and the organization.

Evaluating Reaction and Learning

The early returns were in: eight weeks after the coaching initiative was launched, the report from the first questionnaire highlighted strengths—and an immediate improvement opportunity. Figure 12.3 shows the reaction data from Questionnaire A. The report summarized the data as follows:

Item	% Favorable
1. My coach and I set objectives for coaching.	77%
2. The expectations from the senior leaders for the coaching initiative are not clear.	54%
3. My coach and I connected and established rapport.	89%
4. I was skeptical that coaching was going to work for me.	72%
5. I was satisfied that the first four sessions provided a strong foundation for our coaching conversations.	83%
6. Conducting coaching over the telephone is very effective for me.	91%
7. The pacing of the coaching sessions is about right; not too fast or too slow.	86%
8. The personal assessment data were effectively explained to me.	89%

Figure 12.3 A Portion of a Report from Questionnaire A: Reaction Data at OptiCom.

1. Only about half (54% favorable rating) of the coaching clients felt that their leaders clearly shared their expectations for coaching. Remember, this is a "reversal" question, so that 46% of the respondents agreed with the negatively stated question.
2. Even after two months of coaching, only about three-quarters (77%) of the clients set objectives for coaching, while about one-quarter (28%) harbored skepticism that coaching is going to work for them.
3. Overall, clients felt very positive about the rapport (89%), pacing (86%), and delivery (91%) of the coaching.

Michael met with Jacqui to review the results and to prepare recommendations for the Leadership Advisory Board. They concluded from the data that the senior leaders needed to immediately share their expectations for coaching with their people who are being coached. This communication was a critical element in the leadership process, and Jacqui was dismayed that these communications were not yet complete. Each coaching client was to base, in part, his or her objectives on meeting these expectations, so it was not surprising to learn that one-quarter of the clients (23%) had yet to set these objectives. This also raised the question as to how these clients

Items	% Favorable	Rank Order
10. I am understanding how to be more effective as a leader.	66%	3
11. I am gaining insights into personal changes that I needed to make to be more collaborative with peers.	54%	4
12. I am learning about the impact my actions have on others.	62%	5
13. Coaching is opening up new ways for me to look at business situations.	77%	2
14. I am understanding how to work more effectively with my peers to accomplish business objectives.	42%	7
15. I am learning how to engage my work team more effectively to achieve goals.	48%	6
16. Coaching is enabling me to explore new ways to increase teamwork.	42%	7 tie
17. I have begun to improve my communication skills.	86%	1

Figure 12.4 A Portion of a Report from Questionnaire A: Learning Data at OptiCom.

had grounded their coaching, given that they had not set objectives. Moreover, for those who did set objectives, it wasn't clear how closely aligned these objectives were to senior leader expectations. Written comments supported the notion that those clients who had neither expectations nor objectives were becoming skeptical that coaching was going to work for them. Jacqui and Michael agreed that this issue had to be nipped in the bud. They recommended to the advisory board that all senior leaders immediately set expectations for their people, based on the guidelines that had been issued some two months before. In this way the evaluation revealed how to increase the effectiveness and value of coaching.

The next question Jacqui raised was what implications this issue had for shaping the early learning experiences of the coaching clients. Figure 12.4 shows the summary of the data for the learning section of the questionnaire. Michael had summarized the data as follows:

1. Overall, the coaching conversations had proven to be rich learning experiences for the clients, with percent favorable

ratings ranging from 42 percent to 86 percent. Keep in mind that not all coaching clients are expected to improve in every item listed in Figure 12.4. So, to have so many items selected at a higher percentage underscores the breadth of what was being learned from coaching.

2. Immediate gains seem to come from learning how to communicate better (86%) and opening up new ways to look at business situations (77%).

3. Two-thirds (66%) of the clients were learning how to be more effective as leaders, but were these areas corresponding to what was most important for the organization (e.g., collaboration and teamwork)?

4. A rank order of the learning areas revealed that peer collaboration (ranked fourth and seventh) and teamwork (ranked sixth and seventh—tie) were not at the top of everyone's hit parade.

A more in-depth analysis showed that those clients who did not have set coaching objectives were also those whose rankings of collaboration and teamwork tended to be lower. This confirmed Jacqui's suspicions: Leaders who did not share expectations for coaching missed an opportunity to influence the early course of coaching. Jacqui had the ammunition she needed to ensure that the advisory board held the leaders accountable to quickly share expectations with their people who were being coached.

Evaluating Application and Impact

Several months had elapsed since Jacqui shared the results of the reaction and learning evaluation with the advisory board. All in all, the senior leadership was very supportive of the coaching initiative and questions were being raised about whether to extend coaching to other groups in the company. This begged the question about what value had been generated so far. With the coaching initiative having been completed for about two months, it was time to conduct the second piece of the evaluation: application and impact.

Thirty coaching clients from the entire group that was coached were selected to participate in this next phase of the evaluation. The evaluator, Michael, scheduled a time to meet with, or in some cases talk with, the coaching clients. Twenty-six of the 30 were available (87% response rate) for the interview. Throughout these 30-minute conversations, Michael followed Interview Guide B (see Figure 12.2) to capture intangible and monetary value. When all of the interviews were complete, Michael grouped and organized the data. Let's look at how Michael conducted the interview for one respondent and then see how all of the data were organized and evaluated.

Figure 12. 5 shows how an ROI interview was conducted with one respondent. The individual ROI was calculated for illustrative purposes. In the actual case study, the ROI was determined only for the entire coaching initiative. That means that all of the data for all respondents are grouped and used for the ROI calculations.

The respondent whose data are captured in Figure 12.5 was a leader of a sales team. As suggested by the answers to Question 1, before coaching, the business situation had become somewhat dicey. The team was not meeting its goals and most salespeople were not achieving their quotas. The leader complained that the salespeople were not focused and motivated, while team members cited the leader's inability to articulate direction as the primary cause of the poor performance. The coach helped the leader get past the emotional baggage and provide the team with a more structured approach to evaluate sales opportunities.

This approach produced immediate results in terms of increasing the productivity of the sales team and increasing sales (according to items checked in Question 2). Each of these sources of value was explored in greater detail, as outlined in Question 3. So, for example, following the logic of letter code B, or team productivity, the respondent estimated that at least one hour per week was saved by each of 10 salespeople and that this productivity gain directly resulted from coaching. Given a compensation rate of $75 per hour, this translated to $750 per week. This amount was not taken at face value; rather, this value of $750 was discounted by two factors: (1) estimating the percentage of this amount that resulted from coaching and (2) the percent confidence of the estimate. These two factors—attribution and confidence—represent the way the monetary benefits are isolated. Specifically, the respondent said that he attributed 60 percent of the $750 to his coaching and that he was 50 percent confident in this estimate. Multiplying $750 × 60% × 50% = $225.

ROI calculations always deal with annualized benefits. Therefore, the weekly amount of $225 must be annualized. This is done by

---

Capturing the ROI of Coaching Worksheet

Instructions: This worksheet is designed to serve as an interview guide for evaluators to assist coaching clients in evaluating the monetary impact of coaching they have received. The ROI may be calculated for each client. Data from all clients are combined to determine the ROI for the entire coaching initiative.

1. Describe the performance improvements you have realized as a result of coaching.

   I have really been able to focus my sales team on the right sales opportunities. Before, many salespeople were struggling with opportunities that, while potentially very big, seemed like a lot of work and went nowhere. I provided the team with an approach to decision making that focused us on the right opportunities and got big results.

2. Identify the potential sources of impact of these improvements. (Please check all that apply.):

   a. Increasing your personal productivity   _____

   b. Increasing the productivity of your work group   ____X____

   c. Increasing sales   ____X____

   d. Reducing cost   _____

   e. Increasing product quality   _____

   f. Reducing cycle time   _____

3. For *each* item checked above, please complete one of the benefits calculations on the following page. Use one letter code for each response. Identify currency used in the analysis: US Dollars

   Determine/use the standard values of the client organization. If these are not known or available, use the following values in calculating the monetary benefits. If the benefits are not in $US, then convert the values to the appropriate currency. All benefits must be recorded in annualized numbers (i.e., a benefit that is recorded in monthly terms will be multiplied by 10.5 months to get to the annualized number).

Compensation rate	= $75 USD
Hours per week	= 40 hours
Weeks per year	= 46 weeks
Months per year	= 10.5 months
Sales margins	= 20%
Cost of money	= 10%

Figure 12.5   Example of Interview Guide B Completion for a Coaching Client at OptiCom.

Benefit Calculations: Please describe the benefit in the left margin.

Letter Code	Estimate Monetary Value of Performance Improvement	Estimate % of Improvement Due to Coaching	State Confidence in This Estimate (on a Percentage Basis: 0% = No Confidence; 100% = High Confidence)

1 hour/per 10 salespeople saved every week 60% due to coaching; 50% confident

<pre>
    B $ 750   ×   60   %   ×   50   % = $ 225
              Based ⎧ Daily   Est. Monetary
              On: ⎪ Weekly   Benefit
              Circle ⎨ Monthly   × (46 weeks   ) = $10,350
              One   ⎪ Quarterly   Annualizing multiplier Annualized benefit
                     ⎩ Yearly
</pre>

Letter Code	Estimate Monetary Value of Performance Improvement	Estimate % of Improvement Due to Coaching	State Confidence in This Estimate (on a Percentage Basis: 0% = No Confidence; 100% = High Confidence)

Sales increase of $50,000/month × 20% margins = $10,000

<pre>
    C $ 10,000   ×   60   %   ×   50   % = $ 3000
              Based ⎧ Daily   Est. Monetary
              On: ⎪ Weekly   Benefit
              Circle ⎨ Monthly   × (10.5 months) = $31,500
              One   ⎪ Quarterly   Annualizing multiplier Annualized benefit
                     ⎩ Yearly
</pre>

4. Determine the cost of the coaching.

$12,000	Professional fees
1,500	Cost of client's time to participate in coaching (hours × $75 or standard value)
800	Materials and assessment
2,000	Travel expenses
200	Telecommunications
2,300	Administration costs (includes cost of evaluation)
= $18,800	TOTAL

5. Calculate the ROI.

Tally the annualized benefits (A through F)   = $ 41,850

Enter the values into the formula:

ROI = ((Benefits − Cost) / Cost) × 100

ROI = (($41,850 − $18,800) / $18,800) × 100 = 123%

6. Identify the intangible benefits.

a. Improved teamwork and collaboration

b. Enhanced leadership skills of the sales manager

c. Improved productivity of the sales support staff

d. Increased customer satisfaction

e. Increased employee satisfaction

Figure 12.5 *Continued*

multiplying $225 × 46 = $10,350. Therefore, the total isolated benefit of team productivity for this respondent was $10,350.

Let's turn now to the second source of benefits: sales increase. Sales increased by $50,000 per month over a seven-month period (five months of coaching and two months that had elapsed before the evaluation). ROI calculations do not include total sales, but rather sales net of the cost to produce sales; in other words, margins. The margin for OptiCom solutions was 20 percent. Therefore, the $50,000 was multiplied by 20 percent to produce $10,000 in monthly benefits. Discounting this amount by the same attribution and confidence factors produced a monthly isolated benefit of $3,000. Annualizing this amount was done by multiplying $3,000 × 10.5 months = $31,500. Determining the total isolated benefits of the coaching for this respondent was done by adding $10,350 + $31,500 = $41,850.

Let's now turn to item 4 in the interview guide and determine the cost of the coaching. The fully loaded cost of coaching includes professional fees, opportunity costs (or the cost of the client's time to participate), materials, travel, telecommunications, administration, and the cost of the evaluation. All of these costs combined for this respondent were $18,800.

Item 5 shows how the ROI was calculated, given the benefits and costs:

$$ROI = ((Benefits − Cost) ÷ Cost) × 100$$
$$ROI = (($41,850 − $18,800) ÷ $18,800) × 100 = 123\%$$

Item 6 summarized the intangible benefits noted by the respondent. These included improved teamwork and collaboration, enhanced leadership skills of the sales manager, improved productivity of the sales support staff, increased customer satisfaction, and increased employee satisfaction. Some of these benefits could, in fact, be explored further to see if these benefits could be converted to monetary value. Improved productivity of the sales support staff, for example, would seem to readily convert to monetary value. It's really a judgment call whether to do this. If the tally of monetary benefits is great enough to demonstrate the value of coaching, then there is little need to take the extra step to convert these additional benefits.

Determining the ROI for the Coaching Initiative

The monetary benefits were tallied for all 26 respondents. Table 12.2 presents the total benefits for the coaching organized by each of the six sources of value. The total of all benefits was $802,000. There were two primary sources of these benefits: team productivity and increased sales accounted for 81 percent of the total ($649,000). Personal productivity, cost, and quality contributed modest amounts, and no monetary benefits were associated with reduced cycle time. There are some possible explanations for these data. First, a high proportion of coaching clients were drawn from the sales area, so it is not surprising that sales benefits were so high. Also, improved teamwork was one of the goals of the coaching initiative, so having this emphasis surface as higher team productivity would seem to be a natural outcome.

There were many product development leaders in the mix of coaching clients, so it initially seemed odd that there were no benefits for reduced cycle time. Upon further examination, it was revealed that these leaders had made significant strides in reducing

Table 12.2 Sources of Value and Total Benefits for the Coaching Initiative at OptiCom

Source of Value	Monetary Benefits
Personal productivity	$82,000
Work group productivity	$284,000
Increased sales	$365,000
Reduced cost	$44,000
Increased product quality	$27,000
Reduced cycle time	$0
TOTAL	$802,000

cycle times for key product processes, but many more months (if not years) would be needed until these reductions would show up in monetary terms. This calls into play the issue of timing the evaluation. In this case the evaluation was conducted too soon for some of these benefits to surface.

Total program costs were tabulated as follows:

Professional fees	$360,000
Cost of client's time	$45,000
Materials	$16,000
Travel	$48,000
Telecommunications	$6,000
Administration and evaluation	$57,000
TOTAL	$532,000

The ROI was calculated to be:

$$ROI = ((\$802,000 - \$532,000) \div \$532,000) = 51\%$$

Intangible Benefits

Intangible benefits are the last, but not forgotten benefits. Several strategically critical but intangible benefits were noted and documented by at least half of the respondents. These included the following:

- More effective planning
- Faster revenue stream
- Increased customer satisfaction
- Reduced market penetration cost
- Increased collaboration between sales leaders and product development leaders

Epilogue: The Final Accounting of Coaching at OptiCom

We are about to close out our saga at OptiCom. There is but one act left. Jacqui was preparing for her presentation to the Leadership

Advisory Board. In part, her presentation was to look back at the successful coaching initiative, and in part, it was to look ahead to expanding the coaching initiative to other areas. Her presentation began by asking: Were the coaching initiative objectives achieved in a way that contributed to achieving the business goal? In order to answer this question, she dusted off her evaluation strategy (see Table 12.1) and noted the actual outcomes. The revised strategy document is presented in Table 12.3, whereby the "plan" entries refer to the evaluation strategy and the "actual" entries refer to what was accomplished by the coaching initiative.

It was clear during Jacqui's presentation that the coaching initiative created real value—both monetary and intangible—for the business in a way that contributed to achieving the business goal. This is where the line-of-sight linkage between the evaluation objectives and the business goal comes into plain view:

- Team productivity increased, as evidenced by $285,000 in value.
- Increased productivity accelerated implementing the market penetration plan.
- Implementing the plan increased sales in the newly penetrated market.

This was a wonderful story for Jacqui to share with the Leadership Advisory Board—with a 51 percent ROI to top it off! Valuable recommendations for expanding the coaching initiative to other groups were also made, including the following:

- Streamline the process by which leaders set expectations for their coaching participants
- Provide more structure to introducing clients to coaching, including a mandatory orientation session. Also, make sure that senior leaders and the Leadership Advisory Board have an early opportunity to meet the coaches, ask questions, and begin to build a business relationship.
- Better utilize company communications to educate the general employee audience about coaching and share success stories

Table 12.3 Final Plan versus Actual Comparison of Results for the Coaching Initiative

Coaching Initiative Objectives	Evaluation Objectives
Plan: Business Unit leaders effectively collaborate across functions to develop market penetration plan *Actual: Collaboration behavior increased and was quickly focused on market planning.* **Plan:** Leaders quickly engage their respective teams to implement penetration plan *Actual: Team performance was demonstrated to be more effective.*	**Plan:** Increased collaboration among leaders as a result of coaching *Actual: More than 70 percent of leaders reported a demonstrated increase in collaboration.* **Plan:** Increased productivity of leader's teams *Actual: Increased team productivity produced $280,000 in value.*

<table>
<tr><td colspan="2" align="center">Isolating the Effects of Coaching
Plan: Expert estimation of impact resulting from coaching by the clients; estimations discounted by error factor.
Actual: Isolated monetary benefits totaled $802,000</td></tr>
</table>

Expected Areas of Improvement
Plan:

More effective planning	Faster revenue stream
Higher leader productivity	Increased customer satisfaction
Higher team productivity	Reduced market penetration cost

Actual Monetary Benefits
Personal productivity: $82,000
Work group productivity: $284,000
Increased sales: $365,000
Reduced cost: $44,000
Increased product quality: $27,000

Actual Intangible Benefits
Reduced cycle time
More effective planning
Faster revenue stream
Increased customer satisfaction
Reduced market penetration cost
Increased collaboration between sales leaders and product development leaders
Bottom Line: Significant contribution to business goals through achievement of initiative goals and earning an ROI of 51 percent.

- Keep the Leadership Advisory Board more informed of how the coaching initiative is progressing and be upfront about problems or potential issues
- In the spirit of continuous improvement, consider team coaching to follow the individual coaching to sustain and increase the gains made in team development.

The Leadership Advisory Board took these recommendations to heart and committed to expanding coaching to the next-level-down group of leaders. Jacqui took a few moments to smell the roses and then got to work on developing the new initiative proposal and evaluation plan.

Building Credibility for the ROI Evaluation

The Leadership Advisory Board at OptiCom readily accepted the notion that coaching could produce tangible, monetary value for the business and that this value could be documented. Unfortunately, this ready acceptance of the tangible value of coaching is the exception, not the rule. In fact, hard-nosed skepticism exists among many organization leaders about whether coaching actually produces monetary value. The best antidote for this skepticism is to build credibility for the ROI evaluation. Coaching sponsors, initiative managers, coaches, and others can use the following five proven credibility builders to soften the blow of even the harshest skeptics:

1. *Tell a story with business value as the punch line.* The trials, tribulations, and ultimate success experienced by Jacqui is a great story, but it is a story that no business leader would be interested in if there was no business payoff. Sometimes, HR or learning and development people are accused of being internally focused. That is, they are perceived as being more interested in their initiatives *per se* rather than how these initiatives impact the business. HR initiatives, such as coaching, are a means to an end, not the end itself. The harsh reality is

that an initiative that has little business value has no business being in the organization. The OptiCom story began with a real business need (market penetration) and ended with meeting this need (increased sales). Jacqui gained tremendous credibility throughout this process and, in the end, earned the right to expand the coaching initiative.

2. *Tackle the isolation issue head on.* The greatest challenge for any evaluation is to isolate the effects of coaching from other potential influencing factors. You know that you have successfully isolated the effects when the business leaders and sponsors agree you have isolated the effects. Isolation is in the eyes of the beholder. Therefore, it is important to address this issue early on—the earlier the better. Meet with the business leaders and share with them the evaluation strategy in which isolation is prominently featured. Put their concerns on the table and address each one. If they have additional ideas for isolating the effects, even better. You know you have gotten past this hurdle when the leaders sign off on the evaluation plan.

   Because so much of isolating the effects of coaching relies on expert estimation, this is often viewed as the soft spot in the evaluation strategy. This is especially true if estimation is the only isolation tool used. Here's a little secret: Business *is* estimation. Anyone who has valued inventory, accounted for goodwill on the balance sheet, or determined the cost of quality knows how critical estimation is as a business tool. All we are doing here is applying estimation as a business tool to isolate the effects of coaching. In fact, we even go beyond what many others do in their valuation of hard-asset initiatives when we account for the error of the estimate. Inventory managers, accountants, and quality engineers typically do not take into account the possibility of error. So in a sense, our use of estimation is more conservative than other estimation techniques, which are commonly used.

3. *Be conservative at each step along the way.* Credibility of the evaluation often depends on the day-to-day decisions made

throughout the evaluation. The golden rule is to always take the more conservative path. The more conservative the evaluation, the more credibility it is likely to have. Here are some guidelines:[1]

- *Always take the lower ends of the estimates.* If product margins range from 20 percent to 28 percent, then take the 20 percent figure. If a coaching client says she saved three to five hours per week, then take the three-hour figure for the ROI calculation.

- *Throw out the extreme high scores.* Before tallying all of the monetary benefits, identify the highest monetary value and discard it from the evaluation. This removes any potential criticism that one extreme score skewed the results. Also, consider validating the higher monetary values. For example, a large rates increase can be validated by reviewing monthly revenue statements.

- *Assume that people who were part of the target population, but who could not participate in the evaluation, created no value from the coaching.* If, for example, 50 people were coached and comprised the target population for the evaluation but only 40 could participate in the evaluation, then assume that the 10 who could not participate created no value.

- *Base the ROI calculation on the costs for everyone in the target population regardless of whether they were included in the evaluation.* So, in this preceding example, the costs would be based on all 50 coaching clients, while the benefits would be drawn from the 40 who were part of the evaluation.

- *Use fully loaded costs in the ROI.* Costs must include more than just the professional fees, travel, and other out-of-pocket expenses. Fully loaded costs also include the following:

[1] Phillips (1997).

- Opportunity costs (e.g., the cost of people's time to participate in the coaching)
- Facility costs (e.g., the use of conference rooms and offices regardless of whether these facilities were charged for)
- Administrative costs (e.g., time and expenses of all staff who worked on the coaching initiative, the time of the Leadership Advisory Board, and others who manage and deploy the initiative)
- Deployment costs (e.g., usage of telephone, conference bridges, video conferences)
- Evaluation costs (e.g., all of the time and materials that were used for the evaluation, even if these resources were internal and there were no direct charges incurred)

- *Communicate these conservative decisions and actions to the business leaders and sponsors.* Don't be shy about sharing each of these decisions with the powers that be. They need to understand how thoroughly you approached the evaluation, and their confidence in the outcome of the evaluation will be enhanced. It will soon become clear that in the final analysis, the bottom-line monetary benefits likely represent the lower end of the benefits realized by the business.

4. *Enlist the support of credible sources.* Business leaders often have a go-to person in the finance department on whom they rely to sort through financial data and reports. Identify this key financial resource and buy him or her lunch every now and then. Share with this person how you are approaching the evaluation and gain his or her perspective on how best to proceed. Gaining early buy-in from this kind of credible resource will pay big dividends later.

5. *Ensure the perceived independence of the evaluation.* In the case of OptiCom, Jacqui had engaged the services of an outside evaluator. This external resource brought with him a tremendous amount of ready-made credibility that cast a positive

halo over the entire evaluation. Also, as an outsider, he was perceived as having little vested interest in the outcome of the evaluation. It is not always possible to engage an external resource, so ensuring the perceived independence of the evaluation is a critical issue. How can this be done? Here are some proven ideas:

- *Engage the internal accounting group to oversee the evaluation.* The accounting group can be brought in at certain milestones to review and sign off on the progress of the evaluation. For example, they could approve the evaluation strategy, certify that all costs and benefits were appropriately determined, and approve the final report.

- *Have another group within the company conduct the evaluation.* The quality group is often well-versed in statistics and data collection and may be willing to serve as an evaluator. The challenge here, of course, is gaining their agreement to serve in this role. Another option is to have them handle only certain aspects of the evaluation (e.g., the data collection), which would be more limited in scope and not place such a big demand on their resources.

- *Engage an outside consultant on a more limited basis.* The outside consultant could be brought in to develop the evaluation strategy, and if, for example, the quality group did the actual data collection, the consultant could come back to write the final report. The consultant would then be in a position to certify the evaluation process and results.

- *Clarify upfront with the business leaders and sponsors who will conduct the evaluation and make sure they perceive no issues with the independence of the evaluators.* The more business leaders buy into the evaluation process, the less concerned they may be with who actually does the evaluation. Enhancing the perceived independence of the evaluation may be increased by emphasizing the integrity and conservative nature of the evaluation process.

13

Evaluating Application-Based Coaching: What Are Leaders Doing Differently?

Knowing something and doing something about it are two different things. People may have gained great insights into their behavior as a result of their coaching sessions, but applying these insights to improve performance is another matter entirely. Sponsors of coaching initiatives who ask: "What are they doing differently as a result of coaching?" are really asking about evaluating application. Evaluations often go no further than application. For most business leaders and sponsors, the real question on their minds is whether they got value for their investment. Seeing people behaving in a more effective way as a result of coaching may be as meaningful to some business leaders as on ROI. These leaders will take the leap of faith and agree that these more effective behaviors will increase business performance. Such was the case with the sales and marketing leader at Frontier Manufacturing.

Setting Expectations for Coaching at Frontier Manufacturing

Before the coaching contract was signed, Paul, the sales and marketing VP at Frontier Manufacturing (fictitious name), wanted to be crystal clear with the coaching vendor and his HR VP that he wanted to see changes in how his 12 regional sales managers (RSMs) led their people and seized market opportunities. "Our salespeople seem to act like they need a written invitation to prospect new customers," Paul lamented. "Our RSMs respond by trying to find an engraver for the invitations. Where's the sense of urgency? Forget the invitations; there's a time when you just have to throw them in the deep end of the pool to teach them to swim."

Coaching (as opposed to some big training program) via the telephone was viewed as the ideal solution, given the individual needs and wide geographic dispersion of the RSMs. Besides, Paul lamented, "I don't want to invest in a big sheep-dipping program that doesn't hit the mark." Paul met with the vendor and the HR VP to set expectations for the coaching initiative. These expectations were made to be a specific part of the contract for coaching 12 RSMs:

1. The RSMs would receive five months of coaching.
2. A follow-up evaluation would be held two months after the coaching was completed to determine how well people have applied what they learned during the coaching. The HR VP and vendor would work out how best to conduct this evaluation.
3. At least 10 of the 12 coaching clients were expected to make significant progress in at least these two areas:
   ▪ Improving their people management skills
   ▪ Increasing the number of prospecting calls by their salespeople
4. The vendor will evaluate these two areas and report back to Paul within nine months as to what kind of progress was made.

The Four Major Decision Areas for Evaluating Application

The contract was signed and the coaching initiative was launched. Later, we will look at the results of the evaluation and explore how best to evaluate application. At this point, however, we have already seen how Paul made some important decisions. Let's discuss the following topics:

- Timing for evaluating application
- Setting targets
- Managing vendors
- Strategies for collecting application data

Timing for Evaluating the Application of Coaching

Evaluating application must be conducted after a reasonable time has elapsed since the people participated in the coaching initiative. The question was: What would be a reasonable time to conduct the evaluation? Answering this question is always a judgment call by the initiative sponsor, coaching leader, and evaluator. Enough time has to elapse so participants have an opportunity to apply what they have learned; however, if too much time elapses, people may forget what they have learned or lose the momentum to try something new. It was decided that the best timing for the evaluation at Frontier would be two months after completion of the coaching. Paul considered this time frame appropriate because he felt this afforded the RSMs enough time for the coaching to spur renewed vigor in prospecting for customers. Any time much longer than this, he reasoned, might unintentionally dissipate any momentum gained from coaching. Everyone knew about the evaluation and that the results were going to be publicly discussed. New customer prospects were routinely posted.

Setting Targets for the Evaluation

In an ideal world, the process of setting evaluation objectives for evaluating application would be the same process that was outlined for evaluating ROI. In reality, though, evaluating application is usually less formal. Business leaders have no expectation of documenting a monetary return, so they don't want to "over-science" the evaluation. That does not mean that there is not a lot on the line—or even on the bottom line. In the case of Frontier, increasing the number of prospects means increasing revenue. Paul is one of those leaders who is willing to keep an open mind that coaching can play a role in producing tangible value to the organization. He knows that if the RSMs change their ways and actively prospect, then revenue will increase. Performance measures that are meaningful to Paul are already in place: total revenue by month, net revenue by month, and the percentage of revenue from new customers. What's needed from the evaluation is the bridge between the coaching experience and the impact on these performance measures, which may take several months to show an impact.

Paul and the HR VP struck a good compromise in their selection of the two application-based objectives: improving people management skills and increasing the number of prospecting calls. Paul was willing to take the leap of faith that achieving these two objectives would eventually impact the business performance measures. On the flip side of this coin, he too realized that *not* achieving these objectives did not bode well for achieving the business results that he and his team needed. This evaluation, then, was a kind of canary in the coal mine: an early indication that more development or other personnel actions would be required to achieve the sales goals.

Managing Vendors to Deliver Application-Based Coaching

Working with vendors to effectively design and implement application-based coaching requires a strong partnership. Most vendors will welcome the opportunity to contribute to the successful application of a program they provide. Here are some tips for partnering with vendors to deliver application-based coaching:

- *Share the application objectives during the request for proposals (RFP) stage.* Vendors will structure their proposed program around the program objectives, so they need to know upfront what these objectives are. Knowing Paul's expectations in advance for improved people management and prospecting skills enabled the coaching vendor to more strongly position coaching to achieve the expected outcomes.

- *Mutually agree on an appropriate role for the vendor.* Paul felt comfortable letting the coaching vendor collect data about how people were applying what they gained from coaching. Other sponsors or leaders might not be so comfortable—after all, the vendor has a vested interest in the outcome of the evaluation. In this case Paul felt that the vendor's evaluation role was appropriate given the more limited scope of the coaching initiative (e.g., 12 people) and the objective nature of one of the objectives (e.g., increase in the number of prospecting calls).

- *Agree in advance on targets for application if targets are to be set.* Many vendors may initially be reluctant to be held partially responsible for how coaching is applied in the organization. After all, they have no real authority in the organization. The stronger the company–vendor relationship, the less reluctant the vendors will be. Emphasize that it is a mutual responsibility and that the vendor will be given the tools and support to live up to its end of the bargain. In reality, almost all coaching clients will apply some aspect of what they gained from coaching to the workplace. So, simply looking at application rates (as is typically the case with conventional training programs) has little meaning. What *is* meaningful is that people have taken actions that achieve organization objectives. In this regard Paul was quite explicit when he stated that at least 10 of 12 RSMs were expected to achieve significant progress.

- *Map out a strategy for taking any necessary corrective actions.* If and when the application of coaching is not meeting expectations, corrective actions must be taken. This is the true test of a partnership: how well the partners handle adversity. Mapping out a strategy in advance enables the company and the vendor to quickly mobilize for action.

Strategies for Evaluating the Application of Coaching

Evaluating how coaching clients acted upon the insights gained from coaching and applied what they learned to the workplace presents some special challenges. First of all, the insights and learnings are unique to each coaching client. This is a different situation than, say, a leadership training program where everyone receives the same experience. Next, the insights and the issues being addressed are often private and not for general consumption. Coaching clients have to feel comfortable in sharing their issues and experiences. In the previous two chapters we talked about the importance of allowing each client to tell a story about his or her experiences. The same consideration applies here as well. Evaluating application really boils down to having the client tell a story and then analyzing this story in more detail.

There are three primary ways to capture the client's story and evaluate the application of coaching:

1. Personal interviews
2. Group surveys
3. Focus groups

Personal Interviews

The most effective approach for collecting data on application is the one-to-one interview, which can be done in person or over the telephone. The interviewer can capture data in the client's, or respondent's, own words and has the ability to probe areas of interest. The interviewer can establish some level of rapport with the respondent and create an environment where the respondent feels comfortable in sharing personal information. The additional probing enables more data to be captured and data that are more in-depth and of higher quality than other means. While this method is the most effective, it is also the least efficient of the three data collection methods, and therefore, the most costly. Because of this factor, clients often turn to other, more efficient methods.

Group Surveys

Written surveys try to accomplish much of what the interview does, yet at a lower price point. These surveys contain all of the right questions (we will get to what these questions are later on in this chapter), although there is no opportunity within the survey itself for follow-up questions or probing of any kind. On the plus side, automated survey research tools allow scores, or even hundreds of respondents to provide data, and have the data analyzed in a matter of a couple of weeks. Surveys offer a standardized approach to data collection and therefore lend themselves to questions with response categories or scales. Analyzing standardized questions reveals summary statements to be made about the entire group of people who were coached. The surveys used in the previous chapter at OptiCom provided many examples of these kinds of questions. In this case study, we found for example that 86% of the respondents were improving their coaching skills as a result of their coaching (cf. Figure 12.4). This was very valuable to learn and contributed to understanding the value that the coaching was creating for the clients and the organization. In the next section of this chapter we will examine a survey that explores the application of coaching in detail.

Focus Groups

Focus groups are facilitated meetings of up to a dozen people that are organized around answering a series of focusing questions. A facilitator leads the group through these questions. Focus group data are generated as the result of a facilitative process and, while guided by the focusing questions, the facilitator has the freedom to go off in many different directions to gather the data that are viewed by the group to be most critical. The big appeal of focus groups is that the dialogue can lead to some interesting and unexpected places. Participants build on one another's comments, tell stories, give examples, and share experiences to create a wealth of qualitative data.

These groups can be used either as a companion to other data collection techniques or alone. The most common approach is to use focus groups as a follow-up to survey data. A survey of coaching clients may not only answer questions—but raise some new and intriguing questions as well. A focus group can explore these new questions and provide a fuller picture of the application of coaching. Focus groups are not suitable to explore individual stories, however; the interactive nature of the focus group conversations does produce rich qualitative data. We will see later in this chapter how this approach was used successfully at Frontier Manufacturing.

Later in this chapter, we see how Frontier successfully used a focus group with Regional Sales Managers to explore application and chart a course of action. Guidelines for successfully using focus groups include the following:

- *When focus groups include only a subset of a greater population, make these groups as representative of the greater organization as possible.* This increases the credibility and quality of the data.
- *Keep the size of the group to 12 people and, if more than 12 people are needed, conduct more than one session.* Groups larger than this size make it difficult for everyone to participate, and groups smaller than this may not provide all of the data required.
- *Ensure that the initiative sponsor and/or business leaders buy into this data collection approach.* This will increase their confidence in the outcomes of the group sessions.
- *Use experienced facilitators and those who are especially quick on their feet.* Work with the facilitator in advance to plan the agenda and outcomes for the session.

Planning the Evaluation at Frontier Manufacturing

Paul had been planning a "Hitting the Mark" session with the RSMs. The purpose of this session was to look at midyear results and to take actions to ensure that annual sales goals are met. The HR VP suggested that this would be an ideal time and place to review the results of the coaching. Paul was initially reluctant to give up floor time at this meeting. With the budget constraints, the RSMs only got together twice a year, so their time together was precious. At the urging of the HR VP, Paul agreed on a two-pronged approach to the evaluation—one that would respect people's time and perhaps even energize them further. First, a written survey would be completed by each coaching client and a group summary of the results prepared. This survey would be completed in advance of the meeting so as to not take up valuable meeting time. Second, one hour of the Hitting the Mark session would be devoted to discussing the results of the survey and delve into how the RSMs are trying new ways to lead their teams and increase prospecting.

Evaluating the Application of Coaching at Frontier Manufacturing

Step 1: Administering and Analyzing the Written Survey

About two weeks before the Hitting the Mark session, the HR VP e-mailed the survey questionnaire to the 12 RSMs. Figure 13.1 presents the survey. All surveys were returned and analyzed. Table 13.1 presents the tabulated results of the survey. Before we examine the results, there are a few technical points to be made:

1. The first item captures examples of what the RSMs are doing differently as a result of their coaching. Each RSM mentioned at least one of the four statements in his or her survey. There were many other examples of application, but these were not included in the data summary sheet.
2. The "yes" responses in item 2 show the percentage of respondents who agreed that their coaching improved effectiveness in each of the three categories mentioned (e.g., self, team, and organization).
3. All of the percentages in Table 13.1 are based on all 12 respondents. In this way, all percentages are comparable. So, for

Name: _____

Please take five minutes to respond to the following questions in preparation for the one-day Hitting the Mark follow-up session. In addition to helping you prepare for this session, your responses will help us to better learn from your experiences and ultimately achieve more as a sales team. Please forward your completed worksheet to human resources at least one week prior to your scheduled one-day follow-up session. Thank you!

1. What are you doing *differently* as a result of what you have learned from your coaching?

   _____
   _____
   _____
   _____
   _____
   _____

2. Have these actions and what you learned from coaching improved:
   a. Your effectiveness as an RSM?   Yes _____   No _____
   b. Your team's effectiveness?   Yes _____   No _____
   c. Your organization's performance?   Yes _____   No _____

3. For each "Yes" answer above, please complete the appropriate set of questions on the following two pages (e.g., a, b, and/or c):
   a. What do you think was the impact of improving *your effectiveness as an RSM?*:
      i. Increased your productivity   _____
      ii. Increased employee engagement   _____
      iii. Improved quality of your work   _____
      iv. Improved decision making   _____
      v. Increased clarity about priorities   _____
      vi. Reduced cost   _____
      vii. Reduced the time to complete project   _____
      viii. Other: _____   _____

      Please describe an example of how you improved you effectiveness as an RSM:

      _____
      _____
      _____
      _____
      _____

Figure 13.1 Hitting the Mark Quick Wins Score Sheet.

b. What was the impact of improving your *team's effectiveness*:
    i. Increased productivity of your team   _____
    ii. Increased team's engagement level   _____
    iii. Increased team's level of prospecting   _____
    iv. Increased team's collaboration   _____
    v. Improved team' communications   _____
    vi. Improved quality of the team's work   _____
    vii. Reduced cost of the team's operations   _____
    viii. Other: _____   _____

Please describe an example of how you improved your team's effectiveness:

_____

_____

_____

_____

_____

c. What was the impact of improving your *organization's performance*:
    i. Increased employee engagement   _____
    ii. Increased sales   _____
    iii. Increased results of prospect calls   _____
    iv. Increased productivity of organization   _____
    v. Increased customer satisfaction   _____
    vi. Reduced cost   _____
    vii. Other: _____

Please describe an example of how you improved your organization's performance:

_____

_____

_____

_____

4. What other benefits have you personally, your team, and/or the organization realized so far from the coaching?

_____

_____

_____

_____

_____

Thank you for completing this survey! We will share the group results with you in the Hitting the Mark session.

Figure 13.1 *Continued*

Table 13.1 Summary of Application Data From Frontier Manufacturing

Hitting the Mark Quick Wins Score Sheet Summary		
1. What are you doing differently as a result of the coaching (examples)? ■ Conducting sales team meetings more effectively (5) ■ I spend more time with the sales reps on customer calls (4) ■ Posting individual and/or team sales performance metrics (3) ■ Implemented a new sales opportunity ranking process (2)		
	Yes	No
2a. Did these actions improve your effectiveness as an RSM?	92%	8%
2b. Did these actions improve your team's effectiveness?	83%	17%
2c. Did these actions improve your organization's performance?	58%	42%
3a: Your effectiveness as an RSM (percent selected item)?		
Increased your productivity?	33%	
Increased employee engagement?	83%	YES
Improved the quality of your work?	42%	
Improved decision making?	75%	YES
Increased clarity about priorities?	75%	YES
Reduced cost?	0%	
3b. Your team's effectiveness?		
Increased productivity of your team?	50%	YES
Increased team's engagement level?	75%	YES
Increased team's level of prospecting?	25%	
Increased team's collaboration?	67%	YES
Improved team's communication?	75%	YES
Improved the quality of team's work?	25%	
Reduced cost of the team's operations?	8%	
3c. Your organization's performance?		
Increased employee engagement?	50%	YES
Increased sales?	25%	
Increased results of prospect calls?	33%	
Increased productivity of organization?	25%	
Increased customer satisfaction?	50%	YES
Reduced cost?	8%	

example, under 3a, 33 percent (or four respondents) indicated that the coaching increased their personal productivity, while, under 3b, 50 percent (or six respondents) indicated that coaching increased the productivity of their teams. This also means that the percentages listed in 3a each must be lower than the percentage value (e.g., 92%) presented in item 2a. Likewise, the percentage values in 3c all must be lower than the 58 percent value in 2c because only those respondents who said yes to 2c went on to address the items in 3c.

What do these results say about the coaching initiative at Frontier? First, as illustrated in Question 1 in Table 13.1, all respondents stated that the coaching positively impacted their behavior (note that respondents could state more than one category). Whether it was conducting sales meetings more effectively (5), spending more time with the salespeople (4) posting performance metrics (3), or implementing new processes (2), the RSMs took a series of actions to improve performance. These actions improved performance across a wide spectrum of the organization. All but one RSM improved personal effectiveness (e.g., the 8% "no" for item 2a) and all but two improved team effectiveness (83%). Seven RSMs believed that their coaching positively impacted the overall performance of the organization (58%).

The increase in personal effectiveness created many benefits. More than 75 percent of the RSMs cited increases in employee engagement, clarity about priorities, and improved decision making. Team effectiveness was boosted by increased engagement, collaboration, and communications. Clearly, coaching had a big impact on the RSMs and enabled them to achieve far more than would have been possible without coaching. The attention now shifts to sustaining these gains and continuing to build on the momentum that has been established. There is more work to be done. Coaching did wonders for improving people management and engagement, but revenue generation seemed to be lagging.

Four questions emerged from the data analysis that warranted further investigation. It was hoped that the answers to these questions would unlock the secrets to increasing revenue. These questions would be brought to the upcoming session for the RSMs to deliberate. Collectively, in a collaborative atmosphere, the RSMs could come up with strategies about how best to move forward. Each question related to one or both of the original initiative objectives: improving people management and increasing prospecting calls. These questions (with the relevant initiative objective in parentheses) were as follows:

1. What does higher engagement levels of the salespeople look like, and how can we better manage our people to continue this momentum (people management)?
2. What best practices can we share about leading our respective sales teams, especially in the areas of people management and prospecting (both objectives)?
3. Why does the impact of coaching on increasing sales seem to be lagging (sales)?
4. What can we do to accelerate the impact on the organization, especially to increase sales (sales)?

Step 2: Conducting the Hitting the Mark Session

Armed with these four focusing questions, the HR VP developed the one-hour agenda for the Hitting the Mark session. The objectives for this session were to:

1. Share ideas, perspectives, and best practices about effectively managing people and increasing sales through prospecting
2. Agree on a plan of action to continue momentum

The agenda is presented in Table 13.2, which used the survey data as a platform to encourage dialogue and information sharing. Each focusing question guided the dialogue of the 12 RSMs to explore key areas that emerged from the survey. Some of the major findings from the session included the following:

Table 13.2   The Agenda for the Survey Feedback Session

Time	Activity	Resources
5 minutes	Overview of team activity	Paul opens activity
5 minutes	Feedback of the survey results Review qualitative and quantitative data; show how the focusing questions emerged from a review of the data.	HR VP facilitates Summary sheet of the data
25 minutes	Focusing Questions Spend about five minutes discussing each question, noting key points and themes.	HR VP facilitates Set of four focusing questions
20 minutes	Open Dialogue Scan the group so that each RSM can express their views on the coaching and its impact.	HR VP facilitates
5 minutes	Next Steps Summarize actions and commitments made during the activity.	Paul closes

- Coaching was highly effective in enabling the RSMs to seek their own solutions to improving how they managed people.
- Immediate gains were realized in improving decision making, setting priorities, and engaging their teams to achieve these priorities.
- Although prospecting calls had increased, the lead times were too long for these prospects to be converted to customers and to show up as increased revenue.
- RSMs agreed that they needed to do more to coach their salespeople on conversion strategies to accelerate the revenue increase.

Epilogue

The experience at Frontier Manufacturing illustrated how a business leader wanted evidence that a coaching initiative changed behavior and had an impact on the organization. ROI data were not needed, in part, because Paul accepted at face value the link between the changed behavior on the part of the RSMs with increasing the number of sales prospects. Monetary value was implied (increased revenue), so there was no perceived need to document this value. It was also clear from the focus group discussion that it would have been too early to conduct the ROI analysis anyway. The lead time to convert prospects into revenue was too long. One important lesson to be learned here is that, regardless of whether ROI data are to be collected, a clear chain of impact must be described: coaching led to behavior changes, which positively impacted the organization.

Conclusion

14

The Value Nexus: Organization Value and Individual Values

The four-quadrant Leading with Insight model presented in the first section was developed based on the experiences of both authors. Each quadrant was illustrated with stories about coaching relationships that really hit home about how the coach and client can achieve extraordinary success. This model has further proven its value in capturing and organizing the data from all of the coaching relationships that the authors have formally evaluated. In this final chapter, we look at all of the coaching relationships in aggregate. The Leading with Insight model provides a platform for this analysis and enables us to gain greater insights into the collective value that coaching provides to the business in addition to the value individuals gain from coaching. This cuts to the heart of Coaching That Counts: how coaching creates value for both the individual and the organization. Let's examine this value nexus and see how coaching creates a win-win situation for both the individual and the organization.

A review of the data reveals six key findings:

1. The perceived effectiveness of coaching increased with the length of the coaching relationship.
2. Less than half of coaching relationships evolved beyond Quadrant 2.
3. The impact of coaching on the business increased as coaching relationships evolved.

4. Monetary benefits produced from coaching increased as coaching relationships evolved.
5. Seventy percent of the monetary value was associated with quadrants 3 and 4.
6. As coaching relationships progressed through the quadrants, the average monetary benefit produced by each client increased.

Each of these findings is examined in detail in the following sections.

Finding 1: The Perceived Effectiveness of Coaching Increased with the Length of the Coaching Relationship

Coaching clients were asked after their coaching relationship had concluded how effective they believed their coaching to be. Figure 14.1 displays the hours of time that people were coached and how

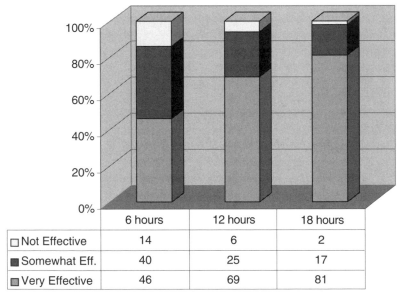

	6 hours	12 hours	18 hours
☐ Not Effective	14	6	2
■ Somewhat Eff.	40	25	17
▨ Very Effective	46	69	81

Figure 14.1 Percentage of Respondents Citing the Effectiveness of Coaching According to the Hours They Spent Being Coached.

effective they believed their coaching to be. This figure clearly shows that those who were coached the longest (e.g., 18 or more hours) rated coaching the highest: 81 percent rated coaching as very effective, 17 percent as somewhat effective, and only 2 percent as not effective. On the other hand, those who were coached the shortest amount of time, (e.g., up to 6 hours) rated coaching as less effective: 46 percent rated coaching as very effective, 40 percent as somewhat effective, and 14 percent rated coaching as not effective.

One implication of the data is that coaching relationships should not be arbitrarily cut short. Coaching relationships should be allowed to run their course regardless of how long this may take. Some organizations, for example, will begin coaching with a pilot program and set a time limit of, say, six months. Coaches and clients will be surveyed or interviewed to evaluate the relative success of the pilot. These data suggest that, by setting this kind of time limit, these organizations may be limiting the effectiveness of the coaching and having the pilots underperform. A more effective approach would seem to be to let the coaching relationships run their course and to conduct an interim evaluation, say after the pilot had been running for three months. This evaluation would go beyond just featuring an effectiveness rating to also include many of the items found in the OptiCom survey (Figure 12.2). This interim evaluation may also uncover some ways to increase the effectiveness of coaching and suggest some midcourse corrections.

Finding 2: Less than Half of All Coaching Relationships Evolved Beyond Quadrant 2

It takes time for a coaching relationship to run the course through all four quadrants. In fact, few coaching relationships complete the cycle. Figure 14.2 shows the percentage of coaching relationships that cover the four quadrants of the Leading with Insight model. This figure shows that, for example, only 15 percent of the total coaching relationships successfully dealt with issues related to "Original Actions" (Quadrant 4). These percentages are cumulative, so the

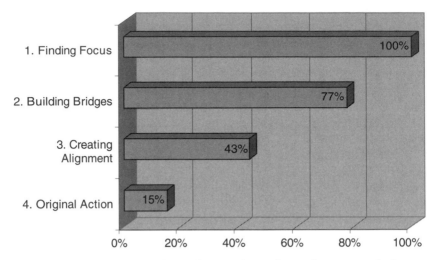

Figure 14.2 Percentage of Coaching Relationships That Covered the Four Quadrants of the Coaching That Counts Model.

15 percent of the relationships related to original actions were also included in the other three quadrants of Finding Focus (Quadrant 1), Building Bridges (Quadrant 2), and Creating Alignment (Quadrant 3). This figure also shows that 43 percent of the relationships dealt with Creating Alignment (and Finding Focus and Building Bridges), whereas 77 percent dealt with Building Bridges (and Finding Focus). All coaching relationships in the data (100%) dealt with issues about Finding Focus.

Of course, not all coaching relationships *should* cover all quadrants. The specific quadrants covered relate to the specific issues the coaching client needs to have addressed. Once these needs are addressed, then the coaching relationship has achieved its goal and the relationship can be concluded. Chapters 3 and 4 offer case studies to this effect for Quadrants 1 and 2, respectively. On the other hand, in most coaching relationships, as one door closes another opens. There may be, for example, a presenting problem that must be immediately dealt with. As this problem is resolved, new issues pop up and the coach and client then tackle these new issues. Each new door that opens deepens the relationship and explores more profound issues. At least four factors limit how the coaching relationship may evolve:

1. *The skill level of the coach.* There is great variability in the education, experience, credentials, and personal development of coaches. Not all coaches are capable of guiding clients through all four quadrants. This opens up a "buyer beware" situation for those people who wish to engage coaches in their organization. Fortunately, groups such as the International Coach Federation (ICF) have established rigorous and consistent criteria for certifying coaches and accrediting coaching schools. An ICF Master Certified Coach (MCC), for example, must have 2,500 hours of documented coaching experience and 200 hours of approved education in coaching. With fewer than 1,000 MCCs in the world, however, there are too few of these coaches to go around. There are other groups and other certifications as well. Some coaching companies will qualify coaches based on a set of skill and experience criteria. It is essential that coaches experience all four quadrants through their own personal and professional development in order to guide clients to do the same. It is important to note that the experiences do not need to be the same. Ever person who goes through the depth of personal and professional development described by the Leading with Insight model will travel his own path; however, the underlying dynamics in each quadrant have similarities that can only be appreciated through experience. The point is for people who hire coaches to explore the qualities and qualifications of the coaches and to know what the coaches bring to the party. As we will see later in this chapter, coaching relationships that cover all of the quadrants tend to generate benefits that are more strategic in nature and result in higher monetary value. In launching a coaching initiative, selecting coaches who do not have the ability to guide their clients in all quadrants may limit the strategic value of the initiative. The added investment in higher quality

coaches may produce a greater monetary return on the investment.

2. *The willingness and ability of the client to explore deeper issues.* Just as variability exists among coaches, so too with coaching clients. Not all clients are willing to dig deeply into their own reactions, emotions, and values, in order to grow and develop. Clients must be deeply committed to their own development to devote the time and energy required to realize results in Quadrants 3 and 4. Not all clients are willing, or in some cases, able to undertake the complex, but deeply rewarding, challenges that are at the core of these later quadrants. Some clients may choose to take a break from coaching after attaining their goals, and will resume a coaching relationship later when they have the need or desire to further their own development.

    Interviews with some clients revealed that they were not willing participants in the coaching initiative. They were told to be coached. In many of these cases, coaching did not go too far. Coaching should always be a voluntary decision. To do otherwise does not serve the person, the coach, or the organization. Even for those who are willing participants in coaching, there is still an initial skepticism that must be overcome. Coaches must, as soon as possible, establish rapport and allow the skepticism to dissipate.

3. *The demands on rapport, intimacy, and trust.* These demands increase as the relationship moves to the higher numbered quadrants. The coaching relationship evolves to the extent that the coach and client infuse this relationship with mutual trust and feel comfortable with higher levels of intimacy. This takes time to happen as the relationship matures, and still many coaching relationships do not mature to the point that a sustained and successful exploration of Quadrant 4 issues can be done. It is a very powerful partnership when both the coach and the client are ready, willing, and able to work their way through to Quadrant 4. The client must trust the coach, and the coach must trust herself. Coaches must be willing to reflect

very clearly the dynamics that they see, including telling clients things that they don't want to hear. It takes a lot of courage on both the part of the coach and the client to step into this revealing place.

4. *Internal versus external coaches.* Many organizations have decided to develop a cadre of internal coaches. These coaches may be hired from the outside and perform full-time coaching services or be drawn internally from the ranks of people in HR, training, leadership development, organization development, or other areas. The rationale for having internal coaches varies among organizations, although cost considerations are usually at or near the top of the list. Full-time professionally credentialed coaches hired into organizations can be as effective as external coaches as long as these internal coaches are perceived to be independent agents with no axe to grind or politically tainted in any way. One of the first decisions to be made, and perhaps one of the most important, is to whom these coaches report. Generally, the higher the reporting relationship, the greater the perceived independence the coaches will be. Having the lead coach of the group report to the CEO is likely the best solution, although this may not be practical in all situations. Alternately, having smaller groups of coaches report to the heads of the business units in which they work may be a good solution.

Let's turn our attention now to internal coaches drawn from the ranks of HR and other groups. People who have been tagged to be coaches are often sent to an external coaching school. This education, while often excellent, needs to be combined with the experience of coaching and being coached. It is surprising how many internal coaches have never received coaching themselves. It takes at least a year or two of full-time coaching to develop the requisite skills and applied knowledge to be an effective coach. Part-time coaches will take longer. Organizational leaders who develop their own internal coaches must recognize the time and resource requirements. It will take time for these newer coaches to develop the skill set, insight, and experience to coach in all four quadrants. To gain the greatest impact from coaching programs it is essential to calibrate the needs of the leaders to be coached with the coaching capabilities of the coaches assigned to work with them. Inexperienced coaches are unlikely to offer the high-quality coaching the leader needs or the high-impact coaching the business requires.

Finding 3: The Impact of Coaching on the Business Increased as Coaching Relationships Evolved

Coaching That Counts is coaching that impacts the organization in addition to the individual. Examples of business impact that were explored in personal interviews with coaching clients included productivity, team productivity, revenue, employee retention, cost reduction, and work quality. During these interviews, which lasted about half an hour, coaching clients were interviewed, and they reported on which particular business areas they believe were impacted. These interviews, and other survey data, provided sufficient information to characterize the coaching relationship in terms of the four quadrants of the Leading with Insight model, as discussed in Finding 2. We learned as we examined this finding that less than half of the coaching relationships reached Quadrants 3 and 4. This is unfortunate, because as we will learn, these latter two quadrants produce a higher percentage of business impact.

Figure 14.3 shows the percentage of respondents who reported their coaching having a significant impact on at least one business impact area according to the four quadrants. Percentages are given for each quadrant. So, in the first quadrant, Finding Focus, 58 percent of those respondents whose coaching relationship was characterized as Finding Focus reported that their coaching impacted a business area. Of those clients whose coaching relationship also addressed Quadrant 2, Building Bridges, 78 percent reported business impact. Of all the clients who Created Alignment (Quadrant 3), 87 percent reported business impact. Every client (100%) who

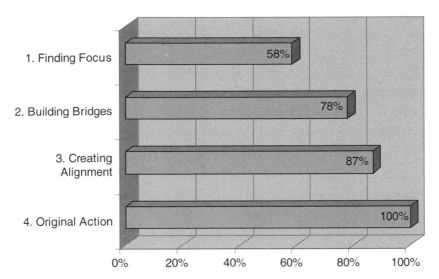

Figure 14.3 Percentage of Respondents Who Said That Coaching Impacted at Least One Business Area According to the Quadrant in Which the Impact Was Made.

engaged in Original Action (Quadrant 4) reported impacting at least one business area. Therefore, the higher the quadrant, the higher the reported business impact.

Earlier in this chapter, we talked about some of the factors that may limit coaching from accessing the higher-level quadrants. An implication suggested by Figure 14.3 is that those who manage coaching initiatives could look closely at these limiting factors. Overcoming these limitations would appear to increase the likelihood of the coaching initiative significantly impacting the business.

Finding 4: Monetary Benefits Produced from Coaching Increased as Coaching Relationships Evolved

In Finding 3, we learned how coaching impacted the business according to the four quadrants. Now we turn our attention to how this impact created monetary benefits. During the interview process, the clients were asked additional questions that explored if, and by how much, the impact on the business produced monetary benefits. These monetary values were determined in much the same way that monetary benefits were identified for OptiCom in Chapters 11 and 12. Every business impact area identified by a coaching client was explored for potential monetary benefits. Of all the respondents interviewed, 57 percent were able to convert at least one impact area to monetary value.

Figure 14.4 shows the percentage of respondents who converted at least one impact area to monetary value for each of the four quadrants. Returning to Finding Focus, 42 percent of these respondents were able to convert the value to monetary terms. These monetary benefits contained the lion's share of the personal productivity benefits that coaching generated. Half of those respondents who added Quadrant 2, Building Bridges, to their coaching relationship were able to identify monetary benefits. Much of the team productivity benefits were captured in this quadrant, as well as in Quadrant 3. The monetary percentage rose to 60 percent for those in Quadrant

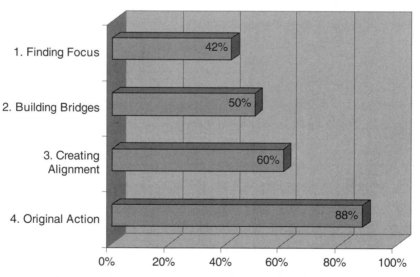

Figure 14.4 Percentage of Respondents Who Said That the Impact of Coaching Created Monetary Value According to the Quadrant in Which the Value Was Produced.

3, Creating Alignment, and to 88 percent for those whose coaching covered all four quadrants. These latter two quadrants contained most of the value gained from revenue increases and employee retention.

Finding 5: Seventy Percent of the Monetary Value Was Associated with Quadrants 3 and 4

In learning about Finding 4, we discovered how the percentages of coaching clients citing monetary benefits increased from 42 percent in Quadrant 1 to 88 percent in Quadrant 4. Let's turn our attention now to the amount of monetary benefit produced in each of these four quadrants. Figure 14.5 shows the percentage of the total amount of monetary benefits produced for each quadrant. The monetary benefits for Quadrant 1, Finding Focus, represented only 2 percent of the total pool of monetary benefits; Quadrant 2, Building Bridges, accounted for 28 percent of the value; Quadrant

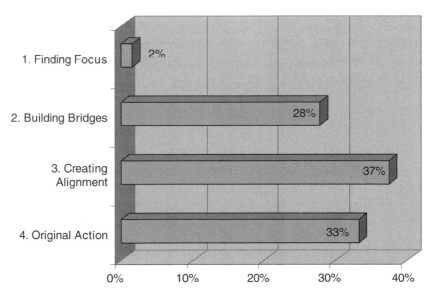

Figure 14.5 The Percentage of Total Monetary Benefits Gained from Each Quadrant.

3, Creating Alignment, accounted for 37 percent; and Quadrant 4 accounted for 33 percent of the total pool of monetary benefits. These data show that 70 percent (e.g., 37% + 33%) of the total monetary value was produced by coaching relationships that accessed Quadrants 3 and 4.

The discussion about Finding 4 indicated a trend whereby the personal productivity benefits tended to surface in Quadrant 1, whereas some of the more strategic sources of benefits, such as increased revenue, tended to come in Quadrants 3 and 4. Although these are tendencies and not steadfast rules, the data suggest that the more strategic benefits may not kick in until coaching relationships go beyond Quadrant 2. Returning briefly to Figure 14.2, we saw that less than half (43%) of the coaching relationships go beyond Quadrant 2 and therefore may not access the more strategic sources of benefits. This reinforces the importance of enabling coaching relationships to move beyond Quadrant 2 whenever appropriate. The implication is that by not doing so, coaching initiatives may leave up to 70 percent of the monetary benefits unrealized.

Finding 6: As Coaching Relationships Progressed Through the Quadrants, the Average Monetary Benefit Produced by Each Client Increased

Figure 14.6 shows the average monetary benefits produced by the client relationships for each of the four quadrants. Those coaching relationships that worked within the first quadrant, finding focus, produced on average $4,454 in benefits. As mentioned earlier, these benefits were largely a result of personal productivity benefits. It is inherently difficult to generate a large amount of monetary benefits from the productivity increases of the individuals being coached. The average benefit produced by those client relationships working in the second quadrant, Building Bridges, bumped to $51,535. As respondents were building bridges, they were also opening new avenues to produce monetary benefits. The average monetary

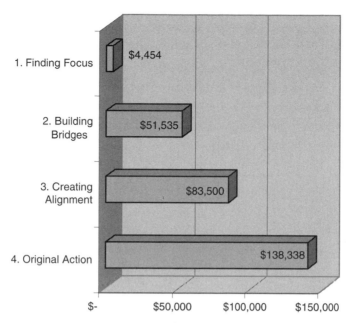

Figure 14.6 Average Monetary Benefit for Respondents According to Benefits Produced in Each Quadrant.

benefit for Quadrant 3, Creating Alignment, increased to $83,500, and the average monetary benefit increased even more for Quadrant 4, Original Action, to $138,338. One reason why these latter two values are so great is that there is simply more of an upside to increasing revenue rather than productivity. Let's now explore in more detail how monetary value can be gleaned from each of the four quadrants.

Four Examples of Monetary Value: Completing the Case Studies from Section One

The following represent four examples of how coaching clients were able to generate monetary benefits that were directly attributed to the coaching they received. Each example is representative of value that was gained from each respective quadrant. We will return to

Section One of this book and complete each of the four case studies by converting the benefits to monetary value.

Quadrant 1: Jane Cites Personal Productivity

During an interview with a researcher, Jane stated that, as a result of her coaching, she was much better able to set priorities and not feel like the victim of an oppressive workload. Her ability to schedule work improved, and she was able to get more done in a shorter period. Jane said that she gained four to six hours per week. Monetary benefits were determined as follows:

1. The first step was to determine the total annualized monetary benefit:
   - Four hours was the lower end of the range that Jane gave, so to be conservative, the lower end of the range is used.
   - $65 per hour was the standard value supplied by HR.
   - 48 weeks was used rather than 52 to account for time away from work.

   $$4 \text{ hours} \times \$65 \text{ per hour} \times 48 \text{ weeks} = \$12,480$$

2. The next step is to isolate the effects of coaching:
   - Jane attributed 80 percent of this improvement to her coaching and was 70 percent confident in this estimate.

   $$\$12,480 \times 80\% \times 70\% = \$6,989$$

   - *$6,989 was added to the benefits pool.*

Quadrant 2: Jack Increases the Productivity of Others to Deliver Client Solutions

In the interview, Jack talked about how coaching improved his ability to build internal partnerships. He was better able to communicate his ideas and gain buy-in. As a result, he was able to more quickly and effectively garner the resources required to address external client needs. Jack was able to give a specific example of how he worked with eight people on a client solution team he assembled. He had worked on five to six such teams since beginning his position. In the particular example he gave, he talked about how the client solution team gained at least 15 to 20 hours per week over the course of the four months the team was working. In fact, the team was originally expected to take the usual six months, customary for this type of work. Monetary benefits were determined as follows:

1. The first step was to determine the total annualized monetary benefit:
   - $70 per hour was supplied by HR for the level of person involved in a client solution team.
   - 15 hours was used because it was the lower end of the range.
   - 48 weeks were used to represent a year.
   - The monetary amount was reduced by 33 percent because the team was operational for only four months.
   - Jack also said that he expected similar gains in team productivity for the other client solution teams he led. To be extra conservative, the gains from these other teams were not converted to monetary value, but rather held as intangible benefits.

   15 hours × $70 per hour × 48 weeks = $50,400

2. The next step was to isolate the effects of coaching:
   - Jack attributed 60 percent of the benefits to coaching and was 90 percent confident in the estimate.

   $50,400 × 60% × 90% = $27,216

   - *A total of $27,216 was added to the benefits pool.*

Quadrant 3: Mark Gains Retention Benefits

In his interview, Mark talked with pride about how he was able to save two talented people from the chopping block. He attributed the retention of these two people to the coaching he received and the increased effectiveness of his team. Monetary benefits were determined as follows:

1. The first step was to determine the total annualized monetary benefit:
   - HR determined the total value of retaining a person at this level to be at least $165,000. This value included the costs to recruit, bring onboard, and train a replacement as well as a conservative estimate of opportunity costs. To be extra conservative, the benefits from only one of the two retained people were included in the analysis.
2. The next step was to isolate the effects of coaching to produce this benefit:
   - Mark attributed 75 percent of the retention benefit to coaching and was 100 percent confident in this estimate.

$$\$165,000 \times 75\% \times 100\% = \$123,750$$

   - *A total of $123,750 was added to the benefits pool.*

Quadrant 4: Clare Increases Revenue in an Emerging Market

Clare was enthusiastic in the interview about how she was able to spearhead a new integrated technology solution for a strategically important emerging market. The first-year revenue from this solution was expected to be at least $10 million. At the time of the interview, the accounts receivable was already more than $5.5 million. Clare and her company had hit a homerun at a time when it was especially needed. The icing on the cake was that this solution was coming in at a healthy margin of 35 percent. Monetary benefits were determined as follows:

1. The first step was to determine the total annualized monetary benefit:
   - $5.5 million was used because this revenue had already been invoiced to clients. While revenue was clearly going over this

amount, and likely to go way over the $10 million projected for the year, the $5.5 million was used to be extra conservative. This was also an issue of timing. Had the value interview been conducted six months later, more of that $10 million could have been used in the value equation. Timing is everything!

- The margin of 35 percent was used because benefits are based on net revenue, not total revenue. In other words, the costs associated with producing the revenue are taken out of the benefits calculation.

$$\$5.5 \text{ million} \times 35\% = \$1,925,000$$

2. The next step was to isolate the effects of coaching:
   - Clare attributed 25 percent of the revenue increase to the coaching she received and was 50 percent confident in her estimate.

$$\$1,925,000 \times 25\% \times 50\% = \$240,625$$

- *A total of $240,625 was added to the benefits pool.*

These examples illustrate how monetary benefits were calculated. There were, of course, significant intangible benefits as well. Some final points to reinforce about how these benefits were determined are as follows:

- Every coaching client was personally interviewed about his or her experiences and probed for examples of application.
- For those who successfully applied what they learned—and this represents the vast majority of coaching clients—we further explored how these applications potentially impacted business results.
- We adopted conservative evaluation procedures and calculations, fully isolated the impact of coaching, and included fully loaded costs.

- The end result was a chain of impact being drawn from the coaching experience to the business impact.
- Monetary benefits were determined consistently across all respondents and adhered to a set of standards.

This research should be viewed as the beginning of a formal exploration of the full value coaching offers. The findings that are offered are not meant to be definitive, but rather the opening to an exciting line of research.

Coaching That Counts

Leadership coaching is coming of age. From the scores of client testimonials, examples of real business impact, and the creation of monetary benefits, it is clear that coaching adds real value for both individuals who are coached and organizations that sponsor coaching initiatives. Both individuals and organizations are well-served by coaching. The success of coaching has attracted attention. This attention has increased the visibility of coaching as well as the expectations of senior business leaders for coaching to deliver a substantial ROI. Coaching has made the transition from a "nice to do" for leaders to a "need to do" for businesses. This transition is healthy, but it also carries responsibilities. Coaches need to be comfortable with the notion that their work will ultimately have to have a tangible impact on the business. Coaching clients will have to apply what they have learned to create this tangible impact. Coaching initiative managers will have to create the environment that supports this higher level of value creation. And the sponsors of coaching initiatives will have to take that initial leap of faith that all of these pieces will come together to create real value in their organizations.

There is no standard roadmap. Each organization and its set of players will have to find their own way of creating value. The key for a coaching initiative—or any strategic change initiative, for that matter—is to firmly link the objectives of coaching to the strategic goals of the organization. Coaching must count in ways that are strategically important and that meet the expectations of senior leadership. By adding monetary benefits and ROI to the vocabulary of those who are involved in coaching initiatives, we are not reducing coaching to numbers, but rather translating the magic and power of coaching into another language: the language of business.

Like with any translation, some information may be lost or changed. The language of business emphasizes monetary value, managing costs, and producing a healthy ROI. The evaluation of coaching that has been conducted to date clearly delivers on these expectations, but this is only part of the story. Intangible benefits represent the other part of the story. Monetary benefits and intangible benefits are like two sides of a coin: both are important. Up until now, the challenge has been that the story of monetary benefits has not been fully told. Business leaders have been left with the impression that intangible benefits represented the limits of what coaching creates. Coaching That Counts changes this scenario and changes the equation for coaching in the minds of business leaders. Coaching is essential in those situations where leaders must be qualitatively more effective and produce results that are more strategic in nature. Coaching That Counts opens the door to exploring and increasing the strategic value of coaching.

The Leading with Insight model clearly demonstrates that coaching adds value by consistently translating deeper levels of insight into business results that deliver increasingly greater strategic value to the business. The relationship between how coaching is delivered in organizations and the value that organizations realize follows the same dynamic. All coaching is not the same. If organizations "go cheap" with poorly trained coaches, fair-weather support for the coaching initiative, and short coaching cycles, the outcomes will be transactional in nature and of little, if any, strategic value. Organizations that invest in quality coaches and coach training, actively support coaching initiatives and take steps to integrate the learning from coaching into the fabric of their organizations will reap the greatest benefits, now, and well into the future. Coaching holds the potential to transform the clients who receive coaching and the organizations in which they work. Realizing that potential requires understanding and respecting the underlying dynamics of successful coaching engagements and developing a solid management and evaluation structure for linking this powerful engine to the strategic intent of the organization. Coaching counts if you do the work and make the investments to make it count.

References and Further Reading

Anderson, M.C. *Bottom-Line Organization Development*, Boston, MA: Butterworth-Heinemann, 2003.

Anderson, M.C. *Strategic Change: Fast Cycle Organization Development*, Cincinnati, OH: South-Western College Publishing, 2000.

Anderson, M.C. "Transforming Support Work Into Competitive Advantage." Spring, 1998, *National Productivity Review.*

Anderson, M.C., Dauss, C., and Mitsch, B. "The Return on Investment in Executive Coaching at Nortel Networks." In: *In Action: Executive Coaching*, Alexandria, VA: American Society for Training and Development, 2002.

Argyris, C. *Reasoning, Learning and Action: Individual and Organizational*, San Fransisco: Jossey-Bass, 1982.

Argyris, C. "Double Loop Learning in Organizations," *Harvard Business Review*, pp. 115–125, 1977.

Bacon, T.R., and Spear, K.I. *Adaptive Coaching*, Palo Alto: Davies-Black, 2003.

Block, P. *Flawless Consulting*, San Diego: Pfeiffer and Sons, 1981.

Campbell, D.T., and Stanley, J.C. *Experimental and Quasi-Experimental Designs for Research*, Chicago: Rand McNally College Publishing Company, 1963.

Carlson, R., and Bailey, J. *Slowing Down to the Speed of Life*, New York: HarperCollins, 1997.

Goss, Tracy. *The Last Word on Power*, New York: Doubleday, 1996.

Hargrove, R.A. *Masterful Coaching*, Revised Edition, San Francisco: John Wiley & Sons, 2003.

Hassett, J. "Simplifying ROI," *Training*, p. 54, September, 1992.

Hawkins, D.R. *Power versus Force*, Sedona: Veritas, 1998.

Hodges, T.K. *Linking Learning and Performance*, Boston: Butterworth-Heinemann, 2002.

Jaworski, J. *Synchronicity*, San Francisco: Berrett-Koehler, 1996.

Kirkpatrick, D.L. *Evaluating Training Programs*, San Francisco: Berrett-Koehler Publishers, Inc., 1998.

Lynch, R.L., and Cross, K.F. *Measure Up! Yardsticks For Continuous Improvement*, Cambridge: Blackwell Publishers, 1991.

Phillips, J.J. *Handbook of Training Evaluation and Measurement Methods*, 3rd Edition, Houston: Gulf Publishing, 1997.

Phillips, J.J. "Measuring ROI in an Established Program," In *Action: Measuring Return on Investment*, vol. 1, pp. 187–197, J.J. Phillips (Ed.), Alexandria: ASTD, 1994.

Reynolds, M. *Outsmart Your Brain!* Phoenix: Covisioning. 2004. (www.outsmartyourbrain.com)

Richardson, C. *Take Time for Your Life*, New York: Broadway Books, 1998.

Schwarzbein, D. *The Schwarzbein Principle II*, Deerfield Beach: Health Communications, 2002.

Wilber, K. *No Boundary*, Boston: Shambhala Publications, 2001.

About the Authors

DR. MERRILL C. ANDERSON

Dr. Merrill C. Anderson is a business consulting executive, author, and educator with 20 years of experience improving the performance of people and organizations. Merrill is currently the chief executive officer of MetrixGlobal LLC, a professional services firm that partners with business leaders to maximize the value of people and change initiatives. He specializes in providing business support groups, such as human resources, corporate universities and training functions, organization development, and quality, with performance-enhancing solutions that increase bottom-line results. He has held senior executive positions, including senior vice president of human resources, chief learning executive for a corporate university, and vice president of organization development, with *Fortune* 500 companies.

Merrill has consulted with more than 100 companies throughout North America and Europe to effectively manage strategic organization change. He has more than 50 professional publications and speeches to his credit, including his most recent book *Bottom-Line Organization Development*, which broke new ground in applying powerful evaluation methodology to increase bottom-line value from strategic change initiatives. Merrill was recognized as the 2003 American Society for Training and Development (ASTD) Return on Investment (ROI) Practitioner of the year. He earned a Ph.D. at New York University. Merrill may be reached at merrilland@metrixglobal.net.

DIANNA ANDERSON

Dianna Anderson is an executive coach and management consultant with more than 10 years of experience guiding individuals and organizations to realize their fullest potential. Dianna is the founder and CEO of Lydian LLC, a company devoted to enhancing business performance and personal satisfaction through coaching individuals, teams, and organizations. Dianna brings to her clients the insight of a professional coach and the practical business focus of a consultant. She works with individuals and organizations to promote personal leadership, authentic relationships, and productive work environments. Before establishing Lydian LLC, Dianna worked as a change management consultant with a global professional services firm, enabling *Fortune* 500 companies to successfully implement strategic change. As a coach and consultant, she has served clients in the chemical, telecommunications, consumer products, automotive manufacturing, financial services, heath care products, pharmaceuticals, and real estate investment industries. Dianna holds the Master Certified Coach (MCC) credential from the International Coach Federation, the highest accreditation available to a professional coach. She is an active member of the International Coach Federation and the president of the Iowa Coaches Association.

Dianna is an Adjunct Professor for the School of Education at Drake University, where she teaches graduate-level courses on coaching. Dianna received her MBA from the Richard Ivey School of Business in Canada. Dianna may be reached at danderson@lydianllc.com.

Index